TAKING THE WHEEL FOR DISCIPLE-MAKING

Volume One

Herb Hodges

Taking the Wheel For Disciple-making

Volume One

©2012 Herb Hodges

ALL RIGHTS RESERVED

No part of this publication may be reproduced, stored in a retrieval system, or transmitted in any form without prior written permission.

Spiritual Life Ministries
2916 Old Elm Lane
Germantown, TN 38138
Herb Hodges -- Executive Director

Web site: herbhodges.com
E-mail – herbslm@mindspring.com

Table of Contents

A Preface of Explanation 5

Introduction ….. ………………………………….. 7

The Christian – A Big Wheel ……………….…. 11

Life's Most Glorious Facts ………………….… 53

God's Saving Secret …………....…………….… 77

Guarding Our Greatest Treasure ………………... 91

A Call for Intercession ……………………….. 99

The Kingdom of Right relationships ..………… 117

Wanted: Seed Sowers ….….…..…..…..……… 135

When Jesus Looks at You ……………………... 147

God's Call to Dedicated Christian Living ……. 167

The Transforming Friendship ….……………… 193

The Closer the Look, The Greater the Book ….. 211

Paying Attention to One Another ….………… 237

The Humans and Divine Ingredients in a True Experience of Salvation ….………………….. 261

The Believer's Lifestyle – The Quiet Time ……. 275

A Preface of Explanation

One of the most commonly asked questions I have faced over the years with regard to disciple-making is the question, "Just what do you teach a disciple or a group of disciples?" It is sometimes phrased, "What do you do in a disciple-making session?" I simply cannot give a stereotyped answer to this question, because I have almost never followed the same pattern twice in teaching disciples. I have often said that discipling is not a "one-way street," that there is reciprocal exchange between discipler and disciple(s). This means that the process is dynamic and alive, never merely the following of a formula or an intended schedule. Many times, I have put aside my plans (sometimes on the spot) and "winged" the session spontaneously. Of course, years of study, teaching, experience and disciple-making may give me something of an advantage at this point.

This series of studies which follow the order of the Navigator's Wheel are an attempt to put working tools in the hands of the aspiring disciple-maker. The long introductory session explains the wheel as a picture of the Christian life, and then explains each of the six parts of the wheel. The "cycles" of the studies should be pursued one by one and in successive order. In cycle one, at least one session should be taught which shows that

Christ Himself is the very life of each Christian. This reflects the *Hub* in the wheel illustration. Then at least one session should be taught which shows *the importance of the Word of God in the daily life of a Christian.* This reflects the *top spoke* in the wheel illustration. This should be followed by at least one session on *prayer in the daily life of a Christian*. This reflects the *bottom spoke* in the wheel illustration. Then, at least one session should be taught which shows the place of *fellowship with other believers in the daily life of a Christian*. This reflects the *left-hand spoke* in the wheel illustration. Then, at least one session should be taught which shows the place of *witnessing and soul-winning in the daily life of a Christian*. This reflects the *right-hand spoke* in the wheel illustration. Then, at least one session should be taught which shows *the obedient Christian in action*. This reflects the *outer rim* in the wheel illustration. This completes one cycle. Then, there are three more cycles which follow the same order (remember that the typical mass transport vehicle, such as an automobile or a bus, has *four* wheels!), though different sessions are taught in each case. There are more than thirty study sessions in the two volumes and each one is important in shaping the life of a disciple with that "form of doctrine" which reveals the Person, the purpose and the truth of God.

As these materials are placed in your hands, I pray that it will be the beginning of an exciting adventure of teaching/training a disciple or a group of disciples, and that you will witness the victory of Total World Impact through generational multiplication as you engage in The Process. If you have not read the book, TALLY HO THE FOX, I encourage you to do so. It will present further concepts concerning the mandate of Jesus to "turn people into disciples in all nations" (Matthew 28:19). May God's Best Blessings and Powerful Anointing rest upon you as you pursue Him and His Purpose for you and others, and may these studies provide the Holy Spirit with "working tools" to quicken your mind, your heart and your ministry.

Introduction

THE IMPORTANCE OF WORKING TOOLS

In disciple-making, it is crucially important to have working tools. How many Christians on a given Sunday emerge from church equipped (through the church service) with working tools by which they can "make disciples"? In an average church service, the number would be – none, zero, zilch! Not one Christian emerges from a typical church service better equipped to make disciples! Why? Because there is *no intention, no vision, no concept, no idea, no strategy, for mastering and retaining the truth received and transferring it to a disciple with accountability to set in motion a chain of multiplication*. Though many Christians are motivated to know God better, honor and worship Him, and concentrate much mental energy in that church service, no viable outcome is expected that would enable him to assist in fulfilling the Great Commission of Jesus in "all nations". This is also true of Sunday School classes, Bible studies, teaching situations, etc., throughout the Christian community.

Let me pose this question to any pastor: If you could know that the sermon you preach next Sunday morning could/would be used deliberately for multiplying disciples who would impact the world to the ends of the earth (distance) until the end of time (duration), would this not be far more satisfying than the mere momentary inspiration of a crowd of people (as important as that might be)? If you knew that the truth you preach next Sunday morning (that very truth repeated in the exact form in which it was delivered) would be powerfully and practically incarnated in a number of persons and repeated again and again through generations of disciples for the purpose of enlarging multiplication of reproducing disciples, would this not be far more gratifying than the relative (relative) "wasting" of that truth by wafting it into the air and (hopefully) into the hearing of an audience of people who will very quickly forget it and never use it for any strategic purpose past the moment of its delivery? It would essentially be the difference between Paul preaching three or four sermons in Thessalonica (Acts 17), and Paul later writing the two letters to the Thessalonians, which have been research territory ever since for sermons, Bible studies, discipling sessions, etc. Surely even Paul himself would prefer the latter result instead of the former.

Many times, when Christians begin to hear and learn about Jesus' specific strategy to "turn people into disciples," with all that this mandate entails and implies, they often jump forth with the question, "How do you do this?" Invariably, they seem to be looking for a "quick-fix" strategy, or an "instant" working plan. This simply will not happen. Jesus spent approximately three years day and night in a close-up, "hands on" relationship with His Twelve—and at the end of the training process, as He was moving toward the Cross, they were still arguing about "who is greatest in the Kingdom!"

The process of disciple-making requires: (1) A clear and full understanding of the mandate of Jesus; (2) A clear strategy for fulfilling the mandate; (3) A steady commitment to the fulfillment of the mandate; and (4) Consistent curriculum which may be used in building disciples. It is the fourth of these requirements that occupies us in this vignette. Systematic curriculum is a primary "working tool" for building disciples. I will frankly say that, without systematic curriculum that is deliberately and strategically transferred through generations of disciples, you will never make disciples after the Jesus

Standard. The Gospel records show every evidence that Jesus used such curriculum in building His Twelve.

When I began to see and realize the strategy Jesus modeled and mandated, I immediately looked for some man who was already pursuing that strategy, and any materials I could find to help me understand it. *I could not find a single such man* (what a tragedy!), but I managed to locate a few published documents on disciple-making. At the time, all I could find was Robert Coleman's <u>The Master Plan of Evangelism,</u> Leroy Eims' <u>The Lost Art of Disciple-making,</u> and Walter Henrichsen's <u>Disciples Are Made, Not Born.</u> I wore these books out, reading each work carefully and then re-reading parts of each over and over. Coleman's book was most instrumental in showing me the model of Jesus (I have re-read all or parts of it again and again, and have re-worked it in my mind many, many times). The other two books helped greatly concerning the method of disciple-making. As I began to re-read my Bible (the primary Textbook for disciple-making strategy and curriculum) through the lens of disciple-making, I found that it was *everywhere* on the pages of Scripture (in both the Old Testament and the New Testament).

The concept of making disciples enlarged daily in my mind and heart, and I am still in hot pursuit of the concept, constantly reading and studying about it. "The final vote of things Christian is cast with the feet," and I began to implement the disclosures God was giving. My understanding was being steadily formed by reading, teaching, discussing, observing many varying ministries, and prayerfully turning all of this over and over in my mind daily.

I ransacked the Gospels, the Book of Acts, and the epistles of the New Testament, looking for the strategy of Jesus and His disciples. I now see that such strategy is everywhere, but I was handicapped by all of the traditional paradigms I had held previously and thus my investigation only slowly disclosed that which is now so very clear and apparent to me. It was only when I began to examine the New Testament emphasis on *transferred truth*, or doctrinal teaching, that I saw how absolutely indispensable systematic curriculum is in building disciples. Every document of the New Testament is laden with doctrinal truth and is incredibly clear in presentation of it. This is especially evident in Paul's epistles, each one of which was written to build disciples. The old clamor for "Christianity without doctrine" is a will-of-the-wisp. No such valid Christianity exists. As I close this brief vignette, let me encourage you to read and study Romans 6:16-18, particularly verse 17, noting the importance of an "exact form of doctrine" in securing victory over sin in daily life. Then read and study Acts 2:42, noting which discipline is recorded first ("the Apostle's doctrine"). Finally, read and study the great Gospel statement in I Timothy 2:3-6, especially noting these words, "God our Savior….desires all men to be saved and to come to the knowledge of the truth." Sadly, we have given all of our attention to getting people "saved" (who can fault this motive?) and have basically ignored God's intent that every saved person be brought to an enlarging and dominating awareness of *His truth* (who can *fail* to see the fault of this omission?) It is my earnest prayer that these studies will be useful in ministering to you personally, and will provide useable working tools to transfer to a disciple with the discipline and accountability that comes through making disciples—so that he will become a link in the chain of multi-generational multiplication of other disciples.

THE CHRISTIAN — A BIG WHEEL

I. THE HUB – CHRIST

II. THE FIRST SPOKE — THE WORD OF GOD

III. THE SECOND SPOKE — PRAYER

IV. THE THIRD SPOKE — FELLOWSHIP

V. THE FOURTH SPOKE — WITNESSING

    A hitchhiker was caught out on a country highway at night. A car pulled up near him and stopped as he waved his thumb to ask for a ride. He ran alongside the car, opened the door, and jumped into the front passenger seat. To his dismay, he found that the car had no driver! However, it began to move forward as soon as he was seated. In a moment, it was moving too fast for him to get out. Three miles later, it rolled to a stop beside a cemetery. The terrified passenger started to open the door and get out when the driver's door opened and a man started to get in. The passenger said frantically, "Mr., you'd better not get in this car; it doesn't even have a driver!" To which the breathless newcomer replied, "Yes, I know; I've been pushing it for the last three miles!" Cars have wheels, wheels are designed to roll, and rolling wheels are supposed to deliver both car and contents to the driver's intended destination.

A wheel is a quite distinctive instrument. A wheel is not made to sit on, to throw, to ride elevators, to hang on trees, to bury, etc. A wheel is more than its separate parts. Several parts are normally joined together to make a wheel. An automobile wheel may be made of a rim, spokes, a hub, and a tire. And it may even have several smaller specialized parts. But it is quite distinctive in components and structure, and it is made for quite distinctive purposes, such as *connection* and *conveyance.*

Dawson Trotman was the founder of the international Navigator's organization, an organization that emphasizes the fulfillment of Christ's Great Commission by making disciples who will impact the world. The well-known pastor and radio preacher, Charles Swindoll, said of Dawson Trotman, "In my opinion, Daws Trotman was the second greatest disciple-maker in the history of Christianity — second only to Jesus Christ, and that includes the Apostle Paul!" That is a stupendous statement, and you may be sure that Chuck Swindoll had weighed his words very, very carefully before he spoke them. If you have read Trotman's life story, you can see why such an assessment might be made. If you have not read it, do yourself an immediate favor — purchase the book entitled <u>Daws,</u> by Betty Skinner, and read and re-read it for the rest of your life. Stand warned, however, that it *is* a biography, and it starts slowly.

The Christian -- A Big Wheel

But when you get into the heart of the book, it will prove to be a life-transformer for you.

Daws Trotman was a very, very creative person. Not only was he a dynamic, driving Christian, but he was exceptionally visionary and inventive as a Christian. He constantly sought means and instruments which could be used to greatest advantage in building men into the disciples the Great Commission calls for. One of the teaching devices he created and used regularly was a *wheel* — that is, the visual, graphic use of a simple picture of a very common wheel.

When Daws Trotman was working with junior high youth, he tried to devise an illustration that would make the basic practical disciplines of the Christian life more vivid to his active young audience.

At first, he used the illustration of a three-legged stool, with the three legs representing the Word of God, prayer, and witnessing. But Daws quickly realized that he did not want to compare the Christian life to sitting on a stool. The Christian life simply should not be lived sitting down! A stool would be great if you were milking a cow, repairing a shoe, peeling potatoes, or playing a guitar. But sitting would never make a good illustration of such an aggressive life as the New Testament called for! He wanted something dynamic, something that moved steadily and with great purpose. Daws said, "I began to think of a wheel, because a wheel is something a boy or a grown man can identify with. Automobiles, bicycles, ships, and trains all use wheels." So the concept of "the navigator's wheel" was born!

Where does a wheel go? It goes wherever the driver, the engine, the power, and the steering mechanism take it. A wheel must remain intact in connection with its power source, but it does not exist to merely remain intact. It is designed to go somewhere and accomplish specific purposes as it does so.

I have a pastor friend whose Datsun automobile has over 375,000 miles on it! How many miles does your automobile presently have on it? How did it get those miles? If it doesn't accumulate miles, it is violating its purpose. Does it "go" just to be going? No, it has specified purposes, such as the delivery of people and cargo to selected places. The purpose of a wheel on a car is to *deliver people to their selected destination.* Question: is God getting *"maximum mileage"* out of our lives? Are we delivering people to **His** *selected destination?* Are we simply "piddling at the purpose," or are we operating at full capacity?

To follow the illustration, the *driver* is Jesus. The *engine* is comprised of all the component parts of the Christian life. The *power* of performance is supplied by the Holy Spirit. The *steering mechanism* is the will of God. The *passengers* are disciples who are being "carried" toward Total World Impact.

The *immediate destination* is the building of one such passenger to the point of multiplying reproduction, the *intermediate destination* is the building of an army of such passengers, and the *ultimate destination* in this life is total world impact. The "out of this world" destination is Heaven itself — for as many passengers as can be won in this life.

In this study, I want to borrow Trotman's illustration and put my own mind to it. This particular wheel has six very important parts. Each part is an absolutely indispensable part of the whole wheel.

The premise of the study is that the Christian life is like a wheel. Since it is a *life*, it insists on total vocational living, that is, living that includes every second of every day after one becomes a Christian.

So it has many aspects and many "angles." However, just as life has several urgent "parts," and each of these specific parts has both *immediacy* and *ultimacy* about it, so it is with the *Christian* life.

Vance Havner wrote, "It's about time we (Christians) cut out the theological *grand opera* and got back to *practicing the scales.*" When the late great Bear Bryant, the legendary University of Alabama football coach, was preparing for his last game as a coach, the Liberty Bowl game in Memphis, Tennessee, he was asked this question by a reporter, "How is it that you always have your teams vying for the national championship when you have no more scholarships available than any other school in the country?" After a few moments of thought, Bear Bryant replied, "Our procedure was always very simple. We recruited the best athletic specimen we could find, got him in the best possible physical shape, and then we taught him over and over and over again *the basic fundamentals of blocking and tackling!*" Christians simply cannot be reminded too often of the basic fundamentals of the Christian life. Any true disciple-making process will build these fundamentals into the disciple — through teaching, reading, modeling, assignments, accountability, etc.

In our daily, physical, earthly lives, the "vital moving parts" are:

1. The essential cardio-vascular functions which supply the living and driving force to all parts of the body;

2. The regular, disciplined eating of wholesome and healthy food, which supplies the necessary nutrients to the entire body;

3. The regular breathing of clean air, which both replenishes and cleanses the entire body;

4. Regular and adequate rest which renews the body;

5. Regular and proper exercise which gives strength and tone to the entire body;

6. The use of the body for some purpose beyond its mere physical functions. Since man is *more than physical*, he needs some *metaphysical purpose* to motivate the proper *use* of his body.

A champion body-builder was returning from a long and strenuous workout in the local health spa. He passed an artist seated beside the sidewalk. The artist was absorbed with canvas, easel, brushes and paints, and was painting a picture. The macho man stopped to observe his work. He said to the artist, "Man, how do you find so much time to do things like that? I spend all my time just keeping fit."

The artist soberly replied, "Fit for what, young man, fit for **what**?" The human body was created by God to be a vehicle, a means of conveyance, like a wheel — not an end in itself.

In this study, we will explore the six "vital parts" of a common wheel. We will see that, since a wheel is designed to move, all these parts are, in one vital sense, "moving parts." And we will see that each of the six parts pictures an absolute essential in the living of a true Christian life. The six vital parts of a wheel are the *hub*, the *four spokes* (a carefully selected number), and the outer *rim*.

I. THE HUB

First, we will examine *the hub* of the wheel. The hub is the operating center of the wheel. In our illustration, the hub represents the operating center of the Christian life. What is the operating center of the Christian life? The answer sounds simplistic, but it certainly is *not* simplistic. In fact, the answer to that question has proven to be subtly elusive to millions of Christians. This was the case in my own Christian life for many years after Jesus Christ saved me. Nobody ever explained the basics of the Christian life to me (!!!). And I have found this to be true of multitudes of born-again people.

The Christian -- A Big Wheel

Our treatment of new-born Christians is often intolerable and unforgivable. While an entire medical science is devoted to the care of infants during the first forty-eight hours after they are born, and this care entails close observation and the rendering of regular services, the Christian community pays no such attention to new-born Christians. Our procedure is more like putting a new-born into a refrigerator than the giving of proper care.

If the proper hub of the wheel is not intact, or is misplaced, the wheel is going absolutely nowhere. Christian, ponder these words carefully. Disciple, ponder these words carefully. Disciple-maker, ponder these words carefully. And remember "the first rule of spiritual life and leadership": Do not assume anything! Do not take anything for granted! Be sure the hub is understood, intact, and in its proper place.

What is the hub of the wheel? What is the operating center of the Christian life. The operating center of the Christian life is ***JESUS CHRIST HIMSELF!*** That sounds simple enough, doesn't it? But the truth is, you can meet thousands of Christians who reveal in a thousand ways every day that this simple, basic truth has never become a practical reality in their lives. In fact, it is evident that most Christians have lived eccentrically as far as this truth is concerned — somewhere away from "ground zero," somewhere off the mark, whether near or far.

We must have a good look at this hub. We must explore it until we cannot mistake what it is, where it is, how vital it is, and how to be sure it is the true operating center of our lives. In order to be sure I am not assuming anything, let me rephrase the last sentence. We must explore Jesus Christ Himself until we cannot mistake Who and what the Bible says He is, where He is, how vital He is, and how to be sure *He is the true operating center of our lives.* This is no idle assignment. This is no spare-time exercise. This is no indifferent task. This is the Top Drawer, Card "A," High Level, Heavyweight Championship vocation of every Christian. If the Christian is wrong here, the wheel will not roll and the intended conveyance will not occur.

We will let the New Testament clearly identify and place the hub of the wheel. It cannot be said too many times: The hub of the wheel is Jesus Christ Himself. The Apostle Paul said, "To me to live is Christ" (Philippians 1:21). Examine these words carefully, technically, and minutely. Jesus said, "Man lives by *every word* that proceeds out of the mouth of God." We must not take liberties with the words of God, either with regard to His *choice* of words or the *arrangement* and *placement* of those words in His communication to us. Note that Paul did *not* say, "To me to live is to *know* Christ." That is a subtle addition, but to have Christ as the operating center does not allow so much as a verb between me and Christ. Similarly, Paul did not say, "To me to live is to *confess* Christ," or to "*live for*" Christ, or to "*serve*" Christ, or even to "*be like*" Christ. Christian, ponder this vital emphasis: The operating center of the Christian life is not any *function*, or *attribute*, or *accompaniment*, or *activity* of the Christian life, as important as they all may be. No, the operating center of the Christian life is Jesus Christ Himself.

He Himself is the Source, the Secret, the Substance and the Strength of the Christian life. And just as the presence and function of the hub are absolutely essential in the proper deployment of a wheel, so the moment-by-moment central presence and essential function of Jesus Christ are absolutely essential in the living of a true Christian life.

Let the New Testament speak for itself in presenting this vital truth. "Christ lives in me," said Paul in Galatians 2:20. "Christ in you, the hope of glory," wrote Paul in Colossians 1:27. "Christ is our life," says Colossians 3:3. These writings in the

New Testament epistles, and many more, are mere echoes of the clearly presented words of Jesus Himself. In John 14:6, Jesus said, "I am the Way, the Truth, and the Life." He did not say, "I am *a* way," or "I am *one* of the ways," or "I am the *best* way," or "I am *one way among many.*" No, all truth is narrow and exclusive — if it is true, then every opposing possibility is false. In a day when pluralism and accommodation are the very order of thought and action (up to the accommodation of Christianity and its exclusiveness in the interest of truth; these are fully rejected by modern humanism), this makes the Gospel of Christ increasingly unpopular. However, popular opinion has absolutely nothing to do with the determination of truth. Truth is absolute, dogmatic, and immutable, public opinion notwithstanding. Jesus Christ is the only Way to God and Life — "no man comes to the Father except by Me," He said.

Then He said, "I am the Truth." The Bible calls Jesus the "Logos" of God. The King James Bible translates this as the "Word" of God (John 1:1-3, 14). However, this word "logos" is the very word from which we derive our English word, "logic." You can see the two words on the page and easily detect the similarity. *Jesus is the Mind of God; Jesus is the Logic of the universe.* To put it personally and practically, the closer you are to Jesus, the more "logical" you are from God's point of view, and the farther removed you are from Jesus, the more *illogical* you are *from God's point of view!*

And, no matter what our response or reaction may be, God's viewpoint is the only one that counts.

Colossians 3:2 says, "In Christ are hidden all the treasures of wisdom and knowledge." Jesus is God's "wisdom-and-knowledge treasure vault." No true wisdom ever derives from any point outside of Christ, and all knowledge — yes, *all knowledge* — is in Him.

Then Jesus said, "I am the Life." "I am the Way, the Truth, and the Life." There are three technical and definitive statements in that compound sentence. Jesus said three things in that sentence, and not merely one. We usually present that sentence as if it meant only one thing, that Jesus is the one and only way to God. It certainly means that, but it also says (and means) a great deal more than that.

Let me explain it a bit further so we can see the clear distinctiveness of each of these brief statements. "I am the Way" in order that human beings may be *saved*; "I am the Truth" in order that human beings may be *sure* they are saved, and *sensible* about it. And "I am the Life" in order that human beings may be *satisfied* just with Me. So this verse is a key example (again, only one among many) of the colossal claims of Jesus Christ.

Think of the actual experiences of Christians with Jesus' words in mind. One hundred percent of all Christians have gotten into Jesus as "the Way" and have been saved. There is simply no other way to be saved. All saved people have received Christ and have gotten into Him as "the Way." However, there is a substantial reduction in experience among Christians with regard to the second statement in the sentence. Though all Christians are in Jesus as the Way, not all (by a long shot) Christians have so adjusted to Him and believed Him as the "Truth" that they are sure they are saved and sensible (Biblically intelligent) about it. What is going on here? The same Divine Person spoke both sentences.

The same Divine authority rests behind both sentences. The same Heavenly "sponsorship" underwrites both sentences. Then why are many Christians not absolutely *sure* they are saved, and even many who are sure they are saved are not Biblically intelligent about it? You see, truth must be known, believed, and (whenever necessary) practiced. If it is not known and believed, the ignorant and unbelieving person has *practically* negated that truth. For him, it is not truth at all. So he can live temporarily as if his decision determined truth. However, all roads, however variant and deviating and wayward, will converge into a Final Meeting with THE TRUTH. In Amos 4:12, the prophet said, "Prepare to meet your God." Some in his listening audience prepared, others didn't — **but they all met God!** Some met Him redemptively to their present and eternal advantage, others only met Him finally to their eternal disadvantage — but *they all met Him*. The unsaved man's reaction to the Truth or rejection of it constitute no determination about the truth at all. Unsaved men do not judge the Truth in their responses and reactions; they only judge themselves.

A man was wandering through the Louvre, the national art gallery of France in Paris. He spoke to a guard in an air of casual superiority: "What's so special about these pictures? In my opinion, they aren't much." The guard replied, "Sir, your opinion doesn't count here. If anything is on trial here, it is not these paintings. It is you!"

C. S. Lewis wrote a book entitled, God In the Dock, showing that the "modern," worldly-wise man has placed God in the prisoner's dock in man's "courtroom," and has dared to pass judgment upon Him as if his (man's) word were final. The Bible calls this, "Man's day" (I Cor. 4:3). Oh, but nothing that mere man does is ultimate. Nothing that man does is final. *Another* Day is coming, and on That Day, the only Standard will be that of THE TRUTH, Jesus Himself. The Bible says that "God has appointed *a Day* in which He will judge the world by that Man Whom He has ordained — and He has given guarantee of this to all men, in that He has raised Him from the dead" (Acts 17:30-31). So if you do not intend to adjust to the truth now, thus forsaking wisdom and choosing in favor of falsehood, then brace yourself, because you will still face THE TRUTH.

Christian, you must apply the same standard to your own life. Though argument tends to make truth academic and legalistic instead of vital and alive, you still must face the Truth in your own experience.

Jesus is the Truth in order that you might be *sure* you are saved, and *sensible about it*. So your vocation only begins when you first accept Jesus as the Truth. Then begins a lifelong investigation of the Truth, a lifelong adaptation of your life to the Truth, and a lifelong propagation and proclamation of the Truth.

If you are not sure you are saved, you should make your first vital adjustment to the truth at this point. "Make your calling and election sure," the Bible says, or "be sure you are saved!" Then, if you are a casual learner of the Truth by picking up bits and pieces through teachers and preachers in church, you have another vital adjustment to make with regard to the Truth. You must daily get into the Bible, the Manual authored by the Holy Spirit, the One who presents and mediates the Truth, and let Him teach you therein the "ways and means" of the Truth.

Finally, in John 14:6, Jesus spoke of Himself as "the Life." He is the Life that we might be *satisfied just with Him*. Are you satisfied with Jesus? Could you be satisfied *just* with Him? None of us could really be confident of our answer to that question unless Jesus was all we had. What if we lost everything but Him? Could we be satisfied just with Him? Paul was! Near the end of his life, he wrote, "I have kept the faith." The faith was all he *had* to keep! He had lost everything else. But Jesus proved to be enough — yes, *more than enough*. One day, we will leave behind everything we built our lives around in this world. Jesus will be all that is left. When we swirl down into the waters of the Dark River of Death, and Jesus is all we have, will we be satisfied? He wants to be *our very Life!* Jesus Himself is the hub of the Christian life.

In John 10:10, Jesus contrasted His Person and Mission with the person and mission of Satan. He said, "The thief (Satan) comes not except to steal, to kill, and to destroy. I have come that men might have life, and that they might have it more abundantly." It is evident that He wants our lives to abound (overflow) with Himself and His eternal quality of life. He is the hub of the Christian life.

II. THE FIRST SPOKE — THE WORD OF GOD

A vital part of any wheel is the spoke that connects the hub with the rim. We want to become deliberately conscious of the functions represented by the four spokes in our illustration. However, the purpose is not to make us self-conscious about these functions. Indeed, the purpose is to make us unself-conscious about these functions. You see, when a wheel is turning quickly and properly, fulfilling the reason for its existence, the spokes become "invisible." All you see is the hub. When the wheel is standing still, the spokes take up a lot of room, and are very evident, but the minute that wheel begins to move rapidly and smoothly, the spokes seem to vanish. The spokes are still there, but you don't see them. The hub becomes pre-eminent. When people look at our lives, and it is our spokes — the daily discipline of our lives — that impress them, we simply are not moving properly!

In our illustration, the spokes represent the direct supply lines of the Christian life, the channels that keep Christ at the center and convey him to the "practicing edge" of the life. The key to the spokes of a wheel is in their connection. Spokes must be connected to the hub and the rim if they are to do their work. When I was a lost high school student, one night, our gang of rowdy guys collected a bunch of old discarded automobile tires, loaded them in the bed of a pickup truck, went up to the top of the steepest hill in my home town (which was located in the mountains of northwest Arkansas!), and started those tires, one by one, rolling down the street on that steep hill. The "Maple Street Hill" was about three city blocks long at that point, and *very* steep. And a University of Arkansas fraternity house was at the bottom of the street, where it made a sharp left turn. So our object was to roll the tires down the hill — and see what happened! Well, *it happened!* Some of them bounced all the way up onto the roofs of houses beside the street. Others smashed into the sides or porches of the houses. I shudder today to think of what might have happened if a car had come around the corner at the bottom of the hill and had started up the hill at the wrong time. A few of the tires, bouncing incredibly high and at great force, bounced onto the roof of the fraternity house at the foot of the hill, and some smashed into the side. What's the point of my story? Simply this: once those tires were released, they were out of control. They rolled through yards, through flower beds, onto porches, onto roofs, and smashed into buildings. The problem? Without proper connection, each tire was without proper direction and function — and was a potential instrument of destruction. When a Christian does not abide in Christ (John 15:1-11), keeping the contact intact, he is constantly in trouble, bumping into other people instead of blessing them, getting into continual difficulty, causing incredible damage, and failing to fulfill the purpose for which Jesus saved him. Remember, the hub is Christ, and constant connection must be maintained with Him through the spokes, the supply lines of the Christian life. Our wheel will have four spokes. The proper function of the wheel will depend on the balance of the four spokes. If any one of the four spokes is

The Christian -- A Big Wheel

missing or is out of proportion, the entire wheel gets out of balance and the wheel bumps down the street. If any one of the four basic disciplines of the Christian life is missing or out of balance, a lop-sided Christian is the result. The lop-sided Christian always seems to be "out of sync"; things do not operate smoothly.

Two of the spokes are *vertical*, and two of them are *horizontal*. The two vertical spokes represent our direct relationship with God Himself. They represent our spiritual intake, our communion with God as we abide in Christ. The two most important means of communion in the Christian life are the Word of God and prayer. Through the Word of God, *God speaks to the Christian*. Through prayer, *the Christian speaks to God*. Since all possibility of relationship, victory, and communion in the Christian life begins when God speaks to you, the uppermost vertical spoke will represent the Word of God.

The Word of God is *absolutely indispensable* in the Christian life. Sinners are saved by means of the Word of God. We are "born again, not of corruptible seed, but of incorruptible, by the Word of God, which lives and abides forever" (I Peter 1:23). The word of God is the very source of all true faith, whether it be "saving" faith or "sanctifying" faith. "Faith comes by hearing, and hearing by the Word of God" (Romans 10:17).

The Word of God is the milk for babies to grow on. "As newborn babes, desire the sincere (pure) milk of the Word, that ye may grow thereby" (I Peter 2:2). And when the Christian moves from milk to the need for meat, the meat also is the Word of God. If you want to see how enthusiastically a new Christian should read, study, and devour the Word of God, just watch a tiny baby sucking furiously on his bottle when he is fed!

Babies also need to learn to walk. "Thy Word is a lamp unto my feet, and a light unto my path" (Psalm 119:105). A baby will need a great deal of instruction and understanding in order to grow properly. "The entrance of Thy word giveth light; it giveth understanding unto the simple" (Psalm 119:130).

Babies also need to be kept clean, and as they grow, they need to learn to keep themselves clean.

Jesus said, "Now ye are clean through the word which I have spoken unto you" (John 15:3). Paul spoke of "the washing of water by the word" (Ephesians 5:26). Sometimes harmful things in the body must be surgically removed. "The Word of God is living and active, and sharper than any two-edged sword, piercing even to the dividing asunder of soul and spirit, and of joints and marrow, and is a discerner of the thoughts and intents of the heart" (Hebrews 4:12).

The one constant need in a believer's life for sanctification and Christ-likeness is regular contact with the Word of God. "We all (Christians), with unveiled face, beholding as in a mirror (the Word of God, James 1:23) the glory of the Lord, are changing into the same image (the likeness of Jesus) from glory to glory (in an ever-progressing way), and this is the work of the Spirit of the Lord" (II Cor. 3:18).

Then the growing Christian is admonished to "herald the Word" (II Tim. 4:2). This he does by giving regular testimony to Jesus and the Gospel. So the Word of God, the first spoke of the wheel, is absolutely essential in living the Christian life.

There are four things that every Christian should do with the Bible every day of his life. He should *know it in his mind.* This means that he will read it every day, saturating his mind with its incredible truth and allowing that truth to fill and condition his mind, his heart, his conduct, and his speech every moment of every day. Inscribed in the flyleaf of my Bible are these wise words:

"Every Hour I Read You Kills a Sin, or Lets a Virtue In, To Fight Against It."

He should *stow it in his heart*. This means that he should seek to understand the mind of God in Scripture. It also means that he should memorize it so he can have it accessible to ready recall at any minute. The benefits of Scripture memory are too many and too great to ignore this discipline. Two of the finest disciples I have ever had, husband and wife, memorized so many verses in just over two years, that they could not hold their Scripture memory cards in both hands! And they never missed the perfect recitation of any verse when I called on them! Today, they are being used of God in incredible ways.

He should *show it in his life*. Dr. J. M. Price, late great Baptist educator, said, "The best binding for the Bible is not Morocco leather, but a human skin!" It should be the daily goal of every Christian to incarnate the Word of God in his own life.

Finally, he should *sow it in his world*. "The seed is the Word of God," Jesus said in Luke 8:11. "The field is the world," He said in Matthew 13:38. "Behold, a sower went forth to sow" should be the biography of every Christian every day. "He that goeth forth and weepeth, bearing precious seed, shall doubtless come again with rejoicing, bringing his sheaves with him" (Psalm 126:6).

Hudson Taylor, the founder of the China Inland Mission, who personally prayed more than a thousand missionaries into inland China, said, "Your spiritual growth as a Christian will be in exact proportion to the amount of time you spend in the Word of God." D. L. Moody, the great evangelist, said, "I prayed for faith, and expected it to come out of heaven and strike me like lightning, but it never came. Then one day, I read in Roman 10:17 that 'faith comes by hearing, and hearing by the Word of God.' So I started reading my Bible daily, and faith has been growing ever since." Is it any coincidence that George Mueller, the renowned man of faith in Bristol, England, whose faith sustained several orphanages without soliciting funds, read his Bible all the way through over seventy-five times — on his knees? Is it any mere coincidence that Dawson Trotman, who later had a world-impacting ministry personally and through disciples whom he had trained, memorized over twelve hundred verses of Scripture within three years of his conversion?

Every Christian should have consistent daily exposure to the Word of God, should practice careful hearing of the Word of God, should render complete obedience to the Word of God, and should make constant confession of the Word of God. Faith *starts* with the Word of God, *stands* on the Word of God, *stays* with the Word of God, *steps out* on the Word of God, *states* the Word of God, and *stops* with the Word of God. I want my life to echo the request of John Wesley, "Oh, God, make me a man of That Book!"

Remember that the Word of God in the believer's life corresponds to food in his physical life.

Job said, "I have esteemed the words of Thy mouth to be more than my necessary food" (23:12).

Jeremiah followed the same theme: "Thy words were found, and I did eat them; and Thy word was unto me the joy and rejoicing of my heart" (Jer. 15:16). Don't kill your appetite for this food of the soul by eating the garbage of the world. A steady diet of the Word of God while walking in the Spirit will secure steady growth in your life.

Remember, too, that this is the *top* spoke on the wheel. Everything else begins here. The initiative to give the Word and speak to us through it belongs to God, but the intake of it is our responsibility. I do not *intend* to spend many days on this earth during the rest of my life without eating physical food, and this spoke of the wheel corresponds in spiritual life to the eating of food in physical life. Should I not determine that I will not spend one day on this earth as long as I live without feeding my spirit on the revealed Word of God in the Bible?

II. THE SECOND SPOKE — PRAYER

The second spoke of our wheel is *prayer*. This spoke is at the bottom of the wheel. The Word of God, the upper spoke, brings the life of Christ in a downward direction to us, and prayer is our response to what He says in His Word. Note that the Word of God basically comes in a downward direction, while prayer is an upward response. This teaches us one of our greatest lessons about prayer. One the best ways to pray is to listen to God in His Word — *and then don't change the subject!* My mother used to tell me that it was impolite to change the subject when someone spoke to you, and the more important the person speaking, the more impolite it was to change the subject. Now apply the illustration. We are often in church services where God speaks clearly and powerfully through a message from the pulpit.

However, the person who leads the closing prayer sounds as if he was asleep or visiting Planet Mars — he never mentions anything God has just spoken to His people! This is a clear example of "quenching the Spirit" by "despising preaching" (I Thessalonians 5:19-20)!

As we begin to explore the place of prayer in the Christian's life, let's establish the principle that a believer's character is fashioned by his communication with God. Communication is one of the vital secrets of *every* healthy relationship. Good communication will transform mere acquaintances into steadfast friends, and will change superficial contact into intimate closeness. Such communication is built if we employ four guidelines:

All relationships thrive on compliments. Mark Twain said, "I can survive for three months on one solid compliment." He was not an exception! Nothing aids a healthy relationship more than an honest compliment. David deployed this principle when he wrote, "Enter into His gates with thanksgiving, and into his courts with praise: be thankful unto Him, and bless His Name" (Psalm 100:5).

If prayer does not begin as a means of worshiping and honoring God, then the first purpose of the Christian life has been omitted. But in reality, praying is more basking in a relationship than it is asking for resources.

All relationships thrive on active listening. Communication is much more than talking! It includes alert listening which conditions the entire relationship. A wise person will give his undivided attention to the other person in a relationship, and as often as possible. Failure to listen is an insult to the dignity and importance of the one speaking. "Be still, and know I am God," He says to us (Psalm 46:10). II Samuel 7:18 says that "King David went in, and sat before the Lord." And though his speech to God is recorded, I am sure that he listened as well. "Stand in awe, and sin not: commune with your own heart upon your bed, and be still" (Psalm 4:4).

All relationships require consistent contact. Consistent contact lets each member in the relationship realize that the relationship is meaningful to all parties in it. However, if contact is not made for long periods of time, the relationship becomes slack and indifferent. If I do not have consistent contact in any of my relationships, the other party feels excluded from my companionship. Problems will develop, whether coldness, indifference, anger, hostility, or whatever.

There are no shortcuts to consistency in a Christian's prayer life. "Life is so daily," bemoaned one cynic. Well, the Christian life is so daily, also. Irregular communication with God testifies to everyone that the relationship is not a priority to you. But regular communication makes your heart, your motives, your thoughts, and your steps line up with God. Also, your faithfulness enables you to have confidence before God. Hebrew 4:16 says, "Let us then approach the throne of grace with confidence, so that we may receive mercy and find grace to help us in our time of need." Consistent communication with God is a necessity if your relationship with Him is to be vital.

All relationships require complete honesty. If dishonesty or deceitfulness creeps in, the relationship is threatened. If these things continue, they are very likely to destroy the relationship altogether. Even so, absolute honesty is the only basis for a good relationship with God. We all know that too many things get into our lives that violate our relationship with God. To try to hide these, or to ignore them (as David did in II Samuel 12), will only deteriorate the relationship. The Christian must "keep short accounts with God," regularly confessing his sins and receiving God's cleansing. I John 1:7 says, "If we walk in the light (practice open, honest communion with Him) as He is in the light, we have fellowship one with another, and the blood of Jesus Christ His Son cleanses (present continuous verb, "keeps on cleansing") us of all sin."

These are wise practical guidelines to follow in our prayer life. Prayer is both a *priority* in our discipleship, and a *proof* of it. We often think of prayer as preparation for the battle, but Jesus showed us that prayer is the battle itself. Prayer was at the very heart of His work while He was on earth, and it is the very heart of His work in heaven today — and it should be at the very heart of our lives and our service for Him.

Where did Jesus sweat great drops of blood? Not in Pilate's judgment hall, or on His way to Golgotha. It was in the Garden of Gethsemane. If we had witnessed His struggle that night, we might have sadly misinterpreted the situation. We might have said, "Why, if He is so broken up when all He is doing is praying, what will He do when He faces a real crisis? Why can't He approach this ordeal with at least the same calm confidence that His three sleeping friends have?" However, when the real test came, Jesus walked to the cross with unbending courage, and His three friends fell apart and ran away!

Prayer is not a request for God to help us in His work; prayer is the work itself!

Luke 18:1 says that "men ought always to pray, and never give up." I Thessalonians 5:17 says, "Pray without ceasing." James 5:16 says, "The effectual fervent prayer of a righteousness man availeth much." In John 15:7, Jesus said, "If ye abide in me, and my words abide in you, you shall ask what you will, and it shall be done unto you." It is obvious that prayer is one of God's primary means of grace.

Contrary to common belief, prayer is the most practical and relevant thing in life. God's wisdom comes in answer to prayer. God delivers us from false judgments and unwise counsel through prayer. Prayer keeps us from majoring on lesser and unimportant things. Prayer allows us to have true perspective in life. If you value your Christian experience, be sure to take prayer seriously.

Martin Luther said, "Prayer is the most important thing in my life; if I should neglect prayer for a single day, I should lose a great deal of the fire of faith." Andrew Bonar said, "The one concern of Satan is to keep the saints from prayer. He fears nothing from prayerless studies, prayerless Christian work, or prayerless religion. He laughs at our toil and mocks at our wisdom, but he trembles when we pray."

Andrew Murray, a giant of the faith, gives this illustration of prayer's importance. "When a general chooses the place from which he intends to strike the enemy, he pays most attention to the points which he thinks most important in the fight. Thus there was on the battlefields of Waterloo, a farmhouse which Wellington immediately saw was the key to the situation. He did not spare his troops in his endeavor to hold that point; the victory depended upon it. And it is the same in the conflict between the believer and the powers of darkness. The inner prayer chamber is the place where the decisive victory is obtained."

Sometime ago, Scott Williams, a dear friend and brother, handed me this poem:

> Last night I took a journey To a land across the seas;
> I didn't go by ship or plane; I traveled on my knees.
> I saw so many people there In bondage to their sin;
> And Jesus told me I should go, That there were souls to win.
> But I said, "Jesus, I can't go To lands across the seas."
> He answered quickly, "Yes, you can — By traveling on your knees."
> He said, "You pray, I'll meet the need. You call and I will hear;
> It's up to you to be concerned For lost souls far and near."
> And so I did. I knelt in prayer, Gave up some hours of ease;
> And with the Savior by my side I traveled on my knees.

As I prayed on, I saw souls saved And twisted persons healed;
I saw God's workers' strength renewed While laboring in the field.
I said, "Yes, Lord, I'll take the job. Your heart I want to please;
I'll heed Your call and swiftly go By traveling on my knees."

We must remind ourselves that we are seeking Total World Impact. We are battling forces of darkness for a world of men, most of whom are without Christ. Archimedes once said, "Give me a fulcrum strong enough, and a lever long enough, and a place to stand apart from that which I am trying to move — and I can move the world." Think of this statement carefully, and let me apply it to our disciple-making, world-impacting goal. The fulcrum is the revealed purpose of God. The lever is prayer. The place to stand — apart from the world — is "in Christ." And if we follow his formula, we can move the world.

Remember that prayer in the spiritual life corresponds to the breathing of good, clean air in the physical life. When a doctor strikes a baby on its backside at birth, that doctor is saying to the baby, "Breathe without ceasing." When the Holy Spirit brings a new Christian to birth, He says to him, "Pray without ceasing."

Harry Denman, the Methodist evangelist, visited a southeastern city for revival services. While he was there, a very gracious Christian couple invited him to be a guest in their home. When the woman showed him to his room, she remarked, "Dr. Denman, this is the room where my grandmother prayed."

Throwing all caution to the winds, Harry Denman turned to her in tender fashion and said, "I'm not interested in where your grandmother prayer. Where do *you* pray?" *This is the crucial question. Do* you pray? Where? Are you systematic and consistent in your prayer life? Do you have a definite time every day for your appointment with God? Are you able to trace any triumphs of God in your life because of prayer? S. D. Gordon said, "Communion and petition store the life with the power and resources of God; intercession lets them out on behalf of others." If you have been converted, for *your* sake, for the sake of *others*, and for the sake of *God* and *His global cause*, practice regularly the ministry of personal prayer.

III. THE THIRD SPOKE — FELLOWSHIP

The third spoke of the wheel is *fellowship* with other believers. We have examined the two *vertical* spokes of the wheel, which represent our direct relationship with God. Now, we will look at the two *horizontal* spokes, which represent our direct relationships with our fellow men. One of the horizontal spokes that powerfully channels the life of Christ to practical personal use is fellowship with other believers.

Recently, I read this riddle: How is it that, in a world that is getting smaller and smaller, people are getting farther and farther apart? The entire world is experiencing a "fellowship crisis." Sadly, the church also often experiences the same crisis. I read of two porcupines in northern Alaska. If they stayed apart, they might freeze to death. But if they got together, they "needled" each other so badly that they could hardly stand it. This is the dilemma which church people often have. One of Satan's primary strategies is to "divide and conquer." Satan tries to turn Christians against one another, because he knows that they will then destroy each other. So Christians who follow Satan's strategy become like the Philistines, who "set ambushments" against each other. And

Satan works through our flesh, so we "just know" that our brothers and sisters are mean, intolerant, and intolerable. Rufus Jones showed perception when he said, "The American churches are like Robinson Crusoe's goat pasture; the fields are so large and the fences so far apart that the goats inside are as wild as the goats outside!" So a great fellowship crisis has developed in the church, and such "fellowship failures" as *criticism and censorship* of brothers and sisters; *coercion* of others to my own understanding, practices and procedures; and *condescension,* or the assuming of a sinful superiority over my brothers and sisters, prevail everywhere.

"To live above with the saints we love, Oh, that will be glory, But to live below with the saints we know, That is often another story!"

Wacky comedian Rodney Dangerfield said, "My wife and I sleep in separate bedrooms, take separate vacations, and eat separately at mealtimes. *We're doing all we can to keep this marriage together!"* Too many Christians are making the same kind of artificial moves to "hold things together."

Obviously, we need to discover the New Testament meaning of fellowship.

It should be evident that fellowship is not the mere gathering of a crowd of Christians.

Fellowship is far more than physical togetherness. A crowd is often nothing more than a large number of "loners" together, and this is just as likely to be true in church as anywhere else. Years ago, David Riesman wrote a book entitled, <u>The Lonely Crowd,</u> and *the title could well describe a Sunday morning crowd of churchgoers!* Furthermore, Christian fellowship is far more than congeniality among Christians. It is more than a warm feeling of personal affinity. Again, fellowship is not the climax of the Christian life. It is not an end in itself. It is a vital means to a number of other things in the Christian life.

Both newborn Christians and veteran believers need rich fellowship with other believers. If a Christian is not given such fellowship when he becomes a Christian, the failure is similar to a mother birthing a baby and putting it in a refrigerator, or out on a doorstep to fend for itself.

I recently picked up a book entitled, <u>Chinese Fairy Tales and Fantasies.</u> It told of a mystical bird that is only half a bird; it had only one eye, one wing, one leg. In order to fly, a "left-hand" bird must find, and cooperate with, a "right-hand" bird. Alone, each is earth-bound, flopping clumsily about. But together, they can soar across the sky. We can only pray that Christians might quickly learn such a lesson. Erich Fromm echoed this need as a universal human need. He wrote, "The deepest need of man is the need to overcome his separateness, to leave the prison of his aloneness. The absolute failure to achieve this aim means insanity. In fact, the word 'idiot' stems from the Greek word for 'a private person.'"

Every Christian should be carefully and extensively taught to live *relationally*. There are two kinds of theology — *revelational* theology and *relational* theology. The purpose of revelational theology is to foster and nurture right relationships (see Matthew 22:37-40). If a believer does not live openly and warmly in relationship with God and other believers, it does not make any difference how much right doctrine he knows and believes. I John 1:3-4 states the ideal: "That which we have seen and heard declare we unto you, that ye also may have fellowship with us: and truly our fellowship is with the Father, and with His Son, Jesus Christ. And these things write we unto you, that your joy may be full."

Too many of our hymns, books, magazines and sermons place an unbalanced and unhealthy emphasis on the isolated believer alone with God. For example, a popular old Christian song entitled "On the Jericho Road," begins with these words, "On the Jericho Road, there's room for just two. No more or no less, just Jesus and you." One wonders where that idea came from. I am certain of this: It didn't come from a visit to the Jericho Road, or from a visit to Scripture! It probably arose from our desire for autonomy, our appetite for personal piety to the neglect of other people, and the general atmosphere of our go-it-alone culture.

The problem we face is not new. During the Middle Ages, there lived a man known as Julian of Norwich. He came to be called, "Saint Julian." While he was very young, his church in the small English town of Norwich recognized his unusual piety and decided to give him the ultimate recognition. On the day of the elaborate recognition and investiture ceremony, Saint Julian was literally sealed into a small room that adjoined the cathedral. The walls enclosed him tightly, with only a small hole in the side. In that small, dark cubicle he would spend the rest of his life praying, administering blessings to passersby, and writing holy literature. Friends, we may be happy that Jesus was not like that, but we must also sadly admit that Julian of Norwich was not the last person to seal himself off from others — even under the pretext of piety, and *even in church.* The community of faith is often saturated with Saint Julians! And not one of us can assume superiority in the matter, because we are all first-graders in the school of relational theology!

Here, as in all matters, we desperately need balance. We have already talked about the believer's time alone with God in the Word and in prayer. Now, we must examine the balancing side of the scale — the great need for what Dr. Luke called ***"the fellowship."***

The Christian -- A Big Wheel

The Old Testament provides a picture of fellowship in one of its "types." The "type" is the Tabernacle which the children of Israel carried with them in the wilderness for purposes of worshiping God wherever they were. The boards of the Tabernacle were closely connected to the foundation, and thus to each other. In the type, the foundation represents Jesus, and the boards might represent all believers. As each believer truly adheres to Jesus by faith, he is necessarily adhered also to the other believers who are in the same relationship.

The first general epistle of the apostle Peter tells us that all Christians are living stones in God's building (I Peter 2:4-8). When an independent stone is made a part of a wall or a building, it normally:

(1) Has other stones around it. Some are *above* it, some are *below* it, and some are *on either side* of it. These are assigned positions, and have nothing to do with rank.

(2) Maintains its identity, though it has lost its isolation and independence. It is now part of a wall or a building, but it can still be clearly distinguished as an individual part of the wall or building.

(3) Lends its ability to carry weight and make a solid wall to all the other stones in the building. Its primary function from the point of its inclusion in the building is to play a role in relation to all other stones in the building.

In his great book, Mere Christianity, C. S. Lewis wrote, "You can get the idea plain if you think of us as a fleet of ships sailing in formation. The voyage will be a success only, in the first place, if the ships do not collide and get in one another's way; and, secondly, if each ship is seaworthy and has her engines in good order. As a matter of fact, you cannot have either of these two things without the other. If the ships keep on having collisions they will not remain seaworthy very long.

On the other hand, if their steering gears are out of order they will not be able to avoid collisions. Or, if you like, think of Christians as a band playing a tune. To get a good result, you need two things. Each player's individual instrument must be in tune and also each must come in at the right moment so as to combine with all the others." Before leaving Lewis' illustrations, let's itemize its parts:

    The Fleet of Ships
    The Band Playing a Tune
    Each ship must be seaworthy
    Each instrument must be in tune
    The ships must keep from colliding
    The instruments must play in unison
    The ships must sail under orders
    The players must follow the musical score

Let me ask you to give yourself a "fellowship test." Read this list of Scriptural injunctions and ask yourself, How well am I warmly and widely fulfilling these in fellowship with other Christians?

    "Love one another" — 12 times in the New Testament (example: John 13:34-35)
    "Receive one another" — Romans 15:7
    "Edify (build up) one another" — Romans 14:19
    "Do not judge one another" — Romans 14:13
    "Serve one another" — Galatians 5:13
    "Bear one another's burdens" — Galatians 6:2
    "Forgive one another" — Ephesians 4:32, Colossians 3:13
    "Submit to one another" — Ephesians 5:21
    "Show hospitality to one another" — I Peter 4:9
    "Lie not one to another" — Colossians 3:9
    "Do not slander one another" — James 4:11-12
    "Do not grumble against one another" — James 5:9

"Forbear (bear with) one another" — Ephesians 4:2, Colossians 3:13

"Minister to one another" — I Peter 4:10

"Teach and admonish one another" — Colossians 3:16, Romans 15:14

"Be humble toward one another" — I Peter 5:5

"Greet one another warmly" — Romans 16:16, I Corinthians 16:20, I Peter 5:14, II Corinthians 13:12, I Thessalonians 5:26

"Honor one another" — Romans 12:10

"Confess your sins one to another" — James 5:16

"Pray for one another" — James 5:16

"Care for one another" — I Corinthians 12:25

"Encourage one another" — Hebrews 3:13, Hebrews 10:25, I Thessalonians 5:11

Look each of these "one another" admonitions up in your Bible, study the concept carefully, and get the feel of the context in which each is found. *This is the **fellowship ethic** of Christianity!* However, most Christians have never noticed this ethic, because they have never read all these passages with this ethic in mind. Dear brother or sister, spend a lot of time mastering the meaning and the practice of these "one anothers." What a vast and incredible difference it would make if Christians started to widely practice this ethic! Let me encourage you to copy the above list and post it in a place where you will see it every day — and ask God for miracle-grace to do what each one tells you. Charles Spurgeon, the great English preacher, said, "Be much with those who are much with God. Make those your companions on earth, who will be your companions in heaven."

Before we leave the second spoke, let me mention some of the vital interpersonal ingredients which help to produce genuine fellowship.

One is *humility*. When humility prevails among believers, Satan is disarmed of the giant weapon of pride. Ego-struggles are replaced with the desire to lift, help and serve. Another ingredient is *honesty*. When honesty prevails, Satan is disarmed of the weapons of deceit, hypocrisy, and growing sin. Another is *humor*. When humor is free, natural, and unstrained, Satan is disarmed of the weapons of stuff-shirt saintliness and cold conviction. Everyone knows that great friction may easily develop among human beings when they are together. Humor acts like a "relief valve" which allows this friction to be reduced. Someone asked Rufus Mosely, "Do you think Jesus ever laughed?" He happily replied, "I don't know, but He sure fixed me up so that I can!" There is hardly anything more wholesome than Christians laughing *at* themselves and *among* themselves. A fourth ingredient that makes for fellowship is *harmony*. When harmony prevails among the people of God, Satan is disarmed of the weapons of strife and divisions. Read through the New Testament sometime soon, looking for the number of plural pronouns that are used for Christians. "We, us, they, them," are common in the New Testament.

Christians are people who are learning to live and serve in the plural! The final ingredient I would mention in the making of genuine fellowship is *helpfulness*. When helpfulness prevails among believers, Satan is disarmed of the weapons of compassion fatigue and despair. Would you rather be among people more characterized by —

    Humility or pride?
    Honesty or deceit?
    Humor or sophisticated coldness?
    Harmony or strife?
    Helpfulness or competitiveness?

The Christian -- A Big Wheel

Have you ever wondered why people in the far north wear more *mittens* in the winter than *gloves?* When people wear gloves, each finger has the protection from the elements by the fabric that surrounds it, but the finger is dependent upon its own heat alone. But when mittens are worn, each finger combines its heat with the heat of all the other fingers, and much greater warmth and health are the result. Christians, we need to take off the gloves and put on the mittens, lending our warmth and health to all other members of the Body of Christ.

Sir Edmund Hillary is renowned as the first man to lead an expedition to the top of Mount Everest in the Himalayan Mountains. He secured a tough Shirpa Indian guide named Tenzing Nordag, and Tenzing proved to be the most outstanding hero of the group. At one crisis spot on the ascent, Hillary slipped and fell into a crevice of the ice. Had he not been attached to the others, he would have fallen into an irretrievable position. However, Tenzing worked slowly and tenaciously for quite a long time, until he had pulled Hillary up again and secured the entire group of climbers. When Hillary was interviewed by reporters later, he mentioned this feat of rescue to them. They hurried to Tenzing and asked about his heroic leadership. In his reply, Tenzing said, "When I was a boy, a veteran climber transmitted to me his love for climbing mountains, and taught me to climb. I have been climbing ever since. Furthermore, I have spent my life training climbers. And it is an unwritten rule among us, that climbers always help each other." The Bible said it long before Tenzing Nordag did: "They helped everyone his neighbor; and everyone said to his brother, Be of good courage." Dear brothers and sisters, we must not only climb the mountain ourselves — we must help all other climbers, and we must spend our lives training mountain-climbers.

G. Avery Lee, in his book, <u>A Fellowship for Sinners</u>, says that the Indian teepee might be used to symbolize the dynamic church. "Each pole in the teepee is held up by all the other poles. Together the poles hold up the teepee. In a church, each Christian serves as a minister or priest to others. Each pleads the case of the other — gives him strength, prays for him, and assists in sustaining his faith."

When this exchange of support takes place and this common ministry is functioning among large numbers of Christians, there you will find a living, energized, growing church.

In Ephesians 3:18, Paul prayed that the Ephesian Christians might "be able to comprehend with all saints what is the breadth, and length, and depth, and height of the love of Christ, which passeth knowledge." Note that it is only "with *all* saints" that any *one* saint can understand the love of Christ!

Fellowship is not an elective in the school of discipleship; it is a required course!

IV. THE FOURTH SPOKE — WITNESSING

The fourth spoke of the wheel is *witnessing* to those who are without Christ. In one version of our Marching Orders, Jesus said, "Ye shall receive power, after the Holy Spirit has come upon you, and you shall be witnesses unto me both in Jerusalem, and in Judea, and in Samaria, and unto the uttermost part of the earth" (Acts 1:8). He first invited His disciples with the words, "Follow me, and I will make you fishers of men" (Matthew 4:19). Paul wrote much later, "We preach Christ, warning every man, and teaching every man in all wisdom, that we may present every man complete in Christ Jesus." Note the two thrusts of the Christian movement: Evangelism and Education. The winning of the lost, and the

The Christian -- A Big Wheel

making of disciples — for the purpose of presenting every man mature in Christ Jesus. What a commanding task!

Evangelism, or witnessing, or soul-winning, is the *fourth spoke* of the wheel. The order is not accidental. The first three disciplines — the use of the Word of God, prayer, and the practice of genuine fellowship — provide the power base from which witnessing is launched. Missionary D. T. Niles said, "Evangelism is an overflow of the Christian's life, not a mere program of activities." The Christian only "abounds" (overflows) if he "abides in Christ." His abiding is enhanced by the Word, prayer, and fellowship. If these are in their proper place and balance, then witnessing is inevitable. *"God tends to use the instrument that is nearest at hand."* Live near to Him, and He will use you to win others. The Holy Spirit is the "Booking Agent" of the witnessing Christian. When the Christian is walking with God, the Holy Spirit is filling him, and the Spirit has ways of drawing the right people into his circles at the most opportune time. I have seen this — and experienced it personally — many, many times. And what a blessing it is when it happens!

In a letter to Sheldon van Aucken, C. S. Lewis wrote, "My feeling about people in whose conversion I have been allowed to play a part is always a mixture of joy, awe and even fear. At such a time, I feel like a boy might feel on being first allowed to fire a rifle. The disproportion between his puny finger on the trigger and the thunder and lightning which follow is alarming. And the seriousness with which the other party takes my words always raises the doubt whether I have taken them seriously enough myself. I think of myself as a fellow-patient in the same hospital as the one to whom I am speaking. I was just admitted a little earlier than he, and thus perhaps can give some advice."

I think Lewis is absolutely right. Steve Brown wrote, "If our sin can't be used as a witness as well as our goodness, we have a serious problem. The church ought to be a fellowship of people who are terribly honest. But instead, we often play a game called let-me-show-you-that-I'm-a-good-Christian."

With regard to witnessing *technique*, the possibilities range from the highly technical (the extensive Evangelism Explosion training, as an example) to the very brief and very simple (the use of the "Four Spiritual Laws" booklet, as an example). Personally, I want to know how to use all of them, and yet not be bound to any one at any time. It is enough to always have on hand a personal favorite. I have used for years and to great advantage the concentric-circle explanation of the nature of man (spirit, soul, and body), showing what it means to be lost, how a person is saved, what happens when a person is saved, and the different kinds of people there are in the world. Another easy-to-use technique for abbreviated contact with a lost person is the "one-verse method." This can take any one of several forms. Here is one which uses Romans 6:23 to maximum advantage. The verse says, "For the wages of sin is death, but the gift of God is eternal life through Jesus Christ our Lord." Note that:

"Wages" are contrasted to "gift"
"Of sin" is contrasted to "of God"
"Death" is contrasted to "eternal life"

And the difference between the two sides is your relationship to Jesus Christ as Lord. This use of one verse can be abbreviated or amplified, as the occasion and the opportunity may call for it.

With regard to witnessing *place*, let me refer you to the study entitled, "Let's Go Fishing!" Someone very wisely said,

"It seems that the alternatives in today's church are either *cop-out, burnout,* or *go out.*"

Two coaches (you would think me biased about the mentality of certain coaches if I told you which sport they coached) went north to fish. They got their equipment, made the trip, found a location, pitched a tent, and cut a hole in the ice. A loud voice broke the silence, saying, "There are no fish under the ice." They were startled. The words were repeated. One of the coaches said quietly, "Is that you, Lord?" The voice answered, "No, this is the manager of the ice-skating arena."

If you discovered a cure for AIDS and someone asked you how many people do you want to receive this cure, you would answer, "Everyone who is infected." Friends, everyone is infected with the disease of sin. When a person is saved, the disease is "in *remission*" (!), and the saved person awaits the final and perfect cure. Meanwhile, he is in a position of perfect security; the disease can still frustrate and contaminate him, but it cannot destroy him. And it is his mission to tell every infected person he meets where he found the Person who arrested him (!) and the cure that arrested his disease! To change the analogy, a Christian lives like one who has been rescued from a burning house. He is overwhelmed with the wonder of being saved, yet he is broken at the thought of loved ones left behind. As long as there is opportunity, he must join the other workers in the Rescue Squad and pluck those still in the house to a place of safety, like "brands plucked from the burning" (Zechariah 3).

A final word needs to be said about *courage* in witnessing. In this day of pluralism, relativism and unholy tolerance, every philosophy, ideology, and religion are perfectly acceptable — except the supernatural Gospel of Jesus Christ. A book of Christian apologetics would be required to show the reason for this strange mixture of tolerance toward error and intolerance toward truth. But the Christian must remember that he does not get his permission from the world; he obeys a Mandate from Heaven's King, One who has "all authority." And he must daily remember that when he witnesses, he is actually *only a second witness.* There is an unfailing law at work whenever a Christian proclaims the Gospel. The one witnessing is never God's first witness in the hearer's life. God Himself is already there before the witness is given. The Holy Spirit has been at work in every unsaved person's life in numerous ways long before a Christian witness speaks the Word of truth to him. So the witness never approaches anyone "cold." It is not possible for a Christian to give the first witness to a lost person. The Christian never arrives in anyone's life before the Holy Spirit does. I never touch someone before God touches him. When God leads us to somebody, He has been there before us. When a lost person is saved, it is only a fulfillment of the Biblical statement which says, "In the mouth of two or three witnesses, a thing will be established."

In the movie musical, Camelot, legendary King Arthur instructed his knights to ask every person they met if they had heard the story of Camelot. If not, they were to tell the story loudly and clearly. Our Lord, King Jesus, has instructed His disciples to ask every person they meet about their relationship with Him. If they are not in a favorable relationship with Him, the disciples are to tell the story loudly and clearly.

A Welsh Christian wrote these words after he had come to North America and visited Niagara Falls many years ago. "The Niagara excites our wonder, fills us with amazement, perhaps awe; but one Niagara is enough for a continent. That same continent, however, requires tens of thousands of silver fountains and lucid brooks; and let me tell you — those clear springs and busy streams, whose names have never been registered in any geography, prove an inestimably greater blessing to the American continent than the mighty Falls whose fame fills the world." In evangelism, the greatest need on earth is an army of ordinary but faithful soul-winners, combining with all others in the army, and giving regular and radiant witness concerning Jesus Christ. This is far more important than the great crusades and the great crusaders, as important as these high-profile leaders and activities may be.

Every Christian is pictured by this wheel. God wants every Christian to be "a big wheel" for Him. But smooth and steady progress is possible on a regular basis in the Christian life only if all the "vital parts" are kept in their respective places and in good working order. The hub of all of it is Jesus Himself. The individual believer's relationship with Him is sustained through the four spokes -- the Word of God, prayer, fellowship, and witnessing. These activities also allow the Life of Christ to reach the rim of the wheel, the productive part of the Christian life, the place "where the rubber meets the road."

An old man had lived alone for several years after the death of his wife. Finally, his children persuaded him to move into an old people's rest home so he could be adequately cared for in the closing years of his life. He finally consented and moved in. The first day he was there, he went down to the cafeteria to eat a meal. He took his plate to a small round table, sat alone, and began to eat, observing his new surroundings as he ate. Just in front of him, he noticed a little lady sitting at the next table alone, and he observed that she kept staring at him throughout the meal. He looked away, looked back at her later, and she was still staring at him. He diverted his gaze from her for a long time, looked back again — and she was still staring at him. This continued until he finished his meal. He took his empty plate back to the counter, placed it there, then turned and boldly walked over to her table. "Ma'am," he said, "I think I detect that you have been sitting there staring at me all during my meal. Why have you been staring at me?" She replied, "Well, I'll declare, sir, you look just like my third husband!" "Your third husband?" he exclaimed in amazement. "Good heavens! How many times have you been married?" "Twice!" she answered. You see, she had **big plans** for him! *However, it would not have made any difference what plans she had for him — if he didn't agree with her plans.* Dear Christian, it is apparent by several considerations that **God has Big Plans for each of His children.** He really wants you to be "a big wheel" in His Big Push as He seeks to drive the Enemy back and occupy his territory. But if this is to happen, you must fully play your assigned role. Is the Hub intact in your life? Are the Supply Lines open? Are you moving for Jesus according to His Specifications? Is the world being impacted in an enlarging way because of your disciple-making activities?

A recent "B. C." cartoon shows one of the aboriginal cavemen standing at the large round rock labeled, "Patent Office." Another caveman has approached with an invention in his hand. The patent officer says, "You're kidding! A perpetual motion machine?" The "inventor" answers, "Yep .... but there's one little snag." The patent officer asks, "What's that?" The inventor wistfully sighs, "It won't start."

What good is a perpetual motion machine if it won't start? What good are all the "vital parts" of the Christian life if they don't function? Christian, it is not necessary to "re-invent the wheel"; it is just necessary to be sure all the parts are in place and the wheel is moving according to the Driver's Purpose.

LIFE'S MOST GLORIOUS FACTS

Romans 8:1-3:

There is therefore now no condemnation to them which are in Christ Jesus, who walk not after the flesh, but after the Spirit. For the law of the Spirit of life in Christ Jesus hath made me free from the law of sin and death. For what the law could not do, in that it was weak through the flesh, God sending his own Son in the likeness of sinful flesh, and for sin, condemned sin in the flesh:

Napoleon Bonaparte once remarked that "there is nothing so stubborn and irresistible as a fact." A detective on a once-popular television show was renowned for his restrictive statement, "The facts, Ma'am (or Sir), just give me the facts; I'm interested in nothing but the facts." Truth is more than facts. Facts are just historically accurate statements, but truth as a category has permanent and determinative dimensions to it. According to Jesus, it is the "truth" that will "set you free." Truth is more than facts.

Gospel truth has many substantial facts at its heart. In fact, it is hard to distinguish in the case of the Gospel between truth and facts. I am calling this message, "Life's Most Glorious Facts." These facts are true.

I. There is a POSITION to EXPLORE, 8:1b

First, there is the fact of an incredible position which every Christian occupies, a position which must be constantly explored. The position is stated in three words in verse one, *"in Christ Jesus."* Jesus Himself initiated this idea of the believer's position in Him in the great fifteenth chapter of the Gospel of John when He used this phrase six times in the opening verses of the chapter: *"in Me." "Every branch* (the symbol in the passage for a Christian) *in Me." "He who abides in Me." "Abide in Me."*

Paul took up this concept as His favorite expression. In fact, in his epistles, he used the phrases "in Him," "in Christ," and "in Christ Jesus" (as in our text) no less than 164 times! A key example is this well-known verse, "If any man is *in Christ*, he is a new creation; old things have passed away, all things have become new." This verse indicates that something experiential (he becomes a "new creature") and something positional (he is placed "in Christ") occurs when a person becomes a Christian.

The concept of the believer's new position was "locked into" Paul at the hour of his conversion. His two leading doctrines thereafter were the doctrine of the resurrection of Christ and the doctrine of the believer's position in Christ. Both of these were initiated into Paul's life, Paul's experience, Paul's heart, Paul's mind on the day of his conversion. When on the Damascus Road, he asked the Divine Intruder, "Who are you?" He answered, "I am Jesus," and Paul's entire life was turned right-side-up. This was the very Jesus whom he knew to have been crucified and buried – but here the dead Jesus was alive and speaking to him *after He had been killed and buried!* So the doctrine of the resurrection was profoundly lodged in Paul when he was saved.

But the Intruder said even more: "I am Jesus *whom you have been persecuting.*" Paul might have answered, "Say what? *Me*, persecuting *you*? I don't even *know* you; I've never *met* you; I have never even *seen* you?" But the Voice clearly said, "You have been persecuting *Me*." So Paul knew immediately, by both intelligence, intuition, insight and illumination, that when anyone touches a Christian, he touches Christ! Christ and the Christian are so identified with each other, in such union, that you cannot deal with one without dealing in the same act with the other. He knew at this moment that every Christian is "in Christ." He knew that a Christian is incorporated into Christ at the moment of salvation, and that incorporation into Christ at conversion means an inviolable identification with Christ thereafter.

Dear Christian, do you realize that the most important thing about you is not *who* you are, or *what* you are, or what you *do*, but *where you are.* The most important thing about you is not your *person*, or your *performance*, or your *product*, or your *social position*; it is rather your *spiritual position*. It is the supernatural and miraculous fact, secured by the grace and power of God, that you are "in Christ Jesus."

Biblically, you are in Christ like Noah and his family were in the ark. The ark is a type of Christ, and it was God who shut them in the ark. So it is God Who, by a miracle of His love, grace and power, places you in Christ at the moment of your conversion – and shuts you in! The storm was raging outside, loosing its full destruction upon the whole unprotected world of men, but Noah and his family had perfect salvation and perfect security inside the ark. In the same way, while the wrath of God abides on everyone outside of Christ today (Romans 1:18, John 3:36), the person who has trusted Christ is in a position of perfect salvation and perfect security "in Christ."

Just as the unintentional manslayer in Israel could be saved by getting inside of one of the "cities of refuge" provided for his sanctuary, safety and security, so the sinner who flees to Christ in faith is saved from the avenging Holiness, Justice and Law of God by getting into the Person of Refuge who was provided for his sanctuary, safety and security. The moment he trusts Christ, he is placed into Christ, thus escaping the destruction invited by his sins, and thus enjoying the provisions of his newfound Savior.

Just as the Israelites in Egypt on Passover night were secure by getting inside a house whose doorposts were sprinkled with prescribed sacrificial blood, so the trembling sinner who takes refuge inside the sanctuary prescribed in His Word and provided through the shedding of His blood, is safe from the Death Angel who will visit every unprotected person with the just wrath of God against sin. This is another Biblical picture of what it means to be "in Christ."

Just as Rahab hid herself in the house with the scarlet thread in the window and thus was secure from judgment, so the believer who seeks resort in Him whose most conspicuous provision is the scarlet sign of His own blood will find himself perfectly protected "in Christ."

Some years ago, while reading a book on the Christian life, I came across this suggestive illustration. "It's as though the whole human race were gathered in a giant Boeing 747 super jet which had been hijacked and was flying full speed to a place we didn't want to go. We land to refuel and are rescued. All who wish can enter another Boeing 747 which immediately takes off and turns back toward the plane's original destination. In Adam, all of us were hijacked, captured and imprisoned by sin. We were subjected to someone whose intentions toward us were evil, and headed for death and punishment. When we became Christians, we changed course.

By turning away from sin and trusting in Christ, a spiritual change occurred that united us with Christ. We deplaned from our seats in Adam, and found our places in Christ. Almost before we knew it, we were forgiven, placed under Christ's protection and governance, given the gift of His perfect righteousness, given His Spirit and His relationship with the Father – in short, we were given the gift of eternal life. Forever after, we are defined by the phrase, 'in Christ.'"

While reading a book by Pastor Rick Yohn, I found another beautiful illustration of our position in Christ. Upon the insistence of his two children, Yohn bought a hamster as a pet for the children. The matter was complicated by the fact that they already had a pet dog, and the dog was excited and aggressive about the new pet which competed with him for the children's attention and affection. The tension was resolved when Rick Yohn purchased a large plastic ball which could rotate with the hamster's movements. The hamster was placed in the big ball and immediately began to play on all the features inside the ball. The dog would animatedly jump around the ball and bark excitedly at the hamster-and-ball arrangement, but after a time, the dog realized that the hamster was unreachable inside the ball and he settled down to his own interests outside the ball. The Christian is like that hamster – he is in Christ, where there are a plethora of "enjoyable features," and he is safe and secure no matter who is outside desiring his discomfort and destruction.

One more matter before we go beyond this point. There is a vocation for the Christian because he is "in Christ." An entire new mental science has developed, entitled "positional awareness." It can be clearly illustrated in the diverse worlds of aviation and sports. In aviation, a pilot is taught to fly by instruments, not just by sight or feeling. He is taught that the position of the airplane in alignment with its flight plan, its received positional signals, and its on-course adjustments to those positional requirements, are all-important if the plane is to be navigated safely and successfully to its intended destination. The same is true of a Christian. He is to live by faith, not by sight or feelings. He is to trust the Flight Plan given in the Word of God and consciously maintain his fixed position "in Christ." This is called "abiding in Me" by Jesus (John 15). I call it "continual centering in Christ." This is the vocation of a Christian after he is saved.

The importance of "positional awareness" can also be illustrated in almost all sports. A coach's admonition to "play your position" is crucial in all team sports, and position is equally crucial in sports which call only for individual participation. The team player who leaves his position may be a hero for one play, but he may be the game-forfeiting goat later. Opponents notice quickly when a position is abandoned, and they will certainly exploit the failure when the game in on the line.

So it is in the Christian life. The position of a Christian is fixed by the grace and power of God at his conversion, and it never varies. He is positionally perfect from the moment of his salvation, but his *practice* often does not match his *position*. He has lost his "positional awareness" and is acting in his own autonomy – and the Enemy will exploit the weakness when the game is on the line! I John 2:27 admonishes us, "And now, little children, *abide in Christ*, that when He shall appear, we may have confidence, and not be ashamed before Him at His coming."

Here, then, is the new position of the believer, a position which needs to be continually explored, explained and exploited in the fellowship of believers.

II. There is a PRIVILEGE (or a PROMISE) to ENJOY, 8:1a

Second, the text informs us of an incredible *promise to be enjoyed.* Romans 8:1 says, "There is therefore now no condemnation to those who are in Christ Jesus." Thank God for texts like this! When a believer first reads such texts, and begins to realize what they mean, he tends to question that they could really be true, and even to doubt their reliability. "This might be true, but surely not for me, and especially at this moment, in this place, and with me in my present condition." We tend to associate the degree of condemnation we experience with the degree of sin and failure we are aware of in our lives at any moment, but this is a total fallacy. Remember that this promise is not based in any way on your practice of the Christian life or on your performance of good deeds (or on the purging of your life of sins and bad deeds), but it is based entirely on your perfect position "in Christ Jesus." "There is ... no condemnation to those who are in Christ Jesus." If your position can vary, your appropriation of this promise can legitimately rise and fall proportionately. But if your position is perfect, so is this promise.

Let me begin to explore this incredible promise of "no condemnation" by examining its opposite. The promise is totally true for every person in Christ, and its opposite is totally true for every person outside of Christ. Here is the opposite truth: "There is now nothing *but* condemnation for those who are *not* in Christ Jesus." This, too, is an absolute truth. You see again that *everything is a matter of position.* Personality counts for nothing here; intelligence quotient counts for nothing here; community or social rank counts for nothing here; vocational position counts for nothing here; service contribution and personal performance count for nothing here. The beautiful fact of "no condemnation" belongs only to the person who is "in Christ Jesus," but it belongs perfectly to him.

Note the clear statements of Jesus at this point. In John 3:16-18, Jesus said, "For God so loved the world that He gave His only begotten Son, that whosoever believes in Him shall not perish, but have everlasting life. For God sent not His Son into the world to condemn the world, but that the world through Him might be saved. He who believes on Him is not condemned, but he who believes not is condemned already, because he has not believed on the only begotten Son of God." So it is not God's initial design to condemn human beings. He did not send His Son to condemn people. Then why are so many people condemned? They are condemned for two reasons: (1) They were already under condemnation when Jesus came; they were *personally* condemned because of what they were (sinners) and because of what they had done (broken God's law in a wholesale manner); (2) Since they confirmed their own condemnation by their response to Jesus when He came, they were *practically* condemned because they rejected the only One who could remove their sin and its condemnation.

Jesus further explained (John 3:19-21), "And this is the condemnation, that light is come into the world (see John 1:4, 6-9, and John 8:12), and men loved darkness rather than light, because their deeds were evil. For every one that does evil hates the light, neither comes to the light, lest his deeds should be reproved. But he who does truth comes to the light, that his deeds may be made manifest, that they are wrought in God." Jesus provided "happy light" on the matter of man's just condemnation because of sin when he said (John 5:24), "Verily, verily, I say unto you, He who hears my word, and believes on Him who sent Me, has everlasting life, and *shall not come into condemnation,* but has passed from death unto life."

In summary, by nature, I am *in myself*, and in *sin* (and theologically, I am *in Adam)*; therefore, I am justly condemned by a holy God who is morally committed to support righteousness and destroy (the unbelievably destructive power of) sin. But *by grace,* I can escape the just condemnation that is due to me because of sin, and be *totally and perfectly justified* before God through faith in Jesus Christ. In that new context, the text is absolutely true: "There is therefore now no condemnation to those who are in Christ Jesus."

I carefully call your attention to what Paul did *not* say here (or elsewhere). He did *not* say, "There is no *cause* for condemnation" in the lives of Christians. Every honest and transparent Christian knows and will admit that there is still plenty of cause for condemnation in his daily life and practice, but the verse still happily declares that "there is now no condemnation to those who are in Christ Jesus." The verse does *not* say, "There are no *complications*" in the lives of Christians, for that certainly is not true. Indeed, the very fact that he is "in Christ" will create further complications for him – as if he did not have enough complications merely because of the calculated risks of daily living! So being "in Christ Jesus" is no guarantee against life's complications. Then, the text does *not* say, "There are no *"conflicts"* in the lives of Christians, for that certainly is not true. As long as "your adversary, the devil, walks around as a roaring lion, seeking whom he may devour," and as long as he is unrestrained as "the accuser of the brethren," every line of communication open to Satan (even his audience with God – see Job 1) will be filled with ceaseless charges and accusations against Christians. And the truth is that every Christian gives him plenty of useable material to work with every day in building his case! He will register his charges before God, before a lost world, and even before the believer himself – and the result for the believer will be incrimination and intimidation if he does not know how to disarm and disqualify "that old serpent, the devil."

What is the believer to do when the devil marshals his valid arguments and states his case? The believer should stand reminded that he has a counselor for his defense, a personal Lawyer, "Jesus Christ the righteous," in heaven to secure his case before God (see I John 2:2). In practical experience, when Satan's accusation reaches the believer, he should reply, "You go talk to my Lawyer!" Satan, the prosecuting attorney, will say, "But you don't have a leg to stand on (snakes know a lot about 'not having a leg to stand on'!); your case is not defensible." Then you reply, "Look, I don't call a lawyer when I don't *need* one; I call a lawyer *when I don't have a good case. That's when I need the best lawyer I can get.*" And, dear Christian, that's why Jesus is called the "Friend of sinners." He has made every provision necessary for the full and total settlement of our sins, the full and total satisfaction of the Holy Law and Perfect Justice of God, and the full and total guarantee of our eternal salvation and security – and He is the Attorney for my Defense and the Guarantor (the "Surety") of my salvation before God now and forever. "Satan, all my dealings with you now will be conducted through my Lawyer; my case rests in His hands. *You go talk to my Lawyer!*" And Satan dares not do that, because it is dangerous for Him to go into the Presence of Jesus. He is over-matched in that Presence, and he knows it. The text does *not* say, "There is no *accusation*" for believers, but never mind; all possible accusations were perfectly settled by our Attorney before court convened! "The Lord is my Lawyer," and He has never lost a case!

Note, also, that the text does not say, "There are now no *consequences*" in the lives of Christians. The fact that there is no condemnation for sin to those who are in Christ Jesus does not mean that sin's consequences are removed from a justified person. The sin may be completely forgiven, the sinner may be completely justified, but this does not prevent the occurrence of serious consequences following the sin.

A father watched sadly as his son rebelled against his authority and went out into a life of serious sin. Every time the boy came home with the signs of sin upon him, the father drove a nail into the door facing at the entrance into the boy's room. Months later, the boy brokenly confessed his sin, asking and receiving God's forgiveness and his father's as well. Both forgave him and the boy was restored to the fellowship of both fathers. The same day, the father removed all the nails from the door facing. When the boy looked at the evidence, he tearfully remarked, "Dad, you removed the nails, but the gaping holes remain." The father gently replied, "Son, that's the way it is with sin. The sin may be forgiven, but the consequences of it cannot be removed." The text does not say, "There are no consequences to those who are in Christ Jesus."

Now, we will examine the promise itself. "There is therefore now no condemnation to those who are in Christ Jesus." Note the two small words that are similar, "now" and "no." "There is *now* no condemnation to those who are in Christ Jesus." This is the promise of a present reality in the life of every Christian. What is life but "now"? Both time and eternity are only a succession of "nows". For a believer in Christ, in *this* now, in *every* now, in *any* now, there is no condemnation.

Though a "guilty" verdict has been declared against every sinner, and though a death sentence has been imposed upon every sinner, God has reversed the verdict and revoked the penalty for those who are "in Christ Jesus." No true believer in Christ has ever faced God's condemnation after his salvation. Because of his position in Christ Jesus the believer is forever placed beyond the reach of immediate condemnation, future condemnation and eternal hell. What a Gospel!

Finally, consider the word "no." "There is now *no* condemnation to those who are in Christ Jesus." The word "no" is a tiny word, but it is a total, complete, absolute word. What a thrilling reality! As a Christian, in spite of the fact that I fully deserve condemnation in myself because of my sins, and in spite of the fact that the sin of any unsaved person would continue in eternity and its judgment would attend it, making hell eternal, nonetheless I am now completely and unconditionally free of condemnation because I am "in Christ Jesus." Thus, I am saved now and forever, and there is no longer any condemnation possible for me.

Firefighters often use a special technique to fight big and stubborn forest fires. They go to a place well ahead of the advancing wall of fire and deliberately set "back fires," fires which burn toward the advancing fire. Then they quench the part of the fire burning nearest them. When the raging flames of the oncoming fire reach the burned-over area, there is nothing flammable left for them to ignite and thus the fire can be brought under control. In the same manner, God exhausted His just condemnation of sin in the infinite death of His perfect Son at Calvary. When a sinner trusts Jesus Christ and His payment for sin, he stands in the burned-over area, where God's wrath against sin has been totally exhausted, and thus he is *free of condemnation*. What a glorious truth! What a great promise to claim! What a great privilege to enjoy!

III. There is a POWER to be EMPLOYED, 8:2-3

Third, the text indicates that there is a great *power to be employed* by every Christian in living the Christian life. "For the law of the Spirit of life in Christ Jesus has made me free from the law of sin and death. For what the law could not do, in that it was weak through the flesh, God sending His own Son in the likeness of sinful flesh, and for sin, condemned sin in the flesh."

What a statement this is! Note that three laws are mentioned in these verses. You've probably heard of the Four Spiritual Laws. Well, there are *three spiritual laws* mentioned in these verses. In textual order, they are: "the law of the Spirit of life," "the law of sin and death," and (simply) *"the* law." The three laws, when arranged in the order of human experience, are slightly different in order. The order of experience is that "the law of sin and death" is experienced first, then "the law" (the law of God given through Moses) is experienced second, then "the law of the Spirit of life in Christ Jesus" is experienced last (this last-named law has operated only in the life of a Christian – with continuing implications), while the other two laws occur automatically in the life of every human being. Let's consider these three laws in the order of human experience.

A. The law that **CONTROLS** *all lost people*

The first law any human being experiences is "the law of sin and death." This law begins to operate in each person's life the moment he is conceived, then it completely governs his life when he is born into human experience on earth. This is the law that *controls* every lost person on earth.

"Sin and death" are always closely connected in the Bible. They are the Siamese twins of human experience. Where sin occurs, death follows. They are like two sides of the same coin. The connection between them is not a chance connection. In the Garden of Eden, God stated a prohibition regarding the fruit of a certain tree; "You shall not eat of it," He said. Then He added, "In the day you eat thereof, you shall surely die." Ezekiel 18:4 echoes this law when it says, "The soul that sins, it shall surely die." Romans 6:23 declares that "the wages of sin is death." Romans 5:12 says that "by one man (Adam) sin entered into the world, and death by sin." James 1:15 says, "Sin, when it is finished, brings forth death." All of these texts express "the law of sin and death." This is a universal law, a law that is self-executing. No sinner has ever survived sin – it always kills him! Even the sinless Son of God did not survive sin when He took it upon Himself on the Cross – it killed Him! The chief illusion of sin-deceived and self-deceived man is, "I can have sin without having death," but that illusion will be quickly dispelled (though his awakening may come too late). Death always follows sin. This is a cause-and-effect law. It is called a "law" because it operates with fixed and regular dependability. It is completely trustworthy and reliable. I repeat: this law, the law of sin and death, controls every lost person on earth.

B. *The law that **CONDEMNS** all lost people*

Next in human experience is "the law," verse three. This is a reference to the law of God mediated to the human race through Moses. This law is recorded in the Old Testament (primarily in the Pentateuch, the first five books), and is summarized in the Ten Commandments (recorded in Exodus 20). This law had several purposes (see the separate study on the law), and one of them is to reveal human sin and point the sinner to the only Savior, the Lord Jesus Christ. The law fully exposes man's moral failure! Several texts of the New Testament clearly state this purpose of the law. In Romans 7:7, Paul said, "I would not have known what sin really was except through the law." Romans 4:15 says, "The law works wrath: for where no law is, there is no transgression."

Galatians 3:19 supports that statement when it says, "Wherefore then serves the law? It was added because of transgressions." Note the word "transgression" in both of these verses. Each word used for sin in the Bible has a very specialized meaning: the word, "sin," for example, means "to miss the mark." "Transgression" means "the deliberate and willful crossing of a prescribed boundary." The seriousness of sin could never have been truly recognized if no standard for righteousness had been given, and that is the purpose of the law. The law helps the sinner realize the heinous nature of his sin, and enables him to recognize the true value of Jesus Christ as Savior. When the law was given, and men continued to sin, they now violated a known standard. Thus, they could recognize the nature of their sin as "transgression." Romans 5:20 says, "The law entered that the offence might abound." The overflowing and deadly nature of sin could never be fully known if the law had not been given. "By the commandment (of the law), sin was recognized as exceeding sinful" (Romans 7:13). So law both aggravated and exposed the sin of man. Though it exposed the moral standard of God, the law could neither prevent us from violating it nor could it provide dynamic so we could fulfill it.

Suppose you are standing near the Rock of Gibraltar at the western end of the Mediterranean Sea, wanting to come to the United States of America. You have a map in your hands, and it gives you directions. But you can't get to your destination by reading the directions on the map. In the same way, the Law of God gives directions, but does not supply the dynamic to bring you to your destination. If you set out swimming, the map cannot "get you there" because it is *weak through your flesh*. What you need is a boat or an airplane which will *cover* you and *carry* you to your destination, and supply all your needs along the way.

So the law of God, which is "holy, and just, and good" (Romans 7:12), was never meant to provide a map to heaven, or a way of salvation, for sinners. Rather, it was to cause the offence of sin to be fully exposed, and to condemn it. The law of God, which is good in itself, became an instrument of condemnation and death to us because of the sinfulness of our lives. Romans 7:13 says, "Sin, that it might appear sin, worked death in me by that which was good."

The text explains the source and cause of man's moral failure. "For what the law could not do in that it was weak through the flesh ..." The problem is not in God's law, which is "holy, just and good" (Romans 7:12), but in the sinner who simply cannot keep the law.

The text indicates that there were two laws in man's experience, and those two laws were in violent collision. The *law of God* required him to do what was *right*; the *law of sin* compelled him to do what was *wrong*. He could neither *fulfill* the law of God, nor *escape* the law of sin. It is no wonder, then that the law is called "the ministration of death and condemnation" (II Corinthians 3:7, 9). The "bottom line" of human experience is that God is the great Plaintiff in the Court of the universe, and He has brought a serious indictment against mankind. Damage has been done by man's moral choice – great dishonor has been brought to the Divine throne, and the moral structure of the universe is seriously threatened by man's sin – and no excuse man can make can erase the guilt of his crimes or evade the penalty they require.

In John Bunyan's Pilgrim's Progress, the author presents several pictures which reveal the hopelessness of trying to save yourself by living by the law. Pilgrim is seeking moral guidance in his pilgrimage, and Mr. Worldly Wiseman counsels him to see Mr. Legality. Mr. Legality, of course, represents the law. When Pilgrim asks directions to Mr. Legality's house, Mr. Worldly Wiseman says, "Do you see yonder high Hill?" "Yes," answers Pilgrim, "very well." Mr. Worldly Wiseman says, "By that Hill you must go, and the first house you come at is his." The narrative then adds, "So

Christian turned out of his way, to go to Mr. Legality's house for help. But behold, when he was got now hard by the Hill, it seemed so high, and also that side of it that was next to the Wayside, did hang so much over, that Christian was afraid to venture further, lest the Hill should fall on his head. There came also flashes of fire out of the Hill, that made Christian afraid that he should be burned." The sinner fails to keep the law because he is "weak through the flesh," and these are the threats of the law against the failing sinner.

Scaled down to its basic statement, Hebrews 10:1 says, "The law . . . can never . . . make . . . perfect." Mark this down: only perfect people are going to heaven! The only standard of entrance into heaven is the standard of perfection. But the law of God given through Moses cannot make sinners perfect, because of the weakness of their flesh. That law only *condemns* sinful men. So all men are condemned by the law.

Martin Luther, in his usual abrupt and candid way, said, "The law of God is a mirror, a hammer and a whip." The law as a mirror reflects our true sinful nature back to us when we look into that mirror. The law as a hammer smashes and shatters self-trust, thus precluding the possibility of self-salvation. And the law as a whip drives us to Christ as our only hope of salvation. In Galatians, Paul said that the purpose of the law was to serve as the sinner's "escort" (KJV, "schoolmaster") to bring him to Christ.

C. *The law that* **COUNTERACTS** *the other two laws*

There is a third and final law in the text, and it is this law that provides the solution to the deadly effects of the first two laws. It is called "the law of the Spirit of life in Christ Jesus." This law *contradicts* and *counteracts* the other two laws. How does this third law *correct* the human failure that is induced by the other two laws?

Note the sharp succession of powerful phrases in the text. "The law could not (save) because of the weakness of the flesh." Theoretically, a person *can* get to heaven by keeping the law. Galatians 3:12 says, "The man that does (all things that are written in the book of the law) shall live in them." However, anyone who hopes to save himself by his own law-keeping should be sure that he fully understands the terms. The terms of self-saving are these: If you wish to get to heaven by your own goodness, then 100% of you (you personally) must keep 100% of the law 100% of the time – from the moment of your conception through the moment of your death. Rots o' ruck! You can dismiss the possibility without another thought, because you not only cannot deserve heaven by your performance, your performance clearly deserves hell! Because of this failure of man, God has graciously acted in love and mercy to redeem helpless, sinful man.

"God sending His own Son." What a world of truth in a phrase? Here we see: (1) The sovereign initiative (grace) of God in acting to save man; (2) The eternal pre-existence of the Son of God; He was "sent" from a previous existence, relationship, status and location; (3) The Deity of the Son of God; He is co-existent, co-efficient, co-equal, and co-eternal with the Father.

"In the likeness of sinful flesh." Again, it is absolutely crucial to note what the text does not say. It does not say that Jesus came "in the likeness of flesh." This would suggest that His humanity was only a "likeness" to human flesh and not really flesh at all. But Jesus came to this world as a real "flesh and bone" human being. Then, the text does not say that He came "in sinful flesh." This would mean that He is a sinner just like you or me. No, the words and the truth about Jesus are carefully guarded words: "God sent His own Son in the likeness of human flesh."

One of the Old Testament types (pictures) of Christ presents a perfect picture of this truth. When the children of Israel had sinned their way into deadly judgment (a plague of venomous serpents was sent among them, and they were dying wholesale by the bite of the snakes), God again provided a gracious remedy. He told them to fashion a serpent of brass and elevate it on a pole in the center of the camp. Then, whoever looked on that serpent would live. God commanded His people to use an exact likeness of the thing that had previously caused their death as the means of their salvation! Even so, Jesus came "in the *likeness* of sinful flesh" in order to bring salvation to us.

"And for sin." This may mean " in reference to sin," or "because of sin," but the Septuagint (Greek) version of the Old Testament uses this same phrase in the sense of "a sin-offering." Jesus came in the likeness of sinful flesh to present Himself as an offering for sin. This is the foundation of the truth of His death for sinners. We are saved only because of His atoning, redeeming death for us.

"(He) condemned sin in the flesh." He condemned the sin in *our* flesh by what He did in His *own* flesh. He "bore our sins in His own body on the tree" (I Peter 2:24), and took it to the place of full and final judgment. Now, "there is no condemnation to those who are in Christ Jesus" (Romans 8:1).

On the basis of these great redemptive truths, the third law can work in our lives. "The law of the Spirit of life in Christ Jesus has made us free from the law of sin and death." This "law of ... life" contradicts and counteracts the *condemnation* of the law of God and the *control* of the law of sin and death. When we trust Jesus Christ as our Savior and Redeemer, we immediately are "made free from the law of sin and death." The verb that is used is an aorist tense, picturing one-time point action. So this freedom is gained in a moment of time.

However, there is also a sense in which the "law of the Spirit of life in Christ Jesus" is *continually* activated in our lives as we walk by faith. Just as it took Jesus Christ and His Death on the Cross to pointedly save me from the penalty of my sin, so it takes Jesus Christ and His saving work to progressively do for me what I cannot do for myself--to set me free day by day and moment by moment from the perversions, the poverty, the power and the pollution of sin.

There are certain fixed laws that operate in the physical universe, and it surely is sensible that there are also fixed laws that operate in the spiritual universe. One of the fixed laws in the physical world is the law of gravity.

On the old "Hee Haw" television show, two hayseeds were lazily lying beside a haystack, each chewing on a piece of straw. One drawled to the other, "What keeps us from fallin' off this world?" The other disinterestedly answered, "The law of gravity, stupid." After a moment of thought, the first asked, "Then what kept us from fallin' off this world before they *passed* that law?" Well, there has never been a time in our history when the law of gravity was not operating. The law of gravity roughly corresponds to the law of sin and death in our text. Both laws pull us down and bind us. Remember, too, that hell is described in the New Testament as a "bottomless pit." If you were thrown into a bottomless pit, what would you do? You would fall! How long? *Forever!* Remember, it is *bottomless*!

In contrast, life in Christ has limitless potential for continuing ascendancy. In his classic, The Great Divorce, C. S. Lewis summarized its possibilities in the words, "Further up and further in." Always! But what changes our direction? What gives the upward momentum? What guarantees the victory today, here and now, since the "law of sin and death," like the law of gravity, is still operating? The answer is found in the third law mentioned in the text.

I travel by airplane into many parts of the world. When I board an airplane, does the pilot press an immunity button that turns off the law of gravity for that particular plane and guarantees that it won't be pulled down? No, the law of gravity continues to work. It doesn't give up and abandon the field when an airplane reaches lift-off point as it completes its taxi down the runway. The law of gravity remains in full operation, but there is another law which is exploited by the pilots on board the plane, an instrument which is designed to overcome the law of gravity by utilizing the other law. That other law is called "the law of aerodynamics."

British Pastor Charles Price gave this illustration. "Three years ago I was speaking in Cape Town on the fact that the Christian life is the consequence of the life of Christ in the Christian. Jesus is not the patron or guru of our Christianity. He is Himself the very content of it, for Scripture says God has given us eternal life and this life is in His Son. A young man in his thirties objected that it all sounded very impracticable. 'You've been saying that it is the Spirit of Jesus Christ living in me who is the source of deliverance and power over the old natural self.' I said, 'Yes". He countered, 'But you haven't told me what I have to do to make it work.

I said, 'Maybe you're asking the wrong question. Not 'What do I have to do?' but 'Who has to do it?'

He replied, 'I'm not a zombie. I don't want to sit back and say, 'Well, it's not me, it's Christ', and hope something will happen.'

He worked as a helicopter charter pilot, and one of his jobs involved flying around Cape Town on a Friday afternoon observing traffic patterns. He suggested I accompany him, so that we could continue the discussion.

So that Friday I found myself getting into a tiny helicopter and feeling quite nervous. 'How does it work?' I asked. He showed me the rotor above me. 'The blades are slightly angled. When the rotor begins to rotate, they push down the air which creates a vacuum which causes a lift.'

I said, 'What's that called?' He said, 'That's what we call the law of aerodynamics.' 'What does it do?' 'Well, it lifts the helicopter off the ground.' 'What happens to gravity?' 'What do you mean?' 'Well—I'm secure with gravity, I'm used to being on the ground. But I don't like this idea of floating in the air.' 'You'll be safe,' he reassured me, and we took off. Sensing an opportunity to reveal the truth, I said, 'What do I have to do though to make sure that it's going to work? Do I have to flap my arms at all?' He laughed, but I continued: 'We were talking about the fact that the source of Christian living is Christ Himself, and that as we live in dependency upon the life of Jesus Christ in us, it is He who enables us to live a Godly life. You're telling me now that this helicopter, when you begin to rotate its blades, begins to bring into force the law of aerodynamics which is more powerful than, and sets the helicopter free from, the law of gravity.' Then I read Romans 8:2 to him. 'That's what I'm telling you about Jesus Christ. When we got into this helicopter, I said to you, 'What do I have to do?' You said, 'Put your seatbelt on and relax.' Don't you see, you've been illustrating what I've been preaching, that there's a more powerful law than the law of gravity—the law of aerodynamics? There's a more powerful law than the law of sin, which otherwise will pull you down. The law of the Spirit of life in Christ Jesus will enable you to overcome the law of sin and death.' The law of sin and death continues to operate for everybody else, but the law of the Spirit of life in Christ Jesus sets every believer free from that law.'

He said, 'I can see that. You are telling me that just as I trusted Jesus Christ to set me free from my sins, as I trusted Christ who enabled me to become a Christian, I am to equally trust Jesus Christ everyday so that His 'Spirit of life' can enable me to overcome all the deadly forces that stand against me and to be the Christian I became when I trusted Him.' I said, 'My brother, you've got it!'"

These are the facts, and there is nothing so stubborn and irresistible as a fact. My heart says, "Give me the truth, Lord, just the truth. I can be content with that."

GOD'S SAVING SECRET

Colossians 1:24-29:

"The church, Whereof I am made a minister, according to the dispensation of God which is given to me for you, to fulfil the word of God; Even the mystery which hath been hid from ages and from generations, but now is made manifest to his saints: To whom God would make known what is the riches of the glory of this mystery among the Gentiles; which is Christ in you, the hope of glory: Whom we preach, warning every man, and teaching every man in all wisdom; that we may present every man perfect in Christ Jesus: Whereunto I also labor, striving according to his working, which worketh in me mightily."

This study focuses on "God's Saving Secret." Note the special word the Apostle Paul uses — the word "mystery," or "secret." He speaks of "the Word of God, even the mystery which hath been hid from ages and from generations, but now is made manifest to His saints: ... which is Christ in you, the hope of glory." The New English Bible translates it like this: "the secret hidden for long ages and through many generations, but now disclosed to God's people" (the ones initiated). So Paul speaks of a "secret" of God, though it's an open secret, a secret to be disclosed to anyone who is truly eager to share it. He defines it like this: "The secret is this: Christ in you, the hope of a glory to come." Look carefully and prayerfully at "God's Open Secret."

I. GOD'S SAVING SECRET CENTERS IN A PERSON

First, we see that God's Saving Secret *centers in a Person*, and depends on a relationship between us and that Person. Here, Paul shows us the *essence* of God's saving secret. The essence of God's open secret is *Christ Himself.* According to the Apostle Paul, the *essence*, the *expression*, and the *explanation* of the Christian faith is Christ Himself. In this place, as in every other part of his writings, Paul's chief emphasis is Christ. Jesus is the sum and the stress of it all! In this most important of all facts, the Christian faith is unique. It is the only religion in the world that rests entirely on the Person of its Founder. A man can be a faithful Mohammedan without concerning himself in the least with the person of Mohammed (and this is a very good thing for Islam, because the life of Mohammed was a shambles from a moral standpoint). A man can be a true and faithful Buddhist without knowing anything whatever about Gautama the Buddha as a person. But it is quite different with the Christian faith. The Christian faith involves nothing *less* and can be nothing *more* than a personal relationship with Jesus Christ Himself.

The fundamental and ultimate issue in *everything* is Jesus Christ. The issue is *not* whether you believe a particular *doctrine*. The issue is *not* whether you practice a certain moral *ethic*. This issue is *not* whether you attend or belong to a *church.* All of these things are very important as addendums to a personal relationship with Christ, but the fundamental issue is, What is your personal relationship right now with Jesus Christ?

A fellow pastor tells of a recent incident in his ministry which reflects this truth. A lady came one day to his study, obviously restless, eager, longing for reality in faith, but disillusioned by what she had seen of Christians and the institutional church. The problem she identified in her life is not an uncommon one. She explained her problem, then she said to the pastor, "I need help, but I don't want you to talk to me about *Christianity.* What I have seen makes it unreal to me. And I don't want you to talk to me about *Christians,* either. The ones I know seem so inconsistent." Now, those limitations would place many Christian witnesses in a very great predicament. But just listen to his glorious answer. He said, "Ma'am, I wish everyone would come to me like that, saying the things you have just said. It would be a great relief. This world is ignorant at this moment of Jesus Christ, because it wastes its time talking about Christians and Christianity. As if there were anything worth talking about except Jesus Christ Himself! I am overjoyed to say to you that I am only too glad to observe the limits of conversation you have so wisely imposed. Let's forget about *Christians,* and *Christianity,* and let's talk about *Jesus Christ Himself.*" And beginning with that introduction, the woman's life began to be changed by a person relationship with Jesus.

Suppose that a certain man realizes that he has a deadly disease. He makes a long trip to a distant city because he has been told that there is a physician there who may be able to cure the disease. When he arrives at the doctor's office, the receptionist tells him, "I'm sorry, but the doctor is out. Would you like to see his assistant?" "No, I want to see the doctor himself." "Would you like to read the latest findings on this disease, published in a recent medical journal?" "No, I would prefer to see the doctor." "May I offer you some medicine which the doctor has prescribed to others with this disease?" "No, thank you, I want to see the doctor first." "Sir, I can introduce you while you wait to a person who was recently cured by the doctor." "Ma'am, I appreciate your interest and offers to help, but I must see the man himself, for myself." Dear friend, if you have never known Christ, do not settle for an assistant (a preacher or teacher or Christian), or the book (even though it is the Bible), or reputable medicines (the gifts and blessings of the Christian life), or the testimony of a person who has cured by Him (a happy Christian). You would be wise to carefully observe each one — and then press right around them to Christ Himself!

Imagine the prodigal son in Jesus' story (Luke 15:11-34) arriving back home after his tragic stint in the far country. Suppose his brother greets him with the words, "Welcome home! *I'm* glad you are home, but *Father refuses to see you.*" Or suppose one of the faithful household servants says to him, "All the *servants* are rejoicing. Your father told us to kill the fatted calf and prepare a feast. He also told us to bring out the best robe and put it on you, and a ring on your finger, and shoes on your feet. However, he still has some issues unsettled in his heart, and he told us to hold the banquet without him, because *he's not ready to see you yet.*" You see, dear friend, the greatest thing Jesus Christ offers, or *has* to offer, is Himself. Without Him, though you have all else, you are desperately poor. But *with Him, though you have little else, you are immeasurably rich in eternity's values.*

God's Saving Secret centers in a Person, and depends entirely on a relationship between the individual and that Person.

II. GOD'S SAVING SECRET CENTERS IN A POSSESSION AND A POSITION

Second, we see in our text that God's Saving Secret *centers in a possession* (the possession of Christ) *and a position* (Christ *in you).* Here, Paul carries us into the *experience* of God's Saving Secret. "The secret is this: Christ *in you,* the hope of glory." Now, not all who profess and call themselves Christians are *in on* this secret. Many hold firmly to the belief that Christ is *for* them, but they have no experience whatsoever of Christ *in* them. And yet, this is the secret of everything Christian — God's *saving* secret, God's *open* secret — "Christ in you."

This is the secret of *beginning* the Christian life. To *begin* the Christian life, you must *receive* the incoming Christ. The Word of God declares in John 1:12 that "as many as *received* Him, to them gave He power to become the sons of God."

It was William Law, a great old English preacher, who said, "A Christ not *in* us is a Christ not *ours*. A Christ not *in* me is a Christ not *mine*." It matters not what you may *believe* with your *head*, or *practice* with your *life*, if Christ is not within you, are no Christian. It is not enough for Christ to be *near* you (indeed, that is always true); He must be in you. Not *there*, but *here!* Not *outside*, but *inside*! You see, when Christ lived in the flesh, He lived *among* men; today He wants to live *in* men.

Late one Sunday afternoon in 1921, Dr. Lyman Abbott, the great Christian writer, sat in the pastor's study of a big eastern church. He was to speak in the evening worship service, reviewing his latest book, <u>What Christianity Means to Me</u>. It was forty-five minutes before time for the service and the church was already packed. The pastor came in and laid his copy of Dr. Abbott's book down in front of the great author and said to him, "Would you please autograph it for me, and write in it the ripest thought that has come to you in your sixty years in the ministry." Then the pastor went out. Thirty minutes later he came back. Dr. Abbott still sat, his pen in his hand, the book open in front of him, and deep in thought. He hadn't written a word. The pastor tiptoed out. Fifteen minutes later he returned. It was time for the service to begin. The ink was not yet dry on the flyleaf of the book. This is what Dr. Abbott had written: "The ripest thought that has come to me in sixty years in the ministry is this: the Christian faith is not a *philosophy* that Jesus came to *teach*; it is a *life* that Jesus came to *impart* and to *infuse* into the experience of individuals." This is the secret — God's open secret, God's saving secret — of beginning the Christian life, to receive Christ into your life and heart.

But this is also the secret of *living* and *sharing* the Christian life. "Christ in you." To *live* and *share* the Christian life, you must *acknowledge* the *indwelling* Christ. It is one thing to receive Christ, but quite another to consciously realize and acknowledge His Presence moment by moment. Yet, the Christian life is nothing less that a moment-by-moment miracle, lived by the power of the indwelling Christ. The "open secret" is that God in Christ is able and willing to move right into the heart of His yielded child and live there, looking out of his eyes, feeling with his hands, talking with his lips, and sharing Himself with others through the believer's life which He occupies.

Captain Reginald Wallis used to define the word "Christian" like this: "Spell out the word C-H-R-I-S-T-I-A-N. Then take the letter 'A' from the end of the word and put it at the beginning. Now what do you read?" The answer, of course, was — "A Christ in." With great earnestness, he would then add: "A Christian is a man in whom Jesus Christ through the Holy Spirit lives, and moves, and has His being."

Every Christmas, I am reminded of Mary's "pattern of incarnation" as a perfect model for our lives. Follow the steps, and you will see the Christian life in miniature. (1) There was an *entrance* of Christ into her. And there must be an entrance of Christ into you that is just as decisive as His entrance into her. His incarnation resulted from the union of two things in her, and His incarnation in us results from the union of Word and Spirit in us. (2) There was an *enlargement* of Christ within her. She carried a growing Jesus in her for nine months, and so we will carry a "growing Jesus" in us throughout our Christian lives. How Mary was stretched and shaped by His Presence in her! She was stretched and shaped personally, socially, mentally, and spiritually (and probably in several other ways as well), and so will we be. You will find that "Christ in you" will do many of the same things to you that Mary's supernatural pregnancy did to her. (3) There was an *expression (exit)* of Christ through (from) her. Even so, when Christ grows sufficiently within us, there will be a regular and growing expression of His Life through us. He will move through us into the world around us just as He moved through Mary into the world around her! (4) There was an *extension* of Christ in an ever-enlarging way around her. After a time, she "lost control" of the One who had come through her. He became "unmanageable"! On occasion, He almost sounded as if He was rebuking her for her attempts to control and restrain Him. Mary suffered some "loss of face" on several occasions because of Him, beginning with His Birth. But she was so visited by Heaven that she never once argued with the negatives of her experience of Him. Even so, He will move into an unhindered expression through us, even if He must rebuke us and discipline us -- and even possibly cause some loss of face on our part -- to "make room" for Himself.

It is a clearly stated rule in the Bible that everything reproduces only *after its own kind*. Thus, only Christ can reproduce Christ. Suppose I suddenly found in my mind a raging desire to reproduce a copy of Raphael's masterpiece painting, "The Transfiguration." You see, when many Christians talk of reproducing Christ, they are speaking of *imitation* instead of *impartation* -- copying Him instead of allowing Him to impart and reproduce Himself in and through them. So I bring out my brushes, my paints, my coloring pencils, my easel, and I set to work. I work for awhile, and realize what a miserable attempt I am making of it. Though I try again and again, I soon become the laughing-stock of all observers. Then I begin to despair of my earlier hope. No matter how well-intentioned I might be, or how hard I might try, the result is always the same — total failure!

But suppose Raphael's spirit and ability could get inside of me! He could gain mastery of my fingers, train my eyes to the delicate perception of proportion and perspective, and he could more and more employ my faculties to his use, until by and by he would perfectly reproduce the masterpiece. Friends, the true Christian life is a masterpiece which only Christ can produce! It is only the Christ within who can produce the Christ without. Once Christ is in you, this is His goal, to so transform you inwardly that He increasingly comes to visibility and activity in the world around — right through you!

A gardener one day rescued a wild briar from the ditch where it had been left to rot and die and he planted it in a flower-bed where he was expecting a crop of flowers in the springtime. An onlooker imagined the briar's reaction in this way: "How foolish," the briar said, "how foolish can a man be? Fancy placing a briar like me in a setting like this! I can produce nothing and I'll be out of place!"

But the gardener knew what he was about. He later returned and made a slit in the briar's stem, grafting into it the stem of a choice rose. Later in the season, as flowers appeared elsewhere, so also were there lovely, perfumed roses on that old briar tree that had been left to rot in the gutter. Addressing the briar with the roses on it, the gardener said quietly, "Now you understand! *I did not plant you there for what you were going to give me, but for what I was going* **to make out of you***! And, even then,* **I had to invest in you everything that I wanted out of you!***"*

This is what Paul means when he states the formula, "Christ in you." Paul never succeeded in explaining it. He frankly called it a "mystery." How one personality can invade another, and live *within* another person, and express Himself through that person, yet preserve that person's essential freedom, is beyond explanation. Yet it happens! This is the *marvelous and mysterious experience* of God's open secret — "Christ in you."

III. GOD'S SAVING SECRET LEADS TO A CERTAIN PRODUCT

Finally, we see that the possession of God's Saving Secret *will lead inevitably to a certain product*. It will always have a certain fixed result. "Christ in you, *the hope of glory*." Now, I think we have made it clear that the Christian Gospel does not just offer a better land in the future, "far, far away." It is not just "a good time coming." It is no mere message, as is often said, of "pie in the sky by and by." It is also God's Good News of present salvation and present help. But there definitely is a future tense of salvation. There is a very, very important future for a Christian. The Christian Gospel is the message of a future glory for those who have Christ in their lives right now. The Christian faith, which is "Christ in you," not only works in this life, but reaches out to the life beyond.

Let me be as clear as I possibly can at this point. This "hope of glory" has both a *present tense product* and a *future tense prospect*. *Now*, the stress in that phase is on the word, "*hope*," but *then*, it will be on the word, "*glory*."

Two children were counting their money. "I have five pennies!" exclaimed one little girl. "I have ten," replied the other. "No, you don't!" protested the first one. "You only have five pennies, too." But the second girl calmly replied, "I only have five pennies *here*, but my father promised me five more *when we are at home together*. So I have ten." Every Christian has a *present-tense glory* right now, and he has a *promise of prospective glory* hereafter — *when he and Jesus are* **at home together.**

The *present tense product* may be explained like this. "Glory" in the Bible is the manifestation of God's character; it is the outshining of God's radiance. "The Word became flesh, and dwelt among us, and we beheld His glory." In other words, we saw the character of God in Jesus. Romans 3:23 says, "All have sinned, and come short of the glory of God." Remember, the "glory of God" is God's own character in demonstration. So, if you are less perfect than God's character, you are a sinner — and each of us qualifies!

So "Christ in you, the hope of glory" is an entire explanation of God's great salvation. You see, when Adam sinned in the Garden of Eden, God's glory, God's character, God's nature — God Himself — departed out of man. In that moment, man died spiritually. In that moment, man also fell back upon his own resources for living. He began to depend on his own body and soul, instead of depending upon God within him. He became "flesh," which is the Biblical word for man acting out of his body and soul, independently of a relationship with God in his spirit. Thus, he was "dead" toward God "in trespasses and sins" (Ephesians 2:1).

Our text tells us that *the only hope* of God regaining his rightful and proper place within man's spirit is by means of *Christ in you*. Without Christ within, each man remains dead toward God, and it is virtually impossible to convince a dead man that he is dead! I say, "virtually impossible" — though God can do it through a miracle! And this is precisely what happens in the miracle of conviction (John 16:7-11). God awakens a dead man to the reality of his own death! Then, he will happily consider the other great miracle of salvation, the miracle of "Christ in you."

But remember that there is also a *future-tense prospect* to the great truth of "Christ in you." What does a Christian have to look forward to in Heaven? Uncertainty? No! Fear? No! Embarrassment? No! You see, *man's* ways lead to a *hopeless end*, but *God's* ways lead to an *endless hope*. According to Ephesians 2:7, every born-again person may expect *eternal kindness* from God. God will never get tired of being kind to me! Why? Because Christ is in me! So God will practice eternal kindness toward His Son and His sons! And I am one of His sons -- a King's kid! Thus, God will never tire of being kind to me. What a prospect!

"Christ in you" is God's provision for you for *time* and for *eternity*, for *earth* and for *heaven*, for *now* and *for then*. The indwelling Christian Himself constitutes the pledge of future glory. "The hope of glory." But is it only a "hope"? Well, even if it is, in the New Testament, the word "hope" has no shadow of doubt, no trace of uncertainty, associated with it. A New Testament hope is "a sure and certain hope." The word "hope" in the New Testament never refers to something that is uncertain, but only to something that is *future*.

When a baby is in his mother's womb before birth, he develops eyes, but there are no colors for him to see! He develops ears, but there are no harmonies for him to enjoy! He develops feet, but there are no paths for him to walk! He develops hands, but there are no deeds of service for him to perform! Just so, man is meant to grow "spiritual organs," to sharpen "spiritual senses" (Hebrews 5:14), while he is here on earth. Do you see why the enlargement of Christ in you is so important on a daily basis? Each saved person is to be in dynamic daily development for His eternal experience of the "glory" hereafter. Each saved person is in "reigning training" right now for His eternal reign with Christ. "Christ in you" now is your present guarantee of an eternity with Him in His heavenly glory hereafter. Hallelujah!

It has been my personal privilege to travel outside the United States over eighty times. Every time I re-enter my homeland after returning from the country I have visited, I eagerly pass through customs, answering any questions in order to get home again. Entrance into heaven might be like that. At re-entry into the United States, the U. S. citizen must fill out a form which asks, "Do you have anything to declare?" Just as there is a pre-determined entrance exam for readmission into the United States, there is a pre-determined entrance exam for admission into Heaven. When you are asked at the Gate of Heaven, "Do you have anything to declare?" you may be sure that the Name of Jesus is going to be like honey on your tongue at that moment! It will be a joy to your heart to declare His Name and announce that His Presence in you is your "hope of glory." As one old preacher said, "Don't miss it if you can!"

Do you know anything about this by personal experience? Can you say, "Christ is in me, the hope of glory?" If not, would you not ....

"Just now, your doubtings give o'er, Just now, reject Him no more; Just now, throw open the door; Let Jesus come into your heart."

As God acts upon you with the miracle of His conviction, as you realize your sin and your need, trust Jesus Christ and Him alone as your only "hope of glory." A foretaste of glory will immediately fill your heart, and the Full Meal in Heaven will be something to experience! *I* have a guaranteed advance reservation. Trust Jesus, and secure your own reservation today.

Perhaps you do not know *how* to trust Jesus to save you. Perhaps you don't know what prayer to pray. Let me help you. Down in your deepest heart, pray a prayer like this:

"Jesus, I have sinned, and I am lost. I cannot help myself; I cannot save myself, any more than I can lift myself by my own shoestrings. But You tell me that You love me, and that You died on the Cross personally for me. You also tell me that You did not stay dead; You arose from the dead. And You tell me that if I will simply trust You — totally depend upon You and You alone to save me — that You will come into my life and forgive my sins and give me Your Gift of Eternal Life. *Jesus, I do now trust You!* **I trust You, and You only, to save me now and forever.** You arose from the dead to guarantee my salvation as I trust You. I trust You, Jesus, right now. Thank You for saving me. Now, take my life and use it for Your purpose. In Your Name, Amen."

Hebrews 7:25 says, "Jesus is able to save unto the uttermost all those who come unto God by Him because He ever lives to intercede for us." And Romans 10:13 says, "Whosoever shall call upon the Name of the Lord shall be saved." This is a very, very serious matter. Call upon Jesus today; trust Him to save You right now.

GUARDING OUR GREATEST TREASURE

Proverbs 23:23:

"Buy the truth, and sell it not."

    Perhaps the greatest ongoing battle being fought on earth today is the battle for truth. The battle rages on many fronts and under many banners. For a Christian, the battle is simplified. The issue is the truth of God pitted against all the ideologies, philosophies and world-views that oppose it. Yes, they *oppose* it, adamantly and aggressively. You see, nothing is more infuriating to the natural human mind than the fact of the extreme narrowness of truth. Many of the opposing views are formidable and mouthed by militants, which increases the necessity of our side being fully armed with apologetic skill *and love*. We are to "speak the truth in love," the Bible says. This is no easy assignment.

    The Bible says that, no matter how a person is thinking before he meets Jesus Christ as his Lord and Savior, his thinking is wrong. He is "futile in his thinking and darkened in his understanding, being separated from the life of God because of the ignorance that is in him due to the hardening of his heart" (Ephesians 4:17-18). Every born-again person knows in retrospect how true that assessment is. In fact, just as only living people can assess death, so only born-again people can realize how ignorant and darkened their minds were when they were without Christ.

Lost people who are entrenched in their self-will and sin follow a succession of downward steps with regard to truth. First, they suppress the truth. Then they exchange the truth of God for a lie. Finally, they insist that their own alternative "truth" is the correct version. This sequence is traced in a horrible passage in Romans 1:18-32, and it can be seen in practical exposure all over the world today.

In contrast, a Christian is a person who has been revolutionized by Divine truth, truth that is both Personal and propositional. Christian faith has a great Personal object (!!), but it also has great propositional content (!). A true Christian will be constantly enlarging his awareness and experience of both the Personal object and the propositional content.

As *Personal*, truth is found in Jesus Christ, Who said, "I am the Truth" (John 14:6). As a circle must have a center, the whole realm of truth must have a point of reference. In the Greek text of John 1, Jesus is called the *logos*, which is the word from which we derive our word, "logic." Jesus *is the Logic of God*. The Apostle Paul called it "the truth as it is found in Jesus" (Ephesians 4:21). When Jesus introduced Himself and placed Himself and His truth on the public market (Luke 4:17-19), He used Isaiah 61 as His own point of reference to define His ministry, and four of the verbs in the text He selected have to do with *teaching*. Christianity is a faith driven by the power of truth. "Faith comes by hearing, and hearing by the Word of God" (Romans 10:17). As *propositional*, truth is found in the Bible, God's own Word. In John 17:17, Jesus said to His Father, "Thy word is truth." The Bible is all true, and it contains all we need to know to "negotiate life in its eternal dimensions" —but not all truth is found in the Bible. Much truth is outside the Bible, and God is the source of all of it. However deep or far the human mind may move in a search for truth, no truth it may find is outside the realm of God. All explorations of "truth" will finally be judged by the question, "Is it true to the Word of God as revealed in Jesus Christ?" Let me make one differentiation before we look briefly at the text: there is a difference between something being *accurate* and something being *true*. Truth is far more and far bigger than mere accuracy. It is accurate that I am over six feet tall, but that does not Biblically qualify to be called "truth." C.S. Lewis helps us when he calls God's truth "true truth."

The tiny text that is at the head of this study gives to each of us a concise command that serves as a guide for our contacts with God's truth. Let me deal with it under several headings.

First, it speaks of a *priceless commodity we are to possess*. "Buy *the truth*." For a Christian disciple, this text reminds us of the vast information gap that characterizes a person when he receives Christ. In another study, I have called it an information *crisis*, and it is exactly that. "He knows nothing as he ought to know," and he will not know what he needs to know unless he daily "buys the truth." Disciple-making, by its very nature, assists the disciple in moving from what he *presently* knows to what he *should* know as a follower of Christ. The disciple-maker will "walk the disciple through the 'purchase process'" by which he 'buys the truth' on a daily basis and with life-transforming results. The discipler will teach the disciple how to appropriate both the Personal truth (how to abide in Christ and be filled with His Spirit) and the propositional truth of God (how to study and incarnate the Word of God). As he grows, the disciple will happily "buy the truth" just as he shops in a market for his favorite item.

In summary, truth is *not variable* and *not negotiable* to a true disciple of Jesus Christ. Someone said, "We live in an age that grants plausibility to every idea and certainty to none." But God's truth is absolute, not relative, whatever the secular mind may think and the secular mouth may argue. And it is not negotiable in that no price will entice the true believer to sell out the truth.

Second, the text suggests *a practical course to pursue with regard to truth.* *"Buy the truth."* This means that a disciple of Christ must take measures to possess the truth. Purchases don't just "happen." Commodities don't fall into the trunk of your car while you are playing in the park or drinking a cup of coffee with a friend. A true disciple will understand how high the stakes are with regard to truth, and will give up anything and everything else to possess truth. Furthermore, he will enlarge his supply of truth at every opportunity, paying whatever price is necessary to stock his mind, his heart and his life with this treasure. He remembers that Jesus said, "You shall know the truth, and the truth will make you free" (John 8:32).

Third, if we are to practice the admonition of the text, there is *a perpetual cost to pay.* *"Buy the truth."* The word "buy" suggests giving up something of value to possess the item. It also suggests an exchange of that valuable thing in order to possess the desirable commodity. It is apparent that truth has a price tag—and it may be exorbitant! "Every road taken is every other road forsaken." When a person consolidates his time, attention, effort and energy to "buy the truth," he won't be found in lesser markets and bartering for lesser commodities.

Finally, the text specifies *a precise caution that must be taken to protect the possession.* *"Buy the truth, and sell it not."*

Just how would a believer "sell" truth? He might sell it by being too *casual* with it. As he neglects it, maintains a casual indifference toward it, or drifts away from it, he is selling the truth.

Then he might sell the truth by *compromising* it. He might twist or distort it in his handling of it, both in public discussion or private consideration, or he might shade it in order to be socially acceptable among co-workers or associates.

He might sell the truth by not *championing it*. If the penetration of Christian truth into the market of world ideas depended totally on you, how much truth would be available for somebody else's "purchase" on the market? The man who refuses to champion truth while still trying to believe it is a coward. He simply walks away from a discussion rather than staying to present the truth. "Peace at any price" calls for too great a price to be paid when truth is the issue.

He might sell the truth by not *communicating* it. The Christian simply remains silent when Jesus and His truth need presentation and expression. "I believe, therefore, I have spoken," but this Christian practices a convenient and self-protective reserve instead of speaking the truth.

Brothers and sisters, God has gone to enormous trouble to make the truth available to us, and we should surely be willing to go to enormous trouble, if necessary, to hear, learn, heed, obey and repeat the truth He has given. A. W. Tozer said, "What divides us Christians is the degree to which we take truth; that is, how fervently we do or don't believe a particular truth," and he was right. In fact, if we genuinely love God (what's not to love?), such a "purchase" will not be seen as trouble at all. It will be viewed as pleasure and not pressure. It will be "an unspeakable joy and full of glory." We need truth more than we need comfort, convenience, happiness, affluence, possessions. "Better to die with a grip on truth than on anything else life offers." The more we "buy the truth," the happier we are. Christians are born (born *again*) to shop—for God's truth. "Buy the truth, and sell it not." Is the possession and practice of Divine truth a priority on your agenda?

Some years ago, I was captivated by the story of a Greenland Eskimo who was taken on one of the American polar expeditions. As a reward for his faithful service, he was brought to New York City for a short visit. He was amazed at all the miracles of sight and sound. When he returned to his native village, he told stories of buildings that rose into the very face of the sky. He spoke of streetcars, which he described as houses that moved along the trail, with people living in them as they moved. He told about mammoth bridges, artificial lights, and all the other dazzling delights of the great metropolis. His people looked at him coldly and walked away. Throughout the village he was dubbed, "The Liar." This name he carried in shame to his grave. Long before his death, his original name was entirely forgotten in the village.

Sometime later, a man named Knud Rasmussen made a trip from Greenland to Alaska. He was accompanied by an Eskimo named Mitek from the same village. Mitek visited Copenhagen and New York, where he saw many things for the first time and was duly impressed. Later, upon his return to Greenland, he recalled the tragic story of "The Liar" and decided that it would not be wise to tell the truth. Instead, he narrated the stories that his people could grasp, shaded them to their understanding, and thus saved his reputation.

He told them how he and Dr. Rasmussen maintained a kayak on the banks of a great river, the Hudson, and how each morning they paddled out for their hunting; ducks, geese and seals were plentiful. And Mitek said they enjoyed the visit with the "natives" immensely.

In the eyes of his people, the truth-teller was a liar, and the man who shaded the truth to fit the minds of the Eskimos was a very honest man. But all the while, truth stood alone, unchanged, unscathed, and largely unknown—but still truth!

"GUARDING OUR GREATEST TREASURE"
(Proverbs 23:23)

I. A Priceless Commodity to Possess

II. A Practical Course to Pursue

III. A Perpetual Cost to Pay

IV. A Protective Caution to Perform

A CALL FOR INTERCESSION

Romans 15:30-33:

"Now I beseech you, brethren, for the Lord Jesus Christ's sake, and for the love of the Spirit, that ye strive together with me in your prayers to God for me; That I may be delivered from them that do not believe in Judea; and that my service which I have for Jerusalem may be accepted of the saints; That I may come unto you with joy by the will of God, and may with you be refreshed. Now the God of peace be with you all. Amen."

    It has been well-said that there are three very important things that largely shape the life of a disciple-maker: (1) His relationship with God; and (2) The fellowship of believers of which he is a part; and (3) The individual disciple's relationship with him. This may be an over-statement, and it may disregard other crucial factors in his life, but the point is still well taken. In the relationship of a disciple-maker and his disciple, nothing is more important than intercessory prayer, the discipler's daily prayer for his disciple.

    Rivet this principle on the wall of your mind; it is universally applicable (no matter what kind of ministry is involved): A true ministry is a miracle of God, and though other vital factors are also involved in such a ministry, it comes only in answer to prayer. The prayer that is necessary is personal prayer by the discipler, and intercessory prayer by as many other believers as possible. In this study, we will examine an example of intercessory prayer. Actually, the text comprises a request by the Apostle Paul addressed to the Christians in the city of Rome, inviting them to support his ministry by their intercession for him. It is a classic Christian call for intercessory prayer, and its lessons are timeless.

I. THE BASIS FOR AN INTERCESSORY PRAYER MINISTRY, 30A

First, we clearly see in this text the *basis* for intercession in the fellowship of believers. In fact, there are *two bases* stated in the text.

Paul uses two strong words to introduce his invitation. In the English Bible (KJV), they are "B" words, "brethren" and "beseech." "Now I beseech you, brethren." The word "brethren" is used for Christians; indeed, for *all* Christians. So this is a general summons to all the Christians in the church of Rome. It is used here to remind these Christians that they are all (and equally) members of the Christian family, the family of faith, and that as such they have full family privileges and full family responsibilities. The other "B" word is the word "beseech." This is a very tender and appealing word. It is the same root form which Jesus used as His title for the Holy Spirit. The word is *parakaleo*, "I beseech you." The word Jesus used as a title for the Holy Spirit is *paracletos*, which derives from the same root word.

You have heard many preachers and teachers preach about the need to be "Christ-like," and even the need to be like God the Father, but how many times have you heard such leaders teach about the need to be like the Holy Spirit? Here, Paul demonstrates a likeness to the Holy Spirit, and he in effect invites all of his readers to seek to grow in that likeness. The words of Paul could be paraphrased, "I tenderly call you alongside of me to make a gentle appeal to you." This is what the Holy Spirit does *for* every believer and *within* every believer. He stands alongside of each of us, to lend the full provision of His Personality to any situation we are in. Here, Paul puts his arm around His fellow-believers in Rome, and tenderly asks them to support Him like the Holy Spirit does. His *appeal* is based on the Spirit's tenderness, and their *response* should be based on the Spirit's tenderness. Actually, it is the Holy Spirit Who is appealing to us today to join Him in His ministry of intercession for believers, and we should respond to the appeal with the same gentle effort as we obey His appeal.

Then Paul states two foundational bases for our prayers of intercession. First, he asks them to pray for him *"for the Lord Jesus Christ's sake."* Note the full title that is used for our Savior. The full title gives great strength to the appeal. He is called "Lord," which is His title as Sovereign Master. He is called "Jesus," which is His title as Sympathetic Man. And He is called "Christ," which is His title as Scriptural Messiah. When all these titles are joined, the full majesty of the Person is intended. What an appeal this should make to every Christian! If this appeal has *no appeal* to you, it is doubtful that you are a Christian.

A business man in Denver, Colorado, was approached in his office one day by two other business men, who made a business proposition to him, seeking to enlist him in a business partnership. However, it quickly became evident that their proposition involved some "shady dealing," some very questionable business practices. He respectfully declined the offer, stating "moral reasons" for his decision. One of the men leaned forward in his chair and indignantly said, "Well, for Christ's sake!" The Christian business man smiled politely and answered, "My friend, I want to thank you for supplying me with the perfect statement of my reason for declining. It is precisely *for Christ's sake* that I cannot engage in such a partnership!" Friends, every decision we make is to be *for Christ's sake*; every action we take should be *for Christ's sake*; every thought we think and every word we speak should be *for Christ's sake.* Thus, Paul's appeal only announces and employs the basic Christian motive; it does not invent it or impose it. Every Christian should respond in full alert and with eager participation when he is invited to do anything "for Christ's sake."

Paul's other foundational base for inviting intercessory prayer for himself and his ministry is stated in this phrase, "and for the love of the Spirit." One translation says, "For the love we bear one another in the Spirit." Now, this is not an ideal to aspire for, this is a spiritual fact. Every born-again person bears love for other Christians in the Spirit. That love may have been violated by carnal selfishness, but it is still present in each believer. Earlier in this same letter (Romans 5:5), Paul said, "The love of God is shed abroad (broadcast, like a sower flinging seeds wholesale in a field) in our hearts by the Holy Spirit Who has been given unto us." *Every believer has been flooded* at the time of his conversion *with the love of God through the incoming and indwelling of the Holy Spirit*. So Paul is simply appealing to the common experience of all Christians as a base for engaging in intercessory prayer.

So Paul makes a powerful appeal to the Christians in Rome to support him through their prayers of intercession for him and his ministry. The grounds of his appeal should be sufficient to enlist every Christian in such a vital ministry.

II. THE BATTLE OF AN INTERCESSORY PRAYER MINISTRY, 30B

Second, Paul exposes to his fellow-Christians in Rome the *battle* of intercession. He says, "I beseech you . . . that ye

A Call for Intercession

strive together with me in your prayers to God for me." The *ministry* of intercession is captured in the words, "your prayers to God for me." The *battle* of such a ministry is revealed in the word translated, "strive together." This is a very militant word. In the Greek text, it is a fifteen-letter word (sunagonisasthai; it's a good thing you don't have to pronounce that to get to heaven!). It is a compound word, made of a combination of a root verb and a prepositional prefix. The prefix is the little word "sun" (pronounced like our English word "soon"), and it means "together with." It is the preposition for mutual action or joint effort. The root form of the verb is the word from which we get our word, "agony."

Now we can see the intense battle that is involved in a ministry of intercessory prayer. Paul literally said, "I tenderly entreat you . . . to strive together with me in your prayers to God for me." What an enlightening sentence! What lessons it reveals about intercessory prayer! Note the phrase, "Strive together *with me*." Here we learn that intercession is not merely a praying of words; it is the taking of a position. It is the experiencing of full identification with another person. It is the fullest and most vital expression of the "inside-out," other-centered, ethic of the Christian life. Every Christian should feature himself as always "striving together with" some other Christian (or a fellowship of Christians) — *for them* (or "for me," as Paul said it). Nothing that a Christian does should be done merely in his own name or for his own advantage. Everything should be done "for the Lord Jesus Christ's sake," and "for *them*."

The root word, "agony," highlights the battle, the struggle, of intercessory prayer. And the words, "together with me," highlight the mutual responsibility of joint effort. No Christian should ever stand alone in the Christian battle.

He should always have the support of other Christians by means of intercessory prayer.

Any large city which features a zoo probably has an animal in its zoo called the *gnu*. I heard of a father gnu who came home from work one day only to have his wife cozy up to him and slyly say, "Honey, I've got *gnus* for you!" One day I visited the zoo in my city and saw the pen which housed the gnus. In the informational plaque on the front fence, this item was posted. "When the gnu is under attack, it falls to its knees and fights from it knees." "The gnu fights from its knees!" How I wish the church was as wise as the gnu! The church will never launch any farther than it can launch from its knees. It will never win any more battles than it can win from its knees. The disciple-maker will never have any more authority than he gains from his knees. We need more "knee-ology" than "theology" in the fellowship of believers today. This certainly does not depreciate theology; it only maximizes prayer.

Furthermore, when Paul used the words, "with me," he let the Roman Christians know that he was not expecting anything from them in his behalf that he was not already doing for them — *and for himself.* Christian, hear this instruction: *pray yourself*, and pray *for yourself*. But do not let self-attention absorb your total prayers. You will never be gratified or fulfilled in your Christian life if you turn prayer into a means of carnal indulgence or self-seeking. In fact, it would be safe to say that your prayer life will soon be a shambles if you only pray for yourself and your selfish concerns. And if your prayer life is *already* a shambles, this is a probable contributing cause. You are reproducing the Adamic (Satanic!) fallacy of prostituting God's resources for your own selfish purposes.

Here is Paul's appeal concerning the battle of intercessory prayer: "I urge you to *become fellow-warriors with me* in your prayers to God for me."

III. THE BLESSINGS SOUGHT IN AN INTERCESSORY PRAYER MINISTRY, 31-32

Third, Paul specifies the *blessings* he hopes to receive because of their intercessory prayers for him. Indeed, these are the specific blessings they are to pray for in his behalf. Verses 31 and 32 supply an incredible education in the Christian life and provide incalculably valuable lessons for the ministry of Christians. The concerns Paul identifies in these verses remain universal needs today for every Christian disciple. Five special spiritual concerns may be detected in Paul's appeal.

First, Paul urges the Roman Christians to pray "that I may be delivered from them that do not believe in Judea" (verse 31a). So we are to invite other Christians to regularly pray for us, that *we would be delivered from the attacks of unbelievers.* The Christian needs protection at every moment from the spirit of unbelief that shrouds the world. However, he must realize that not all unbelief is outside the church. Not all unbelief is practiced and expressed outside the fellowship of "believers"!

Some years ago, while waiting for several hours in the Dallas/Fort Worth airport, I had the happy surprise of getting to visit with five of the Dallas Cowboy football players. They were on their way to Nashville to participate in an off-season basketball competition as the Cowboys' *basketball* team. I had the opportunity to witness to three of them about Christ. When I asked the best-known one of the five, a star Cowboy running back, "Do you know Jesus Christ personally? Have you been saved?" he answered, "Well, I'm a believer, but I am not living it right now." Ponder his words carefully. They contain a subtle but devastating contradiction. The word "believer" comprises a present-tense definition. You may call a one-time killer a "murderer," but it is not proper to call a one-time believer a "believer." A Christian should only be called a believer if the first exercise of faith changed his life into one of continual belief. The star running back would have been more accurate to say, "I believed in Christ . . ." No *"believer"* could accurately say, "I am not living it right now." Believers always behave accordingly! In fact, you believe only what you behave. To call yourself a "believer" (a present-tense confession) and not be living it (a present-tense violation) is a total contradiction. The practice cancels the profession.

However we may interpret that story, the spirit of unbelief is a constant threat to a Christian's life, and this is doubly true for the Christian who is fully engaged in active Christian ministry. We must keep ourselves alert to the attacks of unbelief which originate from *outside* the Christian community, to the attacks of unbelief which arise from *within* the fellowship of believers, and to the attacks of unbelief which assault us *inwardly* through our own flesh.

The word that is translated "delivered" in Paul's request ("that I may be delivered from unbelievers in Judea") is a strong and radical word. It might better be translated, "rescued." What a powerful picture is conjured by that word. The word "rescue" presupposes a serious and threatening danger. A person not in danger does not need rescue, but a person under threat is in immediate need of rescue. No wonder the New Testament presents such graphic pictures of the Christian life in terms of warfare, battle and combat!

As a pastor, I had the privilege of winning a man to Christ and baptizing him. The man was totally blind, the victim of an enemy sniper while he was serving in the United States armed services in the South Pacific. A lull had occurred in a fierce battle, and he stood to his feet to stretch his body, when an enemy sniper's bullet smashed through the front of his face, rendering him totally blind. It was an incredible blessing to be used of God to bring him from spiritual blindness to spiritual sight. Friends, unbelief is like that sniper, and its attacks are like that sniper's bullet, ready always to handicap and incapacitate you as a Christian. The interceding discipler should pray daily that God will deliver his disciple and all others believers from the attacks of unbelievers.

Second, Paul urges the Roman Christians to pray *that his ministry will be accepted by the people* (verse 31b). He asks them to pray that there will be a high confidence level between him and all other believers. Here are Paul's words: "Pray that my service which I have for Jerusalem may be accepted of the saints." Paul was probably talking about an offering collected for the poor saints in Jerusalem, but the same prayer must be prayed for all of our service in the fellowship of believers. A disciple must pray that the ministry of his disciple-maker must be fully accepted by him and others, and that as he himself begins to minister to others, his ministry will be accepted by them. The word translated "accepted" in this verse literally means "well-received with favor." Every Christian should regularly pray this prayer for his own ministry and for the ministries of all other Christians he knows. In the Christian community, one brother's success is everybody's victory. We must get beyond the selfishness of thinking only of our own ministry, and of being jealous only for our own success.

A ministry rendered by one believer must be accepted by other believers. How many times have committed believers tried to minister, only to have their ministry rejected or rebuffed by invulnerable or self-righteous saints. Christian, let this acceptance begin with you. Don't say, "But I don't *like* him," or "I don't like some things about him." Your dislikes of a brother or sister may be an exposure of your character flaws, not a testimony of his capability. You see, you tend to "read" a leader through your own self-image. If your self-image is low, you tend to lower others in your thinking. You tend to attribute your weakness or your sin to others around you.

Whatever may be the cause of rejection of a brother's ministry, pray that it will be overcome and the individual ministries of brothers and sisters will be accepted in the Body of Christ.

Third, in a discipler-disciple relationship, each should pray for the other that he will have *a joyful life and ministry* (verse 32a). Paul appealed to the Roman Christians to "pray that I may come unto you with joy." What a difference is made when a Christian is joyful in life and ministry! May God help the joyless discipler or the joyless disciple! An old Puritan wisely said, "Joy is the infallible sign of the presence of God." Samuel Shoemaker, who mentored me through several of his books, wrote, "The greatest symptom of true spiritual life is not faith, or love, but joy." C. S. Lewis demonstrated his awareness of this great truth when he entitles his autobiography, Surprised By Joy.

However, we find to our dismay and disappointment that many Christians seem to live every day as if they are wound up as tight as a rigid guitar string. They don't seem to be able to bend, so they break themselves and often try to break others as well. Let me ask you a serious question: Is your faith a *pressure* or a *pleasure* to you? Is your faith a *load* or a *lift* to you? Is it a *burden* or a *blessing?* Psalm 16:11 says, "Thou will show me the path of life; in Thy presence is fullness of joy; at Thy right hand there are pleasures forevermore." If I do not experience this fullness of joy and these durable pleasures, I am living away from God's presence, removed from the blessing that comes from His right hand. I need to learn to *relax* and *celebrate* in every situation. Relaxation is a crucial aspect of the faith that rests fully in Jesus Christ, and celebration should be a continual exercise in the life of every Christian.

So every disciple should pray daily that those who minister to him and those to whom he ministers may have a joyful life and ministry.

As far as I am aware, one of the greatest lessons the Holy Spirit has taught me in my "field-training" as a Christian is the lesson of unconditional praise. Nearly a quarter of a century ago, I experienced a time of deep depression which was induced by circumstances in my life at that time. In fact, I thought my life was under threat because of the depth of the depression. It was just at that time ("in the nick of time," as Hebrews says) that God broke into my experience with the lesson of praising Him all the time about everything. At first, the practice was very awkward, but when I obeyed Him with my praise, the depression disappeared like mist in the bright morning sun. So I know how important joy is in a believer's life. Every disciple should pray daily that those who minister to him and those to whom he ministers may have a joyful life and ministry.

Fourth, in a discipler-disciple relationship, each should pray for the other that *he will live in the will of God* (verse 32b). Paul asks his readers to pray "that I may come unto you with joy *by the will of God."* Paul's frame of reference for everything in life was the will of God. To the Apostle, mistakes in tactics, the carrying out of details, may be forgiven, but a mistake in strategy, the large-scale blueprint for living, can't be forgiven. That large blueprint is called "the will of God." A wise Christian said, "To not do the will of God is like cheating at a game of solitaire." The individual cheats only himself.

The will of God may be divided into two sub-categories: the known (revealed) will of God, and the unknown (unrevealed) will of God. Over and over again, the Bible says, "This is the will of God." However, there still seems to be a great deal of fuzzy thinking among Christians about the will of God. Christians seem to be preoccupied with aspects of the will of God that God has not revealed. Whom do I marry? Where shall I live? Which job shall I take? There is no clearly revealed statement in Scripture by which you may always make these choices. However, this rule will stand: If you want to know the will of God for your total life, then do the will of God in the areas where you know the will of God. Jesus said, "If any man will do His will, he shall know..." (John 7:17). If you will give great care to fulfilling the "known" will of God, He will clearly disclose to you His "unknown" will. Furthermore, the will of God is not so much the fulfilling of an action or series of actions, but rather it is a carefully designed relationship between Christ and the individual believer. You, dear Christian, **are** the will of God! You are God's project! He wants to change your character in order to control your conduct!

Imagine a wheel constantly going round and round. If you were on the edge of that wheel, you will go around with it. But if you get on the hub, the middle of the wheel, what happens? Everything revolves around you because of your position on the wheel. Prayer is a primary means by which we discover and occupy our center, our axis, the God in Whom we are to abide.

In the classic <u>One Day in the Life of Ivan Denisovich</u>, the story of life in a Russian prison camp, fellow inmates saw a prisoner praying. They loudly ridiculed him, saying, "Your prayers won't get you out of prison." The prisoner answered, "I'm not praying to get out of prison, but to do the will of God." This should be the priority of every Christian's life — to do the will of God. In this great passage about intercessory prayer, Paul indicates that every believer should daily pray for others — especially disciples praying for their disciplers and

A Call for Intercession

disciplers praying for their disciples — that they will live moment by moment in the will of God.

Finally, in a discipler-disciple relationship, each should pray for the other that *he will be refreshed himself, and that he will have a refreshing ministry* (verse 32). Paul asked the Roman Christians to "pray that I may with you be refreshed." Note the terms "that I may" and "with you." Paul desires refreshment for himself *and* for them. Is this important? You see, everybody who touches your life either refreshes you or drains you. This is also true of everyone whom *you* touch. You will either refresh them or drain them. Every Christian should aspire to be a *blessing* to others, not a *burden* or a *blot*, nor even a mere *blank*. One of the most elevating sentences in Paul's letters is this one: "Onesiphorus has often refreshed me, and was not ashamed of my chain" (II Timothy 1:16). Paul was in prison, and needed whatever encouragement he could receive. It seems that one of his fellow believers often came to see him, and his presence was like a tonic to Paul's spirit.

It should be the passionate desire of every Christian to encourage other Christians every time he contacts them. He should pray that he will be an encourager and that other Christians will commit themselves to the same ministry.

We have seen in this text the *basis* for an intercessory prayer ministry, the *battle* of such a ministry, and the *blessings* that should be sought through such a ministry.

IV. THE BENEDICTION SECURED BY AN INTERCESSORY PRAYER MINISTRY, 33

Finally, we see in this text the *benediction* secured by an intercessory prayer ministry. Paul concluded this passage with this benediction: "Now the God of peace be with you all" (verse 33). Sinful human beings sometimes ask God, "Where are you?" But this was the question God asked Adam. The question is not, Where is God, but rather, where is man in reference to God? Though God is omnipresent (everywhere), He may be far from the heart of a human being. God said, "You shall seek Me, and find Me, when you shall search for Me with all your heart."

The greatest subjective blessing received through a ministry of intercession is a visitation from God Himself. The greatest blessing is the presence of God with the intercessor. Prayer is not a means to get *our* will done in Heaven, but it is a means by which God gets *His* will done on earth. Prayer is not primarily an adjustment of God to ourselves, but an adjustment of ourselves to God. Prayer is primarily intended, not to *change* God's mind, but to *find* it, and enable us to *do* it. A Christian should not pray, "Lord, please do for *me* what *I* want," but "please do *with* me what *You* want." True prayer is made up more of self-surrender than self-assertion.

However, true prayer always attracts the presence of God to the one praying. Just as a person's lungs become filled with oxygen through breathing, so a Christian's spirit is filled with "the God of peace" through praying. Prayer may not be a time in which we seek to change God's attitude toward us, but rather a time when we seek to change our attitude toward Him. However, God draws remarkably near to us, and seems to show us great favor, in response to our prayers. What a "coincidence": the more I pray, the more spiritual power I have! The more I commune with Him in person, the more He comes upon me with power! *He smiles most easily upon the person who is nearest at hand.* So every Christian should master the ministry of intercession because of the benediction it brings to his own life.

A famous painting hangs on the wall of an art gallery in Madrid, Spain. It shows a peasant farm worker who has been plowing a field with a plow and a yoke of oxen. The peasant is caught at mid-morning kneeling in a fresh furrow for a time of prayer. A church and steeple in the background of the picture suggest that the church bell has peeled out the hour of prayer. The farm hand has laid his plough across a fresh furrow and has gotten on his knees to commune with God. But we, the observers, know something he does not know. While he is kneeling in prayer, an angel has come down out of the skies and has picked up the plow, and is completing the plowing of a row at the far end of the field. The angel is turning the oxen to plough another row, and the peasant doesn't even know it. Underneath the painting is this caption: **"NO TIME LOST"**. You see, when a Christian prays, he doesn't really lose time; *he gains eternity*. And this is especially true when He joins God in His interest for *others*. May we say with Samuel, "God forbid that I should sin against the Lord in ceasing to pray for you" (I Samuel 12:23).

Additional Thoughts, Quotes and Illustrations on Prayer

When the door of a steam room is left open, the heat inside rapidly escapes through it; likewise, a man, in his willingness to speak about everything in his conversations with other men, dissipates his experience of the presence of God through the door of speech, even though everything he says may be good.

Leo Tolstoy tells the story of three hermits who lived on an island. Their prayer was simple like they were simple: "We are three; You are three; have mercy on us. Amen." Miracles sometimes happened when they prayed that way. The bishop heard about the hermits and decided that they needed guidance in proper prayer, and so he went to their small island. After instructing the monks, the bishop set sail for the mainland, pleased to have enlightened the souls of such simple men. Suddenly, off the stern of the ship he saw something skimming over the surface of the water. It came closer and closer until he could see that it was the three hermits running on top of the water. Once on board the ship they said to the bishop, "We are so sorry, but we have forgotten some of your teaching about prayer. Would you please come back and instruct us again?" The bishop shook his head and replied meekly, "Forget everything I have taught you and continue to pray in your old way."(Richard Foster)

Prayer takes place in the middle voice. In grammar the active voice is when we take action, and the passive voice is when we receive the action of another, but in the middle voice we both act and are acted upon. We participate in the formation of the action and reap the benefits of it. We neither manipulate God (active voice) or are manipulated by God (passive voice). We are involved in the action and participate in its results but do not control or define it (middle voice). (Eugene Peterson)

Prayer should be nestling before it becomes wrestling. God's hands are our cradle. (Unknown source)

Prayer begins with the Lord, not with us. It is *He* who talks with me first. In the beginning, with the Father and the Holy Spirit, prayer was His idea, not an idea created by either our casual or crisis needs. Because it is His idea, prayer means more to Him than it does to us. Like parents accepting long distance collect calls from their children, even though it cost them money, the conversation will mean more to the parent than the child. (Dan Crawford)

The Christian who becomes *personal with* God will become *powerful for* God. (Source unknown)

When a Christian continues in prayer, the appropriate notice is not so much, "Quiet. Man At Prayer," but "Look Out! God Is At Work!" (Melvin Banks)

Picture Heaven as like a catalogue order center, full of angels reading requests. "This one says, 'I want to be happy in the future.' One angel says, "What exactly does that mean?" "I don't know," another answers. "What shall I do with it?" "Put it in the 'hold' file with all the rest. Someday these humans will learn to be specific," as he marks another request "Incomplete." (Laura Beth Jones)

Prayer opens the sluice-gates between us and the Infinite. It brings the frail wire into contact with the battery. It links together man and God. (John Henry Jowett)

The practical outcome of Communion ends with Commission. (E. Stanley Jones)

"To believe is to pray, and to cease to pray is to cease to believe." (C. S. Lewis)

THE KINGDOM OF RIGHT RELATIONSHIPS

Matthew 22:34-40:

"But when the Pharisees had heard that he had put the Sadducees to silence, they were gathered together. Then one of them, which was a lawyer, asked him a question, tempting him, and saying, Master, which is the great commandment in the law? Jesus said unto him, Thou shalt love the Lord thy God with all thy heart, and with all thy soul, and with all thy mind. This is the first and great commandment. And the second is like unto it, Thou shalt love thy neighbor as thyself. On these two commandments hang all the law and the prophets."

Scan the entire chapter for a moment. Jesus is getting near the end of His ministry. The shadow of the Cross is already dark on the near horizon of His life. The redeeming Events are coming soon now.

Three great questions are asked of Jesus in Matthew 22. Verse 15 mentions the Pharisees, and verse 16 the Herodians. The Pharisees were religious fanatics who favored Israel. The Herodians were Jewish political fanatics who favored Rome. Normally, these two parties were bitter enemies, but it is incredible to see how a common enemy will make bitter enemies into uneasy friends. The Pharisees and Herodians united in this chapter against Jesus. Then the Sadducees are introduced in verse 23. The question of the Pharisees and the

Herodians is recorded in verse 17: "Tell us therefore, What thinkest thou? Is it lawful to give tribute unto Caesar, or not?" The nature of the question suggests that it originated with the Herodians, the political party. Jesus' wisdom is on high profile as He answers the first question (verses 18-22).

The second question is recorded in verse 28. This question was asked by the Sadducees, who did not believe in a life after death. So their question was designed to trap Jesus into some inconsistency in His view of immortality. Jesus accuses them of an erroneous question because they did not know the Scriptures, "nor the power of God." He disarmed their evil intent while dealing with their question. "And when the multitude heard this, they were astonished at his doctrine" (verse 33).

Verse 34 introduces the third question. The first question was *political*, the second was *theological*, and the third is a *legal* question. This question was asked by one of the Pharisees, one who apparently had been delegated to speak for the group. He is identified as "a lawyer" (verse 35). That is, he is an expert in the law, and he asked a question concerning the law. "Master, which is the great commandment in the law?" The word translated "which" in this question is not the word for *quantity* (which one law emerges from the many as the most dominant), but the word for *quality*. What is the quality of the greatest commandment in the law? That is, what kind of commandment do you think is the most important kind in the law?

Note the nature of these questions. All of them, though this may not have been recognized by the questioners, have to do with relationships. The first question has to do with the relationship of *religion and the state* (we call it "church and state"). The second question has to do with the relationship between *this life and the next one*. The final question has to do with the relationship of *man and law*.

Note this principle: Jesus' answers are always bigger than our questions. The lawyer asked for one commandment, and Jesus gave two. He asked a legal question, and Jesus gave a relational answer. Jesus disregarded the apparent intent of the question, and expressed the content of God's revelation. God's revelation is always bigger than any question man may ask about it. The answer to any such question is not in a stated answer. The "answer" is not in the "answer"! The "answer" is in a relationship!

Reinhold Niebuhr, the great Christian theologian, and Abraham Heschel, the leading Jewish thinker, were engaged in conversation. Niebuhr asked Heschel, "Do you really try to obey all of those dietary laws of the book of Leviticus?" Heschel answered, "Yes, I do — every one of them." "Why?" Niebuhr asked, "Why would you keep those old archaic laws today?" Heschel's answer was a classic. It also constitutes a good example of faith. He replied, "My friend, you may not understand or appreciate my answer, but I try to keep all the dietary laws of the book of Leviticus *simply because I do not understand them!*" What an insight! What an example of faith! In other words, I have discovered that God is much, much smarter than I am, and when He speaks, He speaks out of His infinite intelligence and wisdom, and He speaks in the interest of my highest good. So though I do not always understand His reasons for the commands, I keep them anyway, in deference to a Higher Intelligence and a Higher Will. Friends, ponder this paragraph until it *reaches your heart!*

Perhaps the most puzzling cartoonist on the current scene is an artist of paradox named Gary Larson, who created a one-frame cartoon called "The Far Side." Larson confessed that it was a difficult task to regularly throw his mind into reverse to create the comic pictures in the cartoon. But sometimes he stays in the world where we live and creates comedy out of stretched situations there. In one of the easier pieces of hilarity, he pictured a very heavy lady buried in a puffy couch, hair in curlers, a broom in one hand, and a telephone in the other. She is surrounded by three large and looming fish bowls, and each bowl shows the exaggerated figures of several marine creatures. Apparently, the fish bowls have created a conversational idea for her. She says to her friend on the phone, "I kissed a frog, it turned into a prince, we got married — and wham! We're stuck with a bunch of polliwogs!" Sooner or later, we all know how that woman felt. Even our best relationships may sometimes seem to be overpopulated with "polliwogs," when all we ever wanted was to be related to handsome princes — and to play that same role to others. But our relationships sometimes become superficial and shallow and are often strained. It is not easy to maintain good relational skills and good relationships. The words of Jesus in our text will challenge and help us.

"Teacher, of what sort is the greatest commandment of the law?" "You shall love the Lord your God with your whole heart (qualitative, not quantitative), and with your whole soul, and with your whole mind. This is the foremost and greatest commandment. And the second is similar, You shall love your neighbor as yourself. On *these two commandments* (this term bears major emphasis in the text, and it is the only emphatic term in the entire passage) hang all the law and the prophets." The word "hang" means to "suspend" something. All the Old Testament revelation of the law and the prophets is suspended upon these two commandments, like a hat hung on a nail in the wall.

I. THE OBLIGATION

First, we note *the obligation* of these commandments. The common word in the two commandments is the word "love."

This is striking, because it means, first, that love is commanded by God, and thus it is *controllable*. Can you imagine someone *commanding* love? And we are even told that not having this love is the greatest and worst sin that we are capable of committing.

You see the contrasting views of Christ and culture when you realize that the world tells us that you cannot legislate love. Why does the world say this? Because it has the wrong definition of love! To the world, love is an emotional experience which you can "fall into" uncontrollably, and *may* fall out of. It just makes common sense that if you can fall into something, you can also fall out of it. But if love is legitimately commanded, it is necessarily controllable. God expects you to control your love! So a different definition of love (the correct one) is necessary. Love is not primarily an *emotion*; it is essentially a *vocation*. True love involves *choice, commitment* and *continuation*. Our society is in trouble in its "love-life" today because commitment is an almost totally lost art among us.

Note also that the obligation is *positive*. This obligation takes us far beyond the ethic that merely says, "I'm OK, because I don't harm anybody." Many say, "I don't do this, and I don't do that — so I'm much better than many believers." A first-grade teacher was asking the pupils' names on the first day of class. One little boy said, "My name is 'Johnny Don't'!" It seemed that all he had ever heard his parents say to him was, "Johnny, Don't", and he thought that was his name! Many people live this way all the time. In their understanding, the whole Gospel is "Johnny, don't." But no life that is merely negative will please God. Negatives are necessary, to be sure, but the negatives of the Gospel merely "clear the decks" for Divine action. The Divine action is to be continual, while the negatives are to be performed in a moment (though they will need to be maintained by a regular discipline).

Again, note that the word for "love" here is *the distinctive Christian word*. The word is "agape" (in both cases). The love that is mandated toward God is *agape*, the love that is declared for self is *agape*, and the love that is mandated for your fellow man is *agape*. So a reasonable definition of *agape* is required. *Agape* is the kind of love which God has for man. *Agape* is self-disinterested, self-giving love. This kind of love has been defined as "the basic disposition of one's whole being to relate to God for His glory and to man for his good." It is *that distinctive love which desires only the highest good for its object* — whether the object be God, self, or others. The fact that God loves you is not a sentimental fact; it means that He desires only your highest good. So He cannot desire anything for you that will compromise holiness, righteousness, or His best dreams for you. And this is the kind of love we are commanded to have for God and others, and it is the kind of love we are expected to have even for ourselves.

There are three kinds of love recognized (though *eros* is not mentioned by name) in the New Testament — *eros*, *philos*, and *agape*. The simple chart on the next page may help us to see the differences in these three kinds of love.

Study this chart thoughtfully and carefully. It is the nature of love to want to possess its object. Love is a combination of two impulses: to give itself for the other, and to have the other for itself. Perfect love is the proper balance between these two impulses: to give and to share for the other, and to have and to hold for oneself. That awful cross on Calvary stands forever as our proof that God was willing to go the full limit in giving Himself. Yet that willingness to give Himself is also coupled with the Divine desire to possess us, the objects of His love. The Son of Man came to seek, and the purpose of that seeking is that He might find, and bring back His people to God; for it is the nature of love to long to possess its object. So the whole point of the Gospel is that God is looking for you, and that He jealously wants to possess and use you.

EROS	*PHILOS*	*AGAPE*
Sensual, usually selfish	Social	Spiritual, sacrificial
When alone, it is *all take*	It is *give & take*	It is *all give*, though it does desire to possess its object
The subject loves because the object is desirable	Subject & object love because of mutual satisfaction	The subject loves only because of his own determination
"I love you *if you will satisfy me,*"or, "*I love me*, and *I want you*"	"I love you *because we are happy together*"	"I love you *in spite of every detriment to my love*"
The object pleases the subject	Mutual pleasure between object and subject	The condition of the object does not matter
Earned by the object	Mutually earned	Not earned at all; indifferent to the merit of the object

A fourth idea about this obligation. *The total personhood of each individual is to be involved in the fulfillment of this obligation.* This requires the cooperation and submission of all faculties that each individual has — heart, soul, mind and strength. Man's response to God's love is to be a total response.

A Dutchman named Jacob Boehmke gave his personal testimony in these words. "I seemed to be like a battalion of soldiers when at ease, marching off in different directions. I was divided within, and a civil war seemed to be always occurring. There was nothing in me to cement me together. The centrifugal force of sin seemed to be hurtling the divided parts away from any integrating center. But God was at work.

One night, when conviction had reached its height, I went into a room alone, got down on my knees, and *accepted Christ unanimously.* At that moment, Jesus Christ made me 'whole.'" And his whole heart, mind, soul and strength were then required to be involved in this mandate to love. Note the threefold occurrence of the word "all" in this commandment. This isolates each category and maximizes the total obligation.

The word "heart" is normally used in the Bible as the driving mainspring of a person's life (just like his physical heart is the mainspring of his material life). The word "soul" is the seat of your emotions. The word is *"psuche";* we get our words "psychology" and "psychiatry" from this word. The soul is apparently an individual's mind, emotions and will acting within. Your soul is your psychological life. The word "mind" isolates your mental faculty, your ability to think reasonably. It is interesting that Jesus apparently added the mind to the list. This command quotes the Jewish "Shema" from Deuteronomy 6:4-5, but Jesus adds the word "mind" to the list stated there. Why? Let me venture an interpretation. Jesus adds the word "mind" because the heart of a man will not long pursue a course which the mind of that man disagrees with. Furthermore, the very strategy of Jesus, that of "making disciples," requires the continual use of a developing and growing mind. If the Gospel is not presentable and persuasive to the best thinking of a man's mind, it should not invite the devotion of his heart. Your "strength" is the total strength of your life — strength of personality, of energy, and of will.

Think of the *practical, personal* applications of this obligation. Our *emotions* are to be *dominated* by love; our *thoughts* are to be *directed* by love; our *actions* are to be *determined* by love; and our *words* are to be *dictated* by love. These, and many more, are the implications of this command.

II. THE OBJECT

Second, we notice the primary *object* of the command. "You shall love *the Lord your God.*" We have some tremendous advantages in helping us to understand this command because this is a direct quote from two Old Testament passages. We must simply go to the Old Testament and check the exact words, find their Hebrew meanings, and we may understand the object we are to love. The first command in our text is recorded in Deuteronomy 6:5, and the second is recorded in Leviticus 19:18.

Note in particular the Person who is identified as the object of our commanded love. "The Lord your God." The word "Lord" is the word "Jehovah," or "Yahweh," the covenant-making God of the Old Testament. The word itself is a compound word comprised of the past, present and future tenses of the Hebrew verb, "I am." So this is the foundation for the revelation of the great "I Am" God who revealed Himself as such to Moses (see Exodus 3). The word indicates that God is always in the Eternal Now, the Eternal Present. Though this includes all tenses to us — past, present, and future — there is only an Eternal Present to God. Isaiah 57 says that God "inhabits eternity." Time is His accommodation of our finiteness, but He inhabits eternity. So the Hebrew word translated "LORD" indicates that He is the great self-consistent, self-sufficient, self-continuous God. He needs not anything from anybody outside Himself — unless He chooses to.

The word "God" ("thy God") is another gigantic word. In the Hebrew, it is the word "Elohim." This is a plural word (!), which certainly accommodates the Christian doctrine of the Divine Trinity. The plural form also compounds the regular meaning of the word. The word means, "powerful," and the plural form elevates it into "Mighty, All-powerful, All-capable, Omni-competent." So the object of our love is to be the One who loves us enough to enter into covenant with us for our good, and is capable of fully carrying out His purposes. He is certainly worthy of our highest and best love. *His* love for *us* was not half-hearted, and He doesn't expect *our* love for *Him* to be half-hearted. *His* love for *us* was whole-hearted, and He expects *our* love for *Him* to be whole-hearted. God left nothing of Himself out of the relationship, and God expects us to leave nothing of ourselves out of the relationship. As He has loved us with His whole Being, we are to "love the Lord our God" with the devotion of *our* whole being.

III. THE ORDER

Thirdly, we note the *order* of these commands. "You shall love ... God ... and your neighbor as yourself." The order of the stated objects is very important. It is the invariable order of Scripture -- God first, then man. For example, reexamine the Ten Commandments, and you will see this order. The first four are an echo of the first commandment stated here, and the last six are an echo of the second commandment stated here. We are to love God first, then our fellow man.

The order helps us to examine ourselves, for it tells us that where there has been no *expression* of the love of God through you *toward others*, there has actually been no *experience* of the love of God *in your own heart*. Linger here and meditate on this truth. **No expression of the love of God toward others means no experience of the love of God in you.** To put it positively, the experience of God's love by you and in you will lead to the expression of God's love through you.

You see, *the concept of relationship* precedes time. Before the world was created, before man was made, God was (always is) a trinity of persons. He has three ways of being God. He is the Father, the Son, and the Holy Spirit. As a Trinity, God has always modeled the meaning of love. He has

The Kingdom of Right Relationships

always provided the perfect model for a society of beings. He has continuously demonstrated relational existence. So relationships have been topmost in God's priorities for all eternity. If there is anything any higher than right relational living, God has not revealed it to us.

Someone said, "Success is 15% product knowledge and 85% people knowledge." It will not make any difference how well we as Christians master our message if we do not love people. "They won't care how much we know until they first know how much we care." The disarming aspect of all spiritual initiative, whether from God to us, or from us to others, is in the love that is shown.

Recently, I heard this sad statistic with regard to the Christian foreign missionary force. When Christian missionaries have returned early from the foreign field, three times as many came back because of problems in relating to other missionaries than those who came back because of problems of culture, learning the language, or adaptation. The lesson? All Christians, however committed they may be, have trouble in relationships. Where is the deficiency? The deficiency usually stems from the sad fact that most Christians have never been truly discipled in building relational skills and in building and maintaining positive, loving, supportive, productive relationships. The Christian community has been fairly efficient in teaching *revelational* theology, but not nearly so effective in understanding and applying *relational* theology.

In a crowd of people, is there usually more *companionship* or more *competition*? I'm sure we would admit that the answer might largely depend on the nature of the crowd and the reason for its assembly. But tragically, many crowds today are conspicuously full of an adversarial attitude. It seems that there is potential violence at every street corner and in every shopping center today. Every person is either a potential friend or a potential foe. If I see people as my adversaries or competitors, I will spar with them mentally and practically. If, on the other hand, I see people as true spiritual assets, I will identify with them, assist in their development, and help them to see and realize their potential. Perhaps the word "assets" is too mercenary, but it is meant in the very best sense.

Years ago, Billy Graham said, "Our alternatives today are few and simple. It is either 'back to the Bible' or 'back to the jungle.' There is no third possibility." No Christian should ever allow an adversarial attitude to prevail within him toward any other human being. However, we must face the fact that this adversarial attitude is natural to the flesh, and that only by the aid of God and His Love can we win over it.

Let me point out that the two relationships commanded in our text might be viewed in the figure of a cross — vertical, then horizontal. Just as with a cross, the vertical shaft (our relationship with God) carries all the weight, and the horizontal arm (true *agape* relationships with our fellow men) stands only because the vertical supports it. Ponder this paragraph carefully, even drawing a cross and labeling its two shafts if necessary. At the top of the vertical shaft, put the words, "God's Love For Man," and draw an arrow pointing down the upper part of that vertical arm. At the bottom of the vertical shaft, put the words, "Man's Love For God," and draw an arrow pointing up the lower part of that vertical arm. On the left side of the horizontal arm of the cross, put the words, "Love For Fellow Believers," and draw an arrow pointing outward away from the center shaft. On the right side of the horizontal arm, put the words, "Love For All Men," and again draw an arrow pointing outward away from the center shaft.

Here we see the four basic relationships of life. They are: (1) The *indispensable* relationship — my relationship with the *Savior*. (2) The *internal* relationship — my relationship with *self*. (3) The *interpersonal* relationship -- my relationship with the *significant other people* in my life. (4) The *involvement* relationship — my relationship with *society*.

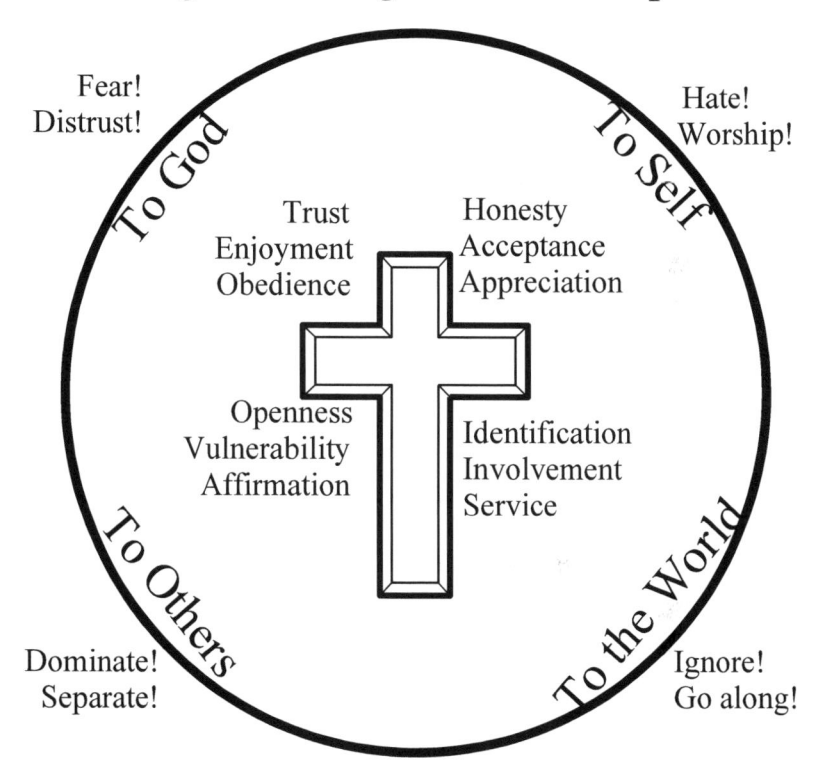

The Kingdom of Right Relationships

Fear! Distrust!
To God
Trust
Enjoyment
Obedience

Hate! Worship!
To Self
Honesty
Acceptance
Appreciation

Openness
Vulnerability
Affirmation

Identification
Involvement
Service

To Others
Dominate!
Separate!

To the World
Ignore!
Go along!

The four basic relationships in life for any human being are recorded inside the circle moving clockwise from the upper left. The four relationships are your relationship *to God*, your relationship to *your own self*, your relationship to *the significant other people in your life*, and your relationship *to the world* or society at large.

The most important relationship in the life of any human being is his *relationship with God*, which is represented in the upper left part of the circle. God's plan is defined inside the circle. First, it is God's plan that every human being live in total *trust* of Him for his entire life. This life then becomes a life of full and perfect *enjoyment*. And each one of us as dependent creatures should live a life of happy *obedience* to God, where both *our* pleasure *and His* are found. Each of these areas might be explored in limitless ways.

Outside the circle, Satan's alternate plan for man's relationship with God may be seen. Since every human being is related to God every moment of every day, either in a good way or a bad way, Satan's plan is to turn man's relationship with God totally sour. He seeks to get man to inordinately *fear* God and to suspiciously *distrust* Him. Every Christian should study this relationship in these areas carefully, because he will see examples of both God's plan in action and Satan's plan in action every day of his life. Indeed, he will know the struggles between the two plans in his own life, also.

The second important relationship in the life of any human being is his *relationship to himself.* God's plan for him is that he live a life of openness, transparency, and total *honesty* in all relational matters in his life. It is God's will that he *accept* himself as God made him, and even that he be honest about himself as he has distorted himself in sin and selfishness — in order that he might present all that he is, good or bad, to God for His purposes to be fulfilled in his life. God expects him to have full *appreciation* of the unique and distinctive way he is made, and that he realize that it is through his unique personhood that God wants to reveal himself to the world.

However, we must remember that there is an alternate plan of Satan for this relationship as well. And we must frankly admit that Satan is a master of distortion in our inner lives. If unchecked, he will twist our view of ourselves and our self-worth until it does not match God's intention or God's revelation. It is Satan's design, first, that we *hate* ourselves.

After all, he tells us, you are worthless and wicked, and the problems will never be solved. So he tempts you to hate yourself. Or he reverses the plan and seeks to get you to *worship* yourself. This is Satan's lifestyle — that of self-aggrandizement and self-exaltation. And he longs to have you made in his image, after his likeness.

The third important relationship in the life of any human being is his *relationship to the significant other people in his life*. God's plan is that he live a life of *openness* with each of these people. It is also God's purpose that he make himself *vulnerable* to them. Vulnerability may be popularly defined as getting out on a limb — and putting the saw in someone else's hands. This does not mean that we court our own disadvantage. It does mean that we would rather allow our own disadvantage than to take selfish or sinful advantage of the others. We would rather suffer hurt from others than inflict hurt on them (see I Peter 2:21-24 for the example of Jesus). Furthermore, God desires that we honestly *affirm* one another in all possible ways. This means that we seek the best, the Christ-like, in the people who are near to us, and that we vocally affirm what we find.

Again, Satan has an alternate plan for our relationships with the significant other people in our lives. If we are alert each day, we will see clear evidence within ourselves and around us in others of Satan's plan. It is Satan's plan that we seek to *dominate* all of those who are near us. He wants us to selfishly control and intimidate as many people as we can. Or he wants us to altogether *separate* ourselves from them. He is in the separation business, and if he can create malicious or suspicious divisions between us, his plan is fulfilled.

The fourth important relationship in the life of every human being is his *relationship to the world*. God's plan for each of us is that we *identify* with the people of society for the sake of representing and serving Christ. Jesus prayed that we would be "in the world but not of it." This means that we are to be totally *involved* in the world, but only for redemptive purposes. We are not to draw our beliefs or attitudes from the world, but we are to become active in it to reach people for Christ's sake. We are to live in the world as Jesus did, as the *servant* of both God and man.

Here also, Satan offers an alternate plan. It is Satan's desire that we *ignore* the world with its massive needs, and be indifferent to it. He offers enough selfish concerns to us to keep us preoccupied with ourselves and our interests so that the needs of the world will go unnoticed and unmet. Or Satan entices us to *go along* with the moral drift and godlessness of a sinful society.

Each believer should do his own lengthy meditating on these four relationships and the two plans for them. He will easily see both God's strategy and Satan's substitute plan in each area. And he must keep himself in the light of God's truth so that he can be a credit to Christ in the Kingdom of Right Relationships.

If God is properly and accurately understood, it should not be at all difficult to trust, obey, and enjoy Him. However, we may need to give disciplined care to the other three relationships. It is very easy for most people, even believers, to be wrongly adjusted to themselves, the significant others in their lives, and the world.

An old and well-known child's fantasy story may help us to understand our vocation in the last three relationships. It is the story of the handsome prince who fell under the spell and the curse of a wicked witch. The witch turned the handsome prince into an ugly frog. The story declared that the frog would remain low and ugly unless a beautiful maiden came along and kissed him. But everyone knows that beautiful maidens just do not go around kissing ugly frogs! But wonder of wonders, one day that is exactly what happened. A beautiful maiden came along, noticed the ugly frog, and planted a big kiss on his ugly lips. When she did so, the ugly frog was instantly transformed into a prince more handsome than he had been before. And of course, in the way of all good, innocent child's stories, the beautiful maiden and the handsome prince fell in love, got married, and "lived happily ever after." Good, happy story!

But most people never detect the meaning of the story. It is actually an illustration of Biblical truth. The handsome prince represents Adam as God created him. The wicked witch represents the devil. The transformation of the prince to a low and ugly frog represents the Fall of man into sin and under the spell of Satan. The beautiful maiden represents Jesus Christ. The kiss represents His embrace of love and grace, and His communication of life to low and fallen men. The restored prince represents the redeemed saint. The marriage reminds us that we are "married unto Another, even unto Him who is raised from the dead" (Romans 7:4). And *we will "live happily ever after"!*

The punch line? What is our relational vocation as Christians living in this fallen world? We are to *go around kissing ugly frogs* — whether the frog be ourselves, a person near and dear to us, or one of the needy sinners-at-large in the world!

WANTED: SEED-SOWERS

Mark 4:26-29:

"And He said, So is the kingdom of God, as if a man should cast seed into the ground; And should sleep, and rise night and day, and the seed should spring and grow up, he knoweth not how. For the earth bringeth forth fruit of herself; first the blade, then the ear, after that the full corn in the ear. But when the fruit is brought forth, immediately he putteth in the sickle, because the harvest is come." (King James Version)

"The Jesus said, "God's kingdom is like seed thrown on a field by a man who then goes to bed and forgets about it. The seed sprouts and grows — he has no idea how it happens. The earth does it all without his help: first a green stem of grass, then a bud, then the ripened grain. When the grain is fully formed, he reaps — harvest time!" (Eugene Peterson translation, <u>The Message</u>)

Let me begin this study with an outline of the parable. First, it reveals *A Simple Procedure, verse 26*. Then, *A Secret Providence* takes over, verses 26b-27. Finally, it closes with *A Sure Promise, verse 28*. *A Simple Procedure, a Secret Providence*, and *A Sure Promise*. These three points may be clearly seen, in order, in the text.

I. A SIMPLE PROCEDURE

Now, let me explain these three points from the text itself. First, a Simple Procedure. A man, possibly a farmer, goes out into a field and casts seed upon the soil of that field.

The verb, "cast," is an aorist tense verb in the original language, and that is very important in understanding the parable. The aorist tense reveals point action, or one-time action. It is like a dot, or a period, on a time-line. It describes action that occurs only one time. So the simple procedure pictured in the parable is that of a farmer who goes out into an open field with a bag of seeds at his belt or in his hand. He gathers a hand-full of those seeds in his fist and flings them wholesale over the soil. He "broadcasts" those seeds as far as he can over the soil of the field. And it must be kept in mind that *he performs this action only one time.* Admittedly, we don't know whether he does it with one sweep of his arm and one opening of his hand, or this is several days' work drawn up into one activity (a time of sowing), but the text clearly pictures his action as one-time point action. I repeat, this is very important in understanding the parable.

II. A SECRET PROVIDENCE

When this one-time action has been completed, then a Silent, Secret Providence takes over. The farmer himself "sleeps, and rises, night and day." The Peterson paraphrase called *The Message* says that after the farmer sows the seed in the field, "he then goes to bed and forgets about it." In other words, he completes the one-time act of sowing the seed in the field, and then he resumes a normal schedule of activities day and night thereafter. He goes to sleep each night, and rises to the particular activities of each new day. It is again very important in understanding the parable to note that the verbs, "sleep" and "rise" are present tense verbs, picturing continuing activity.

Again, Eugene Peterson captures the idea vividly and accurately in his translation called The Message, when he translates, when "the seed (is) thrown on a field . . . the man then goes to bed *and forgets about it."* In fact, the text pictures day after day in succession in this man's life — he sleeps each night and rises up to the business of each new day. He sows the seed once — and then goes about his daily business as if he has totally forgotten the sowing of the seed.

However, though he now disregards the seeds and the soil, a silent, secret providence has taken over. "The seed sprouts and grows — and he has no idea how it happens." Again, the verbs are present tense verbs, picturing continuing action. "The seed *keeps on* sprouting and *keeps on* growing," and the ironic fact is added, "and he has no idea how it happens." The pronoun "he" bears major emphasis in the sentence, which means, "He *himself* (the very one who sowed the seed, mind you!) doesn't have the slightest idea how it (the growth of the plant from the seed) happens." So, while he is just "minding his own business," day after day and night after night, a secret providence has taken over and a great crop is grown.

III. A SURE PROMISE

The text then concludes with a Sure Promise. *"For the earth brings forth fruit of herself,"* Jesus said (King James Version). Again, The Message translation vividly declares the meaning: *"The earth does it all without his help: first a green stem of grass, then a bud, then the ripened grain. When the grain is fully formed, he reaps — harvest time!"* We cannot hear this statement too many times:*"The earth brings forth fruit all by itself"*! Again, a grammar lesson is absolutely vital. The term translated *"all by itself"* bears major emphasis, which means that the Holy Spirit has, if effect, shouted these words from the page. Reread this sentence aloud, and shout these words: **"All by itself!"** It will help you to know what the word actually is. It is the Greek word, *"automate."* We derive our word *"automatic"* from this word. Now the promise is seen in its full assurance; it is indeed a sure promise! Once the seed has fallen on the soil, *"the earth brings forth fruit automatically!"*

Every farmer loves the harvest season of his farming year. He loves to look upon the golden grain in the fields on the day before the harvesting process begins. He moves diligently, efficiently and eagerly into the time of harvest, knowing that his income and livelihood depend on that harvest. However, every farmer also knows that he cannot get to "point B" on the calendar of his farming year — the time of harvest, without going through "point A" — the time of sowing. A profitable harvest will come only after seed has been properly sown. There simply will be no desirable harvest unless the appropriate seed is sown.

Everywhere I move in churches over this land, people are lamenting the sad moral and spiritual decline of this nation. The question, "What is happening?" sounds out consistently. The question, "What is wrong?" is asked monotonously. If *(since)* this text is correct, the answer is simple: There is far too little one-on-one sowing taking place on the soils of men's hearts. The entire problem may be reduced to this simple statement: the harvest is potentially plentiful, but actually pitiful — because of the failure of Christians to consistently, continuously, compassionately sow the seed on the soil where the crop must be raised.

According to Jesus, the soils represent men's hearts, and *each man's heart* is the field for sowing the Gospel seed. Earlier in this same chapter (Mark 4), Jesus had told the "parable of the sower," or the parable *of the soils*, and He tells us that the soils represent men's hearts individually, and the reception of the seed into the soil represents each man's response to the Gospel when he hears it. But it must be noted in each of these two parables that one man did the sowing, and he did it close-up and hands-on. The sowing was not accomplished by a piece of mechanized farm equipment or from an airplane (this type of evangelism is actually caricatured in Joe Bayley's <u>The Gospel Blimp</u>) or by a "piped in" technique. It was done by a farmer whose feet had carried him out into the field, and whose hands held the seed and applied it to the soil. In other words, these parables basically picture personal evangelism, whether one-on-one or wholesale.

Every wise farmer knows that he is in partnership with God and His providence as he waits for a crop, but he also knows that he is himself a crucial part of the miracle merely by sowing the seed on the soil. So farming is a "co-op" activity. "The Farmer's Co-op" is not merely the name of a business; it is the formula for a miracle! And while even the seed is stored with life by the hand of God, the farmer must release it from *his* hand if there is to be a harvest.

Our parable is a bit strange in that the farmer engages in sowing just one time and then forgets the action he has taken. This is the whole point of the parable. Once the seed strikes the soil, *the harvest is automatic.* Now, every farmer knows that not every seed sown will be a part of the crop, but he also knows very well that, without the sowing of the seed, no reaping will occur. Every Christian should know that not every testimony given to a lost person will produce the fruit of eternal life, but he also knows that, unless the testimony *is* given, eternal life will never enter any human heart. "Faith comes by hearing, and hearing by the Word of God," and Christians have been assigned to speak the faith-stimulating Word which echoes the truth of God's Word in their experience. When they do so speak, the harvest is automatic. So where are the seed-sowers?

I want to spend the remainder of this study illustrating the truth of this parable from my own experience. I have seen the truth of this parable demonstrated and proven many, many times. In fact, I could write a substantial book about experiences which prove the accuracy and faithfulness of these words of Jesus. I will confine myself to just one of the many possibilities.

Let me begin by telling you, from a human standpoint, how I became a Christian. My personal testimony is replete with several substantiations of the truth of this parable. The part of the story with which I have become familiar begins before I was born (a long, long time ago!). The story begins on a street in the city of Chicago. A man with a German name and background, Joe Beine, had left his daily workplace at "quitting time" one afternoon, had stepped onto a wide, busy sidewalk, and was moving through the crowd toward his home. Suddenly, his shoulder struck the shoulder of a man facing in the opposite direction on the sidewalk, and the bump was hard enough to turn each of them toward the other. Joe later told me that he did not remember a single word being spoken by either of them at any time during their momentary encounter. The man had a slip of paper between the fingers and thumb of one hand, and was passing out such pieces of paper to anyone on the sidewalk who would receive one. When they turned to face each other, the man simply thrust the leaflet into Joe's hand. Joe thoughtlessly took it, quickly put it in his shirt pocket, and moved silently on down the sidewalk.

When he arrived home a short while later, his wife was cooking the evening meal, so he went upstairs and took a quick bath. Then he put on leisure clothes for the evening and started down to supper. As the passed the bed, he picked up the clothes he had removed and put them in a clothes hamper at the closet door. When he turned again to go down to supper, he noticed that the piece of paper he had placed in his pocket had slipped out onto the bed. He reached down casually, picked it up, and glanced at the front side of the leaflet. He later said, "I had not scanned one paragraph of it before I knew that I needed what it was offering more than I needed life itself." Of course, the leaflet was a Gospel tract. Joe Beine stood beside the bed and read it — twice. Then, he got down on his knees, read the "instructions" on the bottom at the back — and was eternally saved beside his bed! Possessed with his experience, he placed the leaflet on the end table beside him.

He stood up, full of a new glory, but when he went downstairs, he discovered that he was too embarrassed to tell his wife what had happened! They finished the evening meal, she washed the dishes, and he went into the den of their home to read the daily newspaper. When she finished the dishes, she went upstairs to change into leisure clothes for the evening as he had done shortly before. You've guessed by now what happened. She saw the leaflet on the end table by the bed, picked it up, read it — and she, too, was saved beside the bed! But she also discovered that she could not immediately tell him about her experience of salvation. In fact, they got all the way to breakfast the next morning before one broke the news to the other. Joe was already seated at the table to eat breakfast, and she was about to be seated, when she suddenly dropped to her knees and began to weep. He rushed around the table and knelt beside her with his arm around her, thinking she was ill. She sobbed, "Honey, there's something I've got to tell you," and she told him what had happened to her the evening before. "You, too!" he responded, half choked with emotion. And thus the *simple procedure* and *secret providence* and *sure promise* crowded together in the experience of two beautifully simple sinners. Now, the story shifts to a scene which occurred many miles away from Chicago and several years later.

The Beine family, now consisting of Marilyn (a daughter), Bob (a son), and Mr. and Mrs. Joe Beine, had moved south to the little mountain town of Winslow, Arkansas, some miles south of Fayetteville, Arkansas, the Ozark mountain town where I was raised.

At the time of this part of the story, Bob Beine was sixteen years old and I was seventeen. It was a very, very hot day in Fayetteville and I had gone to the city swimming pool for a swim. I was on the side of the pool with many, many kids of all ages. Morally and spiritually, I was a renegade sinner at the time, full of the devil. This problem was compounded by the fact that I had a terrible sense of self-worth and thus was always trying to perform and prove myself. I loudly said something I thought was very clever, wanting all the kids around me to hear it, took God's Name in vain, coupled it with a "damn," and dived into an opening in the water of the pool. I came to the surface and came swimming back to the edge of the pool, proud of my cleverness.

Bob Beine (whose name I barely knew, if at all) had been standing a few feet away at pool side, and he heard my blasphemous words. He moved down the side of the pool until he stood over the place where I was preparing to climb out of the water. He extended his right hand, and I took it, assuming he was just helping me from the water. However, when he had assisted me out of the water, he didn't let go of my hand. Instead, he held it tightly right up near his own chest. When I had brushed the water out of my eyes with the other hand, I looked into his face, wondering why he did not let go of my hand. He looked into my eyes and gently said, "Herb, do you know that you just 'damned' the only Person who ever loved you enough to die for you?" That was all that was said between us. I laughed like I thought he was being clever and jerked my hand away, immediately diving back into the water.

However, I could not get rid of his words as easily as I got rid of his hand. For nine months, I carried that sentence in my heart, creating increasing conviction. "Herb, you just 'damned' the only Person who ever love you enough to die for you." Then, on my eighteenth birthday, a man told me how to receive Christ into my life as my own Savior, Lord, and Friend. I did not fully understand everything, but I knew I desperately needed what he was offering. So I trusted Jesus Christ to save me, and He came into my life. But the stimulus for my decision came from one sentence spoken by a sixteen year old boy — who later did not even remember speaking that sentence!

    I have now been a Christian for just over fifty years. I have been incredibly privileged to influence many people toward Christ. But the thought remains: every person whom I influence and "win" to Christ, every person whom God uses me to enlist and train in the Christian movement, every person whom my trainees enlist and train, *will line up at the judgment seat of Christ behind a man whose name we don't even know, a man who did nothing but place a piece of paper in another man's hand.* That man probably did not even know the principle, that when the seed reaches the soil, the harvest is automatic. But it is God Who governs those matters, and they do not wait on the intelligence of the sower, and they cannot be deterred by his ignorance. To God be the glory. Now, *where are the seed-sowers?*

WHEN JESUS LOOKS AT YOU
JOHN 1:42

I. He Looks With a Double Optic in His Eye

  A. He saw Simon as he was.

  B. He saw Peter as he could be.

II. He Looks With a Divine Optimism in His Heart

  A. A realistic optimism.

  B. An idealistic optimism.

  C. Both idealistic and realistic optimism.

III. He Looks With a Definite Objective in His Mind

  A. An objective for the maturing of the man

  B. An objective for his mission in the Christian movement

  C. An objective for the multiplication of the man and his ministry

WHEN JESUS LOOKS AT YOU

John 1:42:

And he brought him to Jesus. And when Jesus beheld him, He said, "Thou art Simon the son of Jona. Thou shalt be called Cephas" (which is by interpretation, A stone).

Perhaps the most loved character in the Bible, apart from Jesus Himself, is Simon Peter. For sheer variety, for contradiction of personality, for mixture of saint and sinner in one person, the story of Simon Peter is unbeatable. Perhaps the reason we like him so well is because he is so much like us. When we read his story, we are looking at a full-length reflection of ourselves. Let's narrow the spotlight of our attention and let it fall on just one small part of his life—his *call* to become a Christian. It's of great interest to me to note the place of Andrew in Peter's conversion. Andrew is mentioned only three times in the New Testament (engaged in some activity), and on all three occasions he is bringing someone to Jesus. It was Andrew who brought the young boy to Jesus with his five loaves and two fishes for the feeding of the five thousand (John 6). It was Andrew who introduced the *Greeks* to Jesus (John 12) when Philip was uncertain. And it was Andrew who introduced his own brother, Simon, to Jesus.

Focus your attention for a few minutes on the words which Jesus spoke to Peter when they saw each other for the first time. "When Jesus beheld him, He said, Thou art Simon the son of Jona: thou shalt be called Cephas, which is by interpretation, a stone." From this verse, we note how Jesus views men.

I. WITH A DOUBLE OPTIC IN HIS EYE

When Jesus looks at you, He always looks at you *with a Double Optic in His eye*. He *sees* "double" when He looks at you. When Jesus Christ looks at your life, He always looks at you with "double vision." He always looks at you "bifocally." He sees not *one* person, but *two*. When Jesus looked at Simon Peter in the moment of their first encounter, He saw *two* People.

First, He saw Simon as he was at that very moment. He saw *Simon*, the real man then existing. And what He saw was by no means a beautiful or pleasant picture. He saw a *cursing*, swearing fisherman. He saw the weak, unstable, undependable brother of Andrew. He saw a man of hot, rash, impulsive nature. Peter had undoubtedly thought a thousand times thoughts similar to those expressed by the poet, Robert Burns, when he wrote, "Oh, that a man would arise in me, that the man that I am might cease to be."

But Jesus also saw something else when He looked at this man. He not only saw the real man, Simon as he was, He saw Peter as he could be. He saw the man that God's grace could make out of Simon. And the two men—what Simon was and what he could be— were so different that each of them required a different name. Looking at this man as he was, Jesus said, "Thou art *Simon*"; looking at him as he could *become*, He said, "Thou *shalt* be called Cephas, a Rock." And every time Jesus Christ looks at a person, He sees not one person, but two. He looked at *Simon* and saw *Peter*; He looked at *Saul* of Tarsus and saw *Paul* the Apostle; He looked at *Jacob* the liar and cheat, and saw *Israel*, the prince with God. And when He looks at you or me, He sees two people -- the one I *am*, and the one He can *make* of me. It was Ralph Waldo Emerson, the famous poet, who put this truth into these poetic lines:

> *"If in a vision you could see*
> *Yourself as the person God meant;*
> *You could never more be*
> *The person you are content."*

It is told that Michelangelo, the great Italian sculptor, seeing a rough and misshapen block of marble which had been cast aside as worthless and useless, seized a hammer and chisel and began to make chips of marble fly in all directions. A friend happened by and enquired what he was doing. His reply was: "I see an angel imprisoned in this block of stone, and I'm just working to let him out." By no fondest stretch of the wildest imagination could any one of us convincingly be called an angel, but at this very moment, Jesus Christ sees the person you could be (and what a great person he sees!) imprisoned in the hard, stony nature of what you are, and He is working at every moment, using His grace and power while preserving your freedom, to uncover and produce "the Possible You." And when He has finished, the *ideal* will have become the *actual*, the *possible* you will be the *real* you! What a plan! What patience and grace and power!

II. WITH A DIVINE OPTIMISM IN HIS HEART

When Jesus Christ looks at you, He looks at you *with a Divine Optimism in His heart*. During the days of His public ministry, Jesus was called "the friend of sinners." His enemies said, "This man receives sinners," and they meant it as a criticism. However, He regarded it as a compliment. He sought close relationships with all kinds of sinners. He cultivated their friendship, not simply because He thought they were worth saving, but because He believed they could be saved. He always looked at human lives with a radiant and invincible optimism. You may look at yourself as hopeless, but Jesus Christ does not. His thoughts, hopes, and plans for you reach as high as the stars.

Now, this optimism of Jesus is a realistic optimism. It is not blind-eyed, as much optimism of today is. It is not like the optimism of Voltaire's <u>Candide,</u> who closed his eyes to the awful facts of a sinful world and declared, "This is the best of all possible worlds." That opinion requires an exceptional amount of blind faith! The optimism of Jesus is not like that. The text says, "Jesus beheld him." It literally reads, "He looked into him," describing the gaze that sees the individuals through and through and reads his character like an open book. Jesus Christ sees you with a kind of "spiritual X-ray vision" (and realizes the full truth about your "X-rated" heart!). In John 2:25, the Bible says that "Jesus needed not anyone to testify to Him about man, for He knew what was in man." Nothing was (or is) hidden or secret from Him. All of man's inner sin and shame lay naked and open to His searching, penetrating gaze. No one knew so much about human nature as Jesus. He knew exactly the kind of man Peter was. When He said to him, "Thou art Simon," it is as if He had said, "I know all about you. I know full well the character associated with that name. I know all that people say about you, and much more besides. I know your reputation on the lake. I know about all your weaknesses. Thou art Simon." But then, His glorious and superb optimism reveals itself. Knowing Simon as He does, He dares to add, "thou shalt be called Cephas, a Rock."

This optimism of Jesus is also an *idealistic* optimism. Could Jesus be anything less than idealistic, and still be Who

He was? This unconquerable, idealistic optimism partially explains the secret of His redeeming power. It was this optimism that helped to redeem and save Simon. When Andrew brought him to Jesus, Simon was perhaps downcast and ready to despair. When Andrew said, "We have found the Messiah," Simon did not think the message concerned him much. If Jesus wanted disciples, it was surely steady, reliable men like Andrew that He wanted, and not weak, unstable men like himself, who would perhaps break down at the first attack of trial or trouble. But the first words Jesus spoke to him put new courage into his heart, new resolution into his soul, for they were words of glorious and splendid hope. "Thou art Simon... thou shalt be Peter!" At that moment, his redemption began. Doesn't our redemption always happen at this point, when we follow the gaze of Jesus, and look right through what we are to what He knows we can become?

This optimism of Jesus explains His ability to save many who seemed utterly beyond saving. He saved publicans and sinners because He first believed they could be saved. Jesus Christ never met a hopeless case. Never does the Bible record a single failure in His ministry. As an example, when Jesus faced Zacchaeus, the wicked tax collector, He said to him, "You are also a son of Abraham," and the little man could hardly believe his ears. Zacchaeus knew that he had sold his Jewish birthright, his spiritual heritage, by becoming a traitor to the hated Gentile Romans. Men had called him every name in the books - cheat, swindler, liar and thief, but no one had ever said such things as this to him before. Lloyd C. Douglas describes what he thinks occurred when Jesus visited Zacchaeus. Jesus, carefully noting Zacchaeus' "moment of truth," says to him, "A great salvation has come to your house today." Then Jesus asks, "What did you see that made you desire this peace?"

Zacchaeus replies, "Good Master, I saw mirrored in your eyes the face of the Zacchaeus I was meant to be."

And think of the boundless optimism He showed with regard to others. He found Mary Magdalene in her shame, and spoke to her a "thou shalt be" of forgiveness and purity. He found Levi in a hard, greedy profession, and spoke to him a "thou shalt be" of sainthood and service. He found Saul of Tarsus a blasphemer and a persecutor, and spoke to him a "thou shalt be" of grace and apostleship.

This optimism of Jesus is both *idealistic* and *realistic* because it is solidly based on the love, grace, and power of God. Jesus was optimistic about Simon because He knew what the grace of God could do in a human life when given a chance. In John 1:12, there is a verse that is often used for soul-winning, but seldom for any other purpose. The verse says, "As many as received Him, to them gave He power to become the sons of God, even to them that believe on His Name." May I, for the moment, drop the last part of the verse, and thus show you a marvelous truth of God? "As many as receive Jesus Christ, to them He gives the power to become!" If ever we are to become what He wants us to be, we must have "power to become," and that power comes only when we "receive" Jesus Christ into the place of absolute, unreserved authority which He desires and deserves in our lives. May God give us grace to let Him be what He should be in us, that we might become what we should be in Him!

III. WITH A DEFINITE OBJECTIVE IN HIS MIND

Finally, Jesus Christ always views men *with a Definite Objective in His mind*. Is Christ's double vision worthless? Is the optimism of Jesus justified? Or is He "shooting for a star" too high to reach? Is there any reachable purpose in this? Yes, there is!

Christ's first object for Peter was an objective *for the maturing of the man* himself. That is, Jesus had an objective for his *person*. At this point, His objective is the same for each believer. He wants to make each believer like Himself! God wants you, dear Christian, to be like Jesus, both here and hereafter. God wants to "conform you to image of His Dear Son" (Romans 8:29).

Follow the history of Simon beginning at the moment described in the text, and you will find a fascinating progression. At first, he acted almost completely out of the "Simon nature," and seldom out of the "Cephas nature." Then, a while later, he shifted back and forth (like sand) between Simon and Cephas. And finally, after years of Jesus Christ culturing his life, he came to act almost completely like "Cephas" (the nature that Jesus Christ developed in him, making him rock-like) and almost never like Simon. And Jesus Christ can do the same for you. Give Him a daily commitment of your life—and watch!

Then Jesus had a definite objective in His mind about Peter's *mission in the Christian movement*, Peter's purpose in life. Jesus had a specific *purpose* for Peter to accomplish. Look at the mighty manner in which Jesus used Peter when he began to fulfill his Divine mission. Peter became the mighty preacher of the Day of Pentecost, and 3,000 (!) people were won to Christ. Peter became one of the two foremost leaders of the Apostles and the early church (Peter the Apostle to the Jews, and Paul the Apostle to the Gentiles). Peter became the writer of two of the great books of the New Testament (I and II Peter), books full of optimism, courage, faith and hope.

Finally, Jesus had a definite objective in His mind about a *ministry of multiplication* which He wanted Peter to perform. Jesus had a plan for Peter's spiritual *productivity*. Remember that His assignment to all of the disciples was "to turn people into disciples," and the mandate He gave and the model He provided both called for a ministry of massive multiplication through each disciple.

How was this plan fulfilled in Peter's life? Who was Peter's disciple? In answering this question, a solid New Testament case could be made for several individuals as Peter's disciples. Apparently, he set the great ministry of Barnabas, a remarkable disciple and disciple-maker, in motion on the Day of Pentecost and immediately thereafter. But Peter's primary disciple seems to have been John Mark, the man with a checkered history in the Gospels and the Book of Acts. Almost all Bible scholars today recognize that the main source for much of the material which Mark incorporated into his Gospel was the teaching he received from Simon Peter in their personal relationship. Simon Peter was an action-oriented person, and Mark's Gospel is an action book. Just a few minutes before writing these words, I came across this line in a commentary on Mark's Gospel: "Mark traveled extensively with Peter as his traveling companion and interpreter." Peter himself called his disciple "Mark my son" (I Peter 5:13). New Testament scholar A. T. Robertson describes John Mark as "a protégé of Simon Peter." He also said that John Mark was "one of Peter's pupils, who as a young disciple must often have sat at his feet to be catechized and taught the way of the Lord." Robertson adds straightforwardly, "Behind John Mark and his Gospel stands the figure of Simon Peter."

Dr. Robertson further says, "It is clear that in Mark's Gospel we have reports that come from an eyewitness, and it is well-known that the eyewitness was the Apostle Peter. Mark has been willing and able to use Peter's eyes for us." Again, "In Mark's Gospel we are dealing primarily with Peter's interpretation of Christ after his reception of the Holy Spirit at Pentecost. It is quite likely that Mark made notes of Peter's preaching from time to time, beginning at an early date, using this and other data for the final book which we possess."

When Peter was released from prison (Acts 12), the first place he thought to go to was "the house of Mary the mother of John whose surname was Mark" (Acts 12:12). Peter had spent many an hour in that same home through the years of John Mark's early life, and a discipler-disciple relationship had developed between them. Mark reveals his vocation of listening, learning, note-taking, and repeating what he was taught in the Gospel that bears his name. Thus, the life and Gospel of his disciple, John Mark, were some of God's chosen means for multiplying the ministry of Simon Peter.

Is there evidence of spiritual multiplication in John Mark's life? Yes, there is. He is described in Acts 13:5 and II Timothy 4:11 as a "helper." That word comes from a captivating Greek word, *huperetes*, which literally means an "under-rower." The "under-rower" kind of helper refers to a person who is willing to remain under the decks on board ship manning the oars while the captain of the ship gets the credit for its speed, determines its destination, and governs its movements. The purpose of the under-rower was to provide the means of transportation that would guarantee that *others would get to their destination.* The word refers to a person who was willing to help another person, willing to assist another person, willing to attend to the needs of another person. It describes a person who sees his relationship to others as that of service. No wonder that Paul said that Mark was "useful to me for service." Knowing what we know about Paul as a disciple-maker and Peter as one trained in the disciple-making process by Jesus Himself, we may be sure than John Mark was fully involved in helping others for the sake of spiritual multiplication—to multiply himself spiritually and to assist them to multiply through many generations. What a curriculum he used, if the Gospel of Mark is any indication! And Mark has certainly been multiplying Himself and the Christian movement through the centuries through that Gospel in the New Testament that bears his name.

It is obvious, then, that the bifocal vision and boundless optimism of Jesus were fully justified in the life of Simon Peter. But what about us? What about you? What about me? Jesus Christ looks at you today bifocally, and with the most blessed kind of optimism. He sees you the way you are — weak, uncertain, unfaithful, ashamed, guilty, prayerless. But He also sees you as gloriously triumphant, powerful, victorious as a Christian. Will you let His view of you be justified?

Margaret Slattery, in her book, <u>Living Teachers</u>, tells of a community in which a stranger came to settle and to practice law. He buried himself in his legal work, and when he was sometimes seen walking through the community in the evenings, he walked alone, with his head down, and with the look of mental distress upon his face. One day he was introduced to a new friend, a local artist. In confidence, he poured out his heart to him, revealing the deep, dark sin that stained his past and was destroying his peace. The artist said nothing, but parted from him and went into his studio. Weeks afterwards, the artist invited his melancholy friend to come in and view a portrait which he had finished, telling him that it was his masterpiece. The man was surprised and pleased that his judgment had been sought by the artist, but when he went into the studio to view the portrait, he was surprised to see that it was a portrait of himself, only now he stood erect and with his shoulders thrown back, and his head up, ambition, desire, and hope written on his face. The lawyer stared at the portrait in silence for a few moments, then with tears streaming down his face, he said, "If you see that in me, then I can see it in myself. If you think I can be that kind of man, then I can be; and what is more, I will be." When I follow the gaze of Jesus as He looks into me, and begin to realize what He sees in me, I want to echo those words: "Lord, if you can see that in me, then I can see it, too. If you believe I can be that kind of man, then I can be; and what is more, I will be by your grace and power."

I would like for you, the reader, to finish the sermon for me. Jesus Christ says, "Thou art _____." You fill in the blank; you know what you are. Be absolutely honest. Weak? Sinful? Guilty? Helpless? Fill in the blank! Then hear Jesus as He says, "Thou shalt be_____." Only God Himself can fill in this blank. "Thou art, thou shalt be." The actual and the possible! The real and the ideal! What is and what is to be! And between these two stands the Lord Jesus Christ, whose Presence is like a mighty bridge flung across the great gulf that separates them. And when you daily surrender and leave the rest to Him, He will carry you across the chasm, and show the world what great things can come to pass! Dear Lord, let the *possible me* that *You* can see be the *actual me* that *everybody can see!*

AN ADDENDUM
"THE PYGMALION EFFECT"

The last time the Chicago Bears were in the NFL Super Bowl, the pre-game hype included the news story of a third-team bench warmer on the Bears team who supposedly sold the Bears' Super Bowl game plan play book to the opposing team, supposedly giving the opponents a great advantage on the playing field in the Super Bowl game. Christians have an Enemy, though he is hardly a bench warmer! Satan has time and time again stolen plays out of the Christian's "game plan play book," and has "sold them" to one opponent after another. Usually, when others run with our plays, the Christian community abandons the play and no longer uses it. So we have the insane situation of Christian enemies (usually cults or cultic religions) using our plays, while the Christian community abandons them altogether!

Let me mention *just one* of these plays. We could call this play the "Pygmalion Effect." This play has been stolen by Mormons, Jehovah's Witnesses, the philosophers of secular humanism, and the New Age philosophers. And the Christian community has largely abandoned it, even showing ignorance of this play as it is used in the Bible. This paper will explore and explain the "Pygmalion Effect."

George Bernard Shaw, the renowned British playwright and social philosopher, wrote a great play named <u>Pygmalion.</u> It was later made into a movie that became a gigantic box office success. The movie starred Rex Harrison and Audrey Hepburn, and it was entitled "My Fair Lady. " It is the story of an English gentleman, Mr. Higgins, who spots a beautiful

Addendum – The Pygmalion Effect

but badly soiled street tramp named Liza Doolittle, and sees in Liza a lady who would do honor to a king's court. Of course, Mr. Higgins' "vision" is solely a matter of flattering faith on his part at the beginning of the story. The story line develops as Mr. Higgins enlists Liza Doolittle into a strenuous program of tutoring and training, a program designed to make of her what Mr. Higgins has envisioned her to be. And, wonder of wonders, she finally emerges as a first-class lady—all because of Mr. Higgins looking through what she was and seeing what she could become.

So what is the "Pygmalion Effect?" A man named Alson Gretha created the popular definition of it in these words: "Treat a person as he *appears* to be, and you will only make him *worse*. But treat a person as if he already *were* what he potentially *could* be, and you will help to make him what he *should* be."

Andrew Carnegie stated the principle in a different way when he said, "Men are *developed* the same way *gold* is mined. When gold is mined, several tons of dirt must be moved to get an ounce of gold, but one doesn't go into the mine looking for dirt. *He goes in looking for gold.*" And it might be added that the gold is in the dirt to begin with only because of a long process of *heat* and *pressure*. Such processes are always present in the production of gold.

Popular literature, the arts, and cultic religion have been much more facile than the church in seeing and using the "Pygmalion Effect." For example, in another hit play and movie, *The Man of La Mancha* (the movie starred Peter O' Toole and Sophia Loren), this theme provided the plot. Based on Miguel Cervantes' classic novel, <u>Don Quixote</u>, the play tells the story of the mystical, idealistic, visionary Don Quixote, who meets in his crusading travels a small-town prostitute named Aldonza. However, because of his visionary idealism, Don

Taking the Wheel for Disciple-making

Quixote refuses to see her as a prostitute. He sees her as a fine, pure, noble lady. He even conveys upon her the name, "Lady Dulcinea." The play is a fine presentation of the character-struggle within the harlot as she cynically rejects his faith, then begins to erratically adapt her understanding to his faith, and at last takes *his faith* as *hers* and is able to *see herself as he has seen her all the time*. In the closing scene, the simplistic Don Quixote is on his deathbed, having spent his energies in his idealistic crusades. As he nears the end, the transformed Lady Dulcinea enters the room, nobly attired as a lady, and showing that her demeanor now matches this understanding. At first, in his semi-comatose state, he does not recognize her. She says gently, "Do you not recognize me, sire? *I am your lady Dulcinea.*" This is another example from the arts of the "Pygmalion Effect."

A popular version of this principal may be seen in the child's fantasy story of the handsome prince, the wicked witch, the ugly frog, and the beautiful maiden. The story is well-known. Once upon a time, there lived a handsome prince, who tragically came under the spell of a wicked witch. The witch placed a curse upon the prince and turned him into a low, ugly frog. The rule of the story is that he would remain an ugly frog unless a beautiful maiden kissed him. But it seemed to be an impossible situation, because beautiful maidens just do not go around kissing ugly frogs. However, the impossible happened! One day, a beautiful maiden spotted the ugly frog, had compassion on him, and planted a loving kiss on his ugly head. Instantly, there emerged from the ugly frog a prince even more handsome than he had originally been! And, as is usual in all good fantasy stories, the maiden and the prince fell deeply in love, married, and lived happily ever after!

This story is a theological parable. The handsome prince represents Adam as God made him. The wicked witch represents the devil, who brought Adam and the entire human race under the curse of sin, reducing him (them) into something lower and uglier than a frog. And man was destined to remain that way had not a Person with "the beauty of the Lord our God" upon Him come to the ugly frog, seen his real worth, and taken him into His love-embrace and planted the transforming kiss of grace upon him. The beautiful maiden in the story represents the lovely Lord Jesus Christ, who disregarded man's ugliness in sin and embraced him in love and grace, kissing his sin and ugliness away on the Cross. The emerging prince is the saved sinner, restored to something more than Adam had been before he sinned. Then the romance of the ages began. The individual believer is "married unto Another" (Romans 7:4), even to Jesus. The bride is to grow in an ever-deepening love relationship with the Groom — *and they will live happily ever after!*

Satan's junk may become the Savior's jewels. The recycled garbage of human sinners will become Jesus's greatest trophies of grace, to whom He will show His kindness forever (Ephesians 2:7).

Another popular version of the "Pygmalion Effect" is the fantasy story of "The Beauty and the Beast." In the story, Beauty bends down to kiss the unlovable beast and transforms him into a prince. However, one of the main features of the story is in the fact that she did not wait until he became a prince to love him; indeed, it was her love that turned him into a prince!

In the book which introduces J. R. R. Tolkien's epic trilogy, The Lord of the Rings, the book named The Hobbit, the noble wizard named Gandalf says to Bilbo Baggins, the hobbit/hero of the book: "There is more to you than you know." This line plays a large part in turning Bilbo into an over-achieving hero. Gandalf's faith and his practice of the

"Pygmalion Effect" turns an unsung hobbit into a crusading champion of right. And the cause of right triumphs over evil because of *faith in a person's **potential*** instead of simply accepting the failures of his past.

In one of Lloyd Douglas' great novels, Jesus asks the transformed tax collector, Zacchaeus, this question, "What caused the change in you?" Zacchaeus responds with a personal testimony of the power of the "Pygmalion Effect" in his life. He says, "Good Master, I saw mirrored in Your Eyes the face of **the Zacchaeus I was meant to be**! And I determined that **if that's the man You see, then that's the man I will be!**" Christian author Walter Wangerin, Jr., said, "The Gospel of Jesus Christ showed me a new me hidden in the shadow of a sinner."

One of the greatest of the old mystical Methodists, Rufus Jones, said that his transformation as a Christian actually began one day when he had misbehaved terribly as a young boy. He expected a severe discipline from his parents. However, they didn't treat him as he anticipated at all. They went with him to his bedroom and gently asked him to get down on his knees with them. Then they prayed aloud. His mother concluded the prayer by saying, "O God, I ask you in the name of Jesus to make our son the boy and the man You intended him to be." Jones said, "That prayer pierced my heart as well as the heart of God, and my transformation began at that moment." The "Pygmalion Effect!"

Now let me recount a few modern testimonies which reveal the "Pygmalion Effect." Author and Christian leader Ron Hembree wrote, "Pastor/psychologist Dr. Richard Dobbins came into my life when I was a total failure. He said to me, 'Ron, I just want to be your friend.' Sometime later, he said, 'Ron, you're too good a man to be haunted by the past. Turn toward the future. *We need you!*" What lectures, advice,

Addendum – The Pygmalion Effect

and admonitions could not do, a gentle man with a warm and healing heart was able to accomplish. I owe him my ministry. He simply *said* — and *proved* — that *he wanted me."* Dr. Dobbins placed faith in Ron Hembree's Christian future, and soon his faith began to become sight! The "thing hoped for," the "thing not seen," became solid substance (Hebrews 11:1).

In the early 1960s, a man brought his young, fat, short, slow son to a Jr. High football field in a small town in Alabama. The boy was marked by such timidity and inability that the rest of the players laughed at him. But his father took the coach out to supper, and said to him, "I want you to see in my boy an All-American football player, and then I want you to do everything possible to make out of him what you see. As strange as it may seem, I have already seen this possibility in my boy, and I will do my part to make it a reality." Five years later, that boy was a High School All-American, and four years after that, he was a college All-American at the University of Alabama. To complete the influence of the "Pygmalion Effect," that boy, whose name is Bill Battle, later became the University of Tennessee football coach.

Friends, isn't it time we took back the play that is *absolutely fundamental* in our "Christian play book," without which we will score few points and win few victories — isn't it time we took it back out the hands of the enemies of the Gospel, and began to "run the play" with regularity and efficiency in the Body of Christ and in our church communities?

Someone said, "People tend to rise to the level of other people's expectations." A Christian should be a clear reflector of the expectations of Jesus — both in the dreams he holds for his own life, and in the hopes he holds for others. Jesus does not look at your failing past so much as he looks at your future potential. Jesus does not look for perfection in you so much as He looks for potential. Dear Christian friend, your potential is as vast as the Person of Christ!

Supportive Quotes

Henry Ford said, "My best friend is the one who brings out the best in me."

Cecil Myers wrote, We are not mere human beings; we are human becomings."

There walks ahead of you (in your future) a far more Christ-like person than you have yet become.

James Moffatt translates a line in I Corinthians 13 in this manner: "Love is eager to believe the best." It has been said that there are two types of people: *plus* people and *minus* people. Minus people always go around subtracting. If anything good is said about a person, they will find a negative punch line to throw in. In contrast, Jesus always added new dimensions to life, new possibilities and new hope. Someone said, "All of us work best in the sunshine of approval." It was said of Jesus, *"In the company of sinners He dreamed of saints."* So everywhere that Jesus went, He diminished the evil and developed the good.

Give Jesus the you that you are, and in time He will give back the you that you ought to be.

There are three persons in every individual: (1) The person whom his associates see; (2) The person whom he sees himself to be; and (3) The person whom Jesus sees. Everything depends on which "you" you center upon. If you are centering on the "you" your associates see, you will be in bondage to what others think about you. You will look around before you act to see what effect your action will have on others — you won't act, you will react. You will become an echo and not a voice. If you center upon the "you" you know, then you will be discouraged. For who has not had some skeleton in his closet — things in his life that make his cheeks burn with shame and humiliation? But there is that other "you," the one that Jesus sees. What a "you" that is! It is a "you" surrendered to God, co-operating with Him, taking His resources, working out life with Him. That "you" will do things beyond your personal capacity, amazing both yourself and others. Dare to tell Jesus today, "I would like to exchange my 'me' for Thy 'me.'"

Illustrations for Reflection:

The Gold Mine.

Suppose you inherit a gold mine. You're overjoyed. You love that gold mine. You can hardly wait to get out there and get to work in it. But the first time you go out to inspect your treasure, the gold says, "How can you love me? I'm all dirty. I'm all mixed up with that awful iron ore, and I have that rotten clay all over me. I'm contaminated with bauxite and mineral deposits. I'm ugly and worthless."

"Oh, but I do love you," you say to the gold. "You see, I understand what you really are. I know you have all these imperfections, but I have plans for you. I am not going to leave you the way you are now. I'm going to purify you. I'm going to get rid of all that other stuff. I see your inherent worth. I know that the iron ore, the clay, and the mineral deposits are not part of the true you - you are just temporarily mixed up with them.

"I warn you, it won't be easy. You will go through a lot of heat and pressure. Left to yourself, you would remain in this dark place, buried in the dirty ore. But I know how to change you from what you are now to what you can be. I will make you beautiful, and you will make me rich."

Not Perfection, But Potential.

Jesus did not see the *perfection*, but He did see *potential* in them. As we seek to make disciples, we should also look for the potential in people. We must look beyond what a person *is* to see what he can *become*. No person should be cemented into his present character and conduct.

Some of the world's most glittering jewels do not shine when they are first discovered. They are only dull stones, and must be cut and ground before they glow with the colors of the rainbow.

See What Is and What Might Be.

We can all learn a lesson from the "four-eyed fish." These odd-looking creatures are native to the equatorial waters of the western Atlantic region. The technical name of this genus of fish is "anableps," meaning "Those who look upward," because of their unusual eye structure. They have 2-tiered eyes. The upper eyes protrude above the surface of the water and enable the anableps to search for food and to spot enemies in the air. The lower eyes remain focused in the water, functioning in the usual fishlike fashion. They see in both worlds.

If we can develop eyes for seeing *what is* as well as *what might be*, we can help others dream.

Just Like Fishing.

Laura Bridgeman was a forlorn little girl who had been born blind, deaf, and dumb. It was Dr. Samuel Howe who took on the task of setting her free. Dr. Howe later said, "It was just like fishing. A man baits his hook, lets down his line, and tries again. For days and weeks I kept letting my line down to Laura. For six months there was no sign of response. Then one day while I was dangling a new bait I felt a sudden tug. I pulled up the line, and Laura's soul came up into the light."

GOD'S CALL TO DEDICATED CHRISTIAN LIVING

Romans 12:1-2:

"I beseech you therefore, brethren, by the mercies of God, that ye present your bodies a living sacrifice, holy, acceptable unto God, which is your reasonable service. And be not conformed to this world: but be ye transformed by the renewing of your mind, that ye may prove what is that good, and acceptable, and perfect, will of God."

Romans 12:1 forms an obvious major turning point in the book of Romans. The first eleven chapters contain an overload of great *doctrinal* truth, the greatest compendium of such truth ever written. But here, Paul turns from *doctrine* and its *appreciation* to *duty* and its *application*. There are actually three great turning points in the book of Romans, each centering around the word "therefore."

The first might be called the great "therefore" of *justification*. Romans 5:1 says, "Therefore being justified by faith, we have peace with God through our Lord Jesus Christ." The doctrine of justification means, positively, that God pronounces a believing sinner (at the moment of his faith) as being as righteous as Christ Himself, as accepted by God as

Christ Himself, and He treats him in His Family with the same privileges as if he were Christ Himself. The doctrine of justification means, negatively, that the believer is not liable to punishment any longer for a single sin of his past, present, or future (!). He is regarded by God as if he had always kept all of God's laws and is entitled to all the privileges due to those who have always kept those laws. This is a breath-taking doctrine, but nothing less than these facts do honor to the full Biblical doctrine of justification. Now, any sin the believer commits inside the Family must be taken up in private with the Father Himself. If the believer will not voluntarily appear in the "washroom" to be cleansed of any sin that occurs in his life, the Father will take him to the "woodshed" to be clouted — but it is now a Family Matter between a child and its Father! Every believer should spend his entire Life on earth studying the infinite implications of his justification.

The second great turning point of the book of Romans could be called the great "therefore" of *identification*. Romans 8:1 says, "There is therefore now no condemnation to them which are in Christ Jesus." The phrase "in Christ Jesus," used by Paul in his letters some 165 times, is the great phrase for the believer's identification with Christ. The doctrine of identification simply means that every believer is incorporated into the personal history of Jesus Himself. This identification begins for the believer at the moment of his salvation. Thereafter, the believer is viewed as having died with Christ, been buried with Christ, risen with Christ, ascended with Christ, and enthroned with Christ. These are not high experiences to be sought after by a believer; these are present-tense realities all the time! Because of his position "in Christ," the believer is as Christ.

The third great turning point of Romans might be described as the great "therefore" of *dedication*. This is the "therefore" of our text. Note carefully and thoughtfully the *order* of the occurrences of these "therefores." This is the necessary order of experience in the life of a Christian.

First is *justification*, the first and greatest word in understanding the matter of *salvation*. Just as there is no beginning to human life without a human birth, there is no beginning to a Christian life without salvation. Then comes the understanding of *identification with Christ*. This identification is perfect from the moment of salvation, but it usually takes a lifetime for the believer to understand it and live by it. This identification with Christ is the foundation of the believer's progressive *sanctification*. During all stages of the process of sanctification, the believer is to engage in *service* to Christ, and the dedication to this service is the great "therefore" of Roman 12:1-2.

As previously suggested, this is the most abrupt and decisive turning point of the book. Here, the book changes directions. *Up to* this point, everything has been moving in the direction of *heaven to earth* and the keynote is *grace. Here*, the direction reverses, and everything moves in the direction of *earth to heaven*, and the keynote is *Spirit-produced, Spirit-filled gratitude*. The suggestion is that Christianity is like breathing. There is an inhaling of the grace of God in Christ. This was symbolized in John 20 when Jesus "breathed on them." The inference seems to be that they were to "inhale" His fullness by faith. The Spirit-filled life is as simple as breathing — and just as crucial! Then, they were to "exhale" both the *waste* (their sins) and the *worship* (the inevitable result of the Christ-life) toward God. The service of a Christian is simply the Christ-life expressed toward God and toward others. The word "therefore" in Romans 12:1 is a coupling-link between the two parts of the total Christian experience, *doctrine* and *duty*,

learning and *living*. I have labeled it "God's Call to Dedicated Christian Living."
Let's study it.

I. THE STATED CAUSE

First, we see the *stated cause* of dedicated Christian living. "I beseech you therefore, brethren, by the mercies of God...." Three vital things demand our attention in this opening statement of Romans 12:1.

Note first that the call is addressed to "brethren." So the first foundational premise of this kind of living is that the participant must be *saved*. He must be born again; he must be a Christian. You see, God makes plans *only* for *His children*. Though God sovereignly determines the place and the destiny of lost people as well as saved, God leaves the devil's children thereafter to their father.

If you are a parent, you know how it is in your own life. You carefully and lovingly plan for your children's future; and while you may be mildly interested in your neighbor's children, you would never think of planning their lives. The person who is outside of Christ has scorned or ignored the thing which God holds dearest, which is the death of His well-beloved Son. So, before such an unbeliever can come into the plan of God and live a useful Christian life, he must face the sin-question and the Son-question.

One day some people asked Jesus directly, "What must we do, to be doing the works of God?"

Jesus answered with equal directness, "This is the work (or will) of God, that you believe in Him Whom He has sent" (John 6:29). You must first come in faith to Christ as Savior and Lord. Then you are God's child and can fulfill His will for a dedicated life.

Jesus said in John 10:3, "He (the Good Shepherd) calls His own sheep by name and leads them out." The day you are saved, you begin to *know* the will of God and *fulfill* the will of God at the same time. God has exclusive and wonderful plans for His children (Jeremiah 29:11), and they are always "good" from God's point of view (Romans 8:28). This call is addressed only to Christians.

Then note that this call is a "beseeching." This word pictures a reasonable, moral, tender appeal.

The Phillips paraphrase says, "I beg you." This does not reduce God's Apostle to a beggar; it simply acknowledges the tenderness and reasonableness of the call. Note the grace and compassion of this call.

Here is the great Apostle Paul, God's Ambassador, on his knees before the Christians of Rome, begging them to do something that they should do without the begging! Indeed, if they knew the full dimensions of the matter, they would be begging God to let them serve Him! Instead, the call is a tender, compassionate entreaty from the Holy Spirit through the Apostle Paul.

The call has a specified basis. "I beseech you...by the mercies of God." The Phillips paraphrase captures the thought beautifully, "I beg you, my brothers, with eyes wide open to the mercies of God, that you present..." The exhortation to "present your bodies a living sacrifice" is to be obeyed with both eyes steadfastly focused on the mercies of God! This entails not a mere awareness of these mercies, not a mere acknowledgment of these mercies, but a full *apprehension* and *appreciation* of these mercies.

Note the argument Paul did not use. He did not say, "I *command* you on the basis of the *law* of God" or "I *threaten* you on the basis of the *wrath* of God" or "I *warn* you on the basis of the *judgment* of God" or even "I *advise* you on the basis of the *wisdom* of God," but rather "I *beg* you on the basis of the *mercies* of God." Note then the argument he *did* use. "With eyes wide open to the mercies of God."

Generally, this phrase, "the mercies of God," refers to God's compassionate considerations which He displays to us all the time. How merciful, gracious, loving and good God has been! Psalm 68:19 says that "He daily loads us with benefits." We are like pack animals, laden with a heavy cargo of "benefits."

He has covered us up with an avalanche of Divine blessings. Specifically, this phrase refers to the justification, sanctification, and glorification which form the subjects of Romans chapters one through eight. All of these infinite and countless mercies form the basis of the Spirit's appeal to us to surrender ourselves happily to God's purpose. If a Christian won't respond to an appeal made on the basis of the innumerable mercies of God, there is little hope for his usefulness. So the call is addressed to brethren, is stated in the form of a tender entreaty, and is based on the great mercies of God.

II. THE STRONG CALL

Next, we note the Holy Spirit's *strong call* to dedicated Christian living. "I beseech you ... to present your bodies a living sacrifice..." The key word at this point is the strong aorist tense, active voice verb, "present." Perhaps it can best be understood by looking back to its Old Testament counterpart, the bringing of a sacrifice to God through the Jewish sacrificial system. The Jewish system of sacrifice knew five kinds of sacrifices, but they could be divided into two basic categories. The first category concerned the sacrifices that were offered to God *to obtain reconciliation*. This category included the sin offering and the trespass offering. These sacrifices were *compulsory* because of the urgent need of the sinner. The other category included the sacrifices offered to God *after reconciliation* for the purpose of *celebrating the reconciliation that had been received*. These were called "sweet savor" offerings, and they were *voluntary*.

The one offering which meets the requirements of Romans 12:1-2 is the "burnt offering," the first of the "sweet savor" offerings. It was called a *"whole* burnt offering," and the word "whole" points out the distinctive feature of this particular offering. This offering was totally consumed by fire, so it was called a "holocaust offering." You see, the demand made in these verses is quite radical! No part of this offering was withheld from total devotedness to God. When a worshiper brought this offering, he released it into the hands of the priest as if he were giving it directly into the hands of God. Highlight the word, *"release."* Release, not *retain. Present*, not *preserve*, the sacrifice. Indeed, the word "sacrifice" here is synonymous with the word "victim." In order to see the real nature of this dedication, join in your mind the words "holocaust" and "victim." You are invited, dear Christian, to be a willing holocaust victim! In a particular instant of time, the worshiper took his hands off of the sacrifice forever by placing it into the hands of the priest. Even so, we are to "take our hands off" of our lives by a once-for-all surrender, or *release*, of ourselves to Him — as a living sacrifice. The aorist tense of the word "present" calls for a commitment made at a crisis point of time. This is the crisis that initiates the stewardship of the total life and personality.

Once this crisis commitment has been made, it need not be repeated; however, it may (and *must)* be *re-affirmed* whenever necessary. Coldness of heart and recurrence of sin make this re-affirmation often necessary. Suppose a married couple breaks into a serious quarrel. Is it necessary for them to be married again in order to be restored? Certainly not, but an adjustment is necessary! If they are wise, they will make mutual confessions and reaffirm their love for each other. The same is true of a Christian who has become cold of heart or corrupt in practice. Confession and cleansing will re-affirm his original release of himself to God.

Remember that this surrender is to a *Person*, and to a *Plan*. It is to be "acceptable unto God," and it will involve you henceforth in the "good, acceptable, and perfect will of God." So surrender to Jesus Christ is not *resigning* yourself to the *worst* (as carnally-minded people will invariably think it is), but *releasing* yourself joyfully to the *Best* (as every spiritual person regularly proves). God is often accused of brutalizing anyone He can get His hands on, but the Bible says that this is the work of the Devil, not God. Jesus said, "The thief (Satan) comes not except to steal (*dispossession* is his first work) and to kill (*death* is a feature work of Satan) and to destroy (his agenda never varies from that of *destruction)*" (John 10:10). However, when a Christian obeys this command to release Himself to God, He is placing himself in the omni-caring and omni-competent hands of the "Lover of his soul."

III. THE SPIRITUAL CHARACTERISTICS

Next, we will examine the *spiritual characteristics* of Christian dedication. Our text presents a veritable flood of ideas which describe the nature of such dedication. These verses are like a diamond which might be turned again and again in the sunlight, with each new turn disclosing new facets of the gem. Look at several of these facets.

First, Christian dedication is *volitional*. It is voluntary. Don't misunderstand this. This surrender is morally mandatory, though not legally compulsory. Remember that it is based on "the mercies of God," not the law of God. The word "present" is the same word that is used five times in Romans six and translated "yield." This word does not express the demand of a tyrant who crushes you, but the gentle entreaty of a Master who loves you.

Second, Christian dedication is *total* in nature. "Present your *bodies* a living sacrifice." Why the "body?" The body of a sacrificial animal denoted the entire animal. In the case of a man, it denotes the whole man (remember the *"whole* burnt offering"). The Holy Spirit does not say, "Present your spirits, your souls, your emotions, your feelings, your sentiments, or your good intentions." Your body is what you occupy as you read these words. It's what you will take to lunch tomorrow. It sat at your breakfast table this morning. You will have it with you seven days a week for the rest of your life. The body you now live in is, if fact, the only body you will ever have.

Even in eternity, you will have the same body, though glorified. Wherever your body goes, you are there. Wherever you are, your body is there. Take a tour through the Scriptures, and look at how many times God talks about the human body. He is apparently very concerned about your body. The reason is simple: If God gets your body, He gets *you!*

The body is the organ of all of life. It is the vehicle of life-expression. You cannot look, speak, touch, hear, smell (in both senses!), write, travel, etc., without using your body. This is a call simply to devote to God all the active powers of your personality. But take nothing for granted here. Many people have yielded themselves to God only in part. The curse of the times among Christians is the curse of partial surrender. Someone said, "Most of our difficulties in living the Christian life arise from our vain attempts to only *half* live it." Florence Nightingale, when asked the secret of her useful life, answered, "I have always worked hard, and I have never refused Jesus Christ anything." This dedication includes the totality of life as we know it.

Third, Christian dedication is *sacrificial* and *radical* in nature. "Present your bodies a living sacrifice." Take a long look at the word "sacrifice." "Fic" is a Latin term which means "to make." "Sac" is the root form of our word "sacred." The word "sacrifice" means to "make sacred." The object is your body, which has always been used for "profane" purposes. "Pro" means "before" or "in front of." "Fane" means a "holy place," such as a temple. So "profane" means "outside the temple." This word described anything that is used for ordinary, natural, fleshly purposes. Before conversion, a person's body is "profane." After conversion, it is to be used for "sacred" purposes. It is to become a "sacrifice" unto God. Note this rule: there is no such thing as *man* making a sacrifice to *God* without that sacrifice *costing man something,* and there is no such thing as *God* making a sacrifice for *man **without it costing Him something***. Read again the story of the awful Cross to see what His coming to you cost Him!

The first impulse of an intelligent Christian may be to ask, What is the word "sacrifice" doing in the New Testament Gospel? Hebrews 10:12 says that Christ's "one sacrifice for sins forever" rendered unnecessary the system of blood sacrifice. Jesus sat down at the right hand of God — the symbol of a finished, accepted atonement. Dr. K. Owen White said that if an artist should set out some day to paint the book of Romans, using one symbol for each chapter, he might have some difficulty deciding on a symbol for some of the chapters, but not in chapter twelve — the symbol would have to be an *altar.* The first eleven chapters of Romans are about the great sacrifice which Christ made to reconcile us to God; now, we turn from His infinite sacrifice to our finite sacrifices. Paul is inviting us to build an altar, climb atop it, and sacrifice ourselves to God!

So here is a call for sacrifice in a system that has no present sacrifices in it. How do we resolve this paradox? There are several keys. One key is that Christian dedication involves a *"living* sacrifice."

The sacrifices of the Old Testament were effective *only* as they were *slain*, but the sacrifices of the New Testament would be ineffective *if* they were slain. The Old Testament sacrifices were alive when presented, then put to death. But the Christian is *still alive* after he becomes the sacrifice. Our bodies are to be presented like those of the Jewish sacrifices, but not like them to be slain; yet like them so completely to be made God's that during their whole life they are as good as slain. The word "living" implies a vast superiority over slain sacrifices.

A second key is found in the distinction between *bringing* a sacrifice which is outside the worshiper, and the worshiper actually *becoming* a sacrifice. *Becoming* a sacrifice instead of *bringing* one! That's a great difference. God does not ask the Christian to *bring* a sacrifice. Much of our stewardship, unhappily, is based on this appeal. Rather, God invites each of His children to *become* a sacrifice.

The third key is seen in the intelligence of the sacrifices. In the old system, the poor dazed animals gave up their lives without understanding, in dumb passivity. But the Christian sacrifice is nothing if it is not conscious, willing, eager, and free. You, dear Christian, are asked to climb up on the altar and become a sacrifice as surely as if you were killed and consumed in flames.

Bishop Taylor-Smith was once asked what was the secret of his consistent spiritual life. He answered, "Every day when I awake, I do something before I get out of bed. I lift up my heart to my Lord, and I say, 'Blessed Lord, this bed is the altar, and my body is the sacrifice. I gladly offer myself up to you, so that for these next twenty-four hours I may be Thine alone, for Thy pleasure and for Thy service.'" This is the idea of the "living sacrifice."

Fourth, Christian dedication is *spiritual* and *moral* in nature. "Present your bodies a living sacrifice, *holy*..." The Greek word is "hagios," which means "set apart" or "devoted." The primary idea is not that of moral purity or freedom from evil. A pagan worshiper, or a pagan temple, or a pagan act, was called holy simply because it was set apart or devoted to a certain purpose. In the Old Testament, places and objects were often called "holy," not because they were pure or sinless, but because they were devoted to a specific purpose (usually the worship of God). So the *presentation* of verse one makes the thing presented "holy," and this word is totally independent of the moral nature of the thing presented when the presentation is made. *However!* It is this very association that produces the "saint," who should become increasingly pure simply by his association with the holy God. So Christian dedication is first a spiritual act of release and surrender, and this allows God to make the dedicated person increasingly pure and less and less controlled by sin. So the physical body of the believer, presented to God and thus made disposable to Him, is *instantly* holy by *presentation* and will become *increasingly* holy by *association*.

Fifth, Christian dedication is *reasonable* in nature. "Present your bodies a living sacrifice, holy, acceptable unto God, which is your reasonable service." The word translated "reasonable" is the Greek word "logikos," the word from which we derive our English word, "logical." The word means "rational, agreeable to reason." The word has two ideas in it. One is that this dedication is not merely external or material. Perhaps, again, Paul follows his analogy. The Christian surrender is in direct contrast to the dumb, thoughtless sacrifices of the Old Testament. The animal sacrifices of the Old Testament were made with no intelligence or decision from the animals concerning the sacrifice. But the Christian's commitment is to be made in full awareness, full intelligence, of all the issues that are involved.

The other idea is that of reasonable succession. If "A" is true, then "B" should follow. If God has done all these things for us, it is unreasonable for us to be indifferent or half-hearted, and it is perfectly reasonable for us to be totally dedicated to Him. The logical result of our reception of all the blessings that come from our union with Christ is to present ourselves unconditionally and totally to God. Another thing requires to be said at this point. There are charges sounding out from every direction in our lethargic, affluent, self-indulgent, self-dominated world that this kind of demand is ridiculous and that this kind of life is "fanatical" and unreasonable. Quite to the contrary, Paul says, this kind of response to the "mercies of God" is **the only one that makes any sense at all!!** This surrender that is total and irrevocable is the only response which is truly *rational*. C. T. Studd, the English cricketer who became one of the greatest missionaries of Christian history, recognized this when he said, "If Jesus Christ be God, and died for me, then no sacrifice would be too great for me to make for Him."

Technically, when Calvary's "Love Offering" is compared to our puny surrenders, our responses should never be called "sacrifices."

"When I survey the wondrous cross, On which the Prince of Glory died, My richest gain I count but loss, And pour contempt on all my pride.

Were the whole realm of nature mine, That were a present far too small; Love so amazing, so Divine, Demands my soul, my life, my all."

That is the best logic, the greatest intelligence, and the highest thoughtfulness in the universe!

Sixth, Christian dedication is *vocational* in nature. The vocation of the Christian life is both negative and positive in its requirements.

Think of the negative demand first. "And be not conformed to this world." The word "conformed" is based on the word, "schematizo," which refers to a person assuming an outward expression that does not come from within him. So his outward *habits* do not match his inner *heart*.

The full word is "sunschematizo." The prefix "sun" is a preposition which means "together with." The entire long word contains the idea of adopting an outward habit, a "scheme," which is patterned after some definite outward model. The outward model (Phillips calls it a "mold") is "this world," or this age. Someone translated it, "Christian, stop masquerading in the mannerisms, speech expressions, styles and habits of this world." Sadly, Christians may dress themselves in this unbecoming masquerade costume, but it always hides the Lord Jesus Christ in the heart of the Christian. The costume, then, becomes an opaque covering through which the Holy Spirit cannot radiate the beauty of the Lord Jesus Christ.

We hear much today about "adjustment," but here is God's call to *maladjustment!* We hear a lot about "integration," but here is God's call for dis-integration, or *spiritual segregation*. We are often urged into social conformity, but here we are urged to become non-conformists. The word "world" here refers to this age and the spirit that governs it (Satan). The verse says, "Be not fashioned together with the spirit of this age." Anything that puts you in identification with this world system places you in a position that is anti-God. The world-system is a whole way of life, under the supervision of Satan, the "god of this world." This world-system is carefully organized to express the philosophy, the "mind" of the Wicked One. Christians are not to permit themselves to be governed by this Master, by this mind, or by this manner of life.

Archimedes said, "If a man could find a fulcrum strong enough, and a lever long enough, and could occupy a position apart from that which he is trying to move, he could move the world!" The dedicated Christian has all three of these necessary ingredients. The *purpose of God* is the fulcrum, the *strategy of Jesus* is the lever, and our text urges us to *occupy a position apart* from that which we are trying to move. When Christians have used these ingredients, the world has always been moved.

The J. B. Phillips paraphrase of the New Testament says, "Don't let the world around you squeeze you into its own mold." The world has a mold much like a gelatin mold, or a cookie mold. You dissolve gelatin in hot water, pour it into a mold, then place it in the refrigerator until it gels. When it congeals, it takes the shape of the mold into which it was poured. In something of the same manner, the world has a mold — a "shape" for our thinking, our values, our pleasures, our dress, our talk, etc.

The world is constantly trying to press us into its mold so that Christians will be indistinguishable from non-Christians. Christians are either like thermometers or thermostats. Thermometers only register the temperature that is around them. They simply reflect their environment. Thermostats, however, regulate the temperature in their surroundings. Though a thermostat is very small in comparison to the size of the house or the appliance it is in, it bears an influence over those things all out of proportion to its size. It actually controls the temperature of the whole house or the appliance. Some Christians only *register* or *reflect* the moral and spiritual temperature of their environment. They conform to the prevailing mores of their society. But other Christians *regulate* the moral and spiritual temperature of their environment.

In order for the Christian to regulate his environment (as "salt" and "light," Matthew 5:13-16), he must not be conformed to the prevailing spirit of that environment. Perhaps Paul is following his symbol of the Old Testament sacrificial system here. In that system, when an animal was yielded to God as a sacrificial victim, it thereby lost its place in the stall and in the market and no longer could be bought and sold there. Its dedication in one sphere implies its final removal from the other. Even so, when the Christian yields himself to God, he thereby loses his place and voluntarily forfeits his "rights" in a godless world.

Now look at the positive demand in the vocation of Christian dedication. "Be not conformed to this world, but be ye transformed by the renewing of your mind." The word "transformed" is "metamorphoumai," which gives us our English word, "metamorphosis." "Transformed" describes a change from within. The world exerts pressure from without, but the Holy Spirit changes your mind and your life by releasing power from within. "Transformed" means that your outward expression is changed to be consistent with your inward nature. Thus, in "metamorphosis", the outward expression more and more reflects the inner nature. Metamorphosis means that the true inward character is being brought to outward visibility. This word is used of Jesus in Matthew 17:2 on the occasion of His "transfiguration." His Deity, hidden in humanity, came bursting forth to visibility, and "His outward expression was changed before them, and His face shone as the sun, and His clothing was white as the light." This word is also used of the progressive change of a Christian in II Corinthians 3:18, and it refers to essentially the same thing as here in our text. To be transformed in the sense of these texts means to be like Christ both inwardly and outwardly. It means that the Christ who is literally in us begins to reveal Himself through us.

It must be remarked that both words, "conformed" (sunschematizo) and "transformed" (metamorphoomai), have to do with an outward expression. The *difference* between the two words is in the respective *originating sources* of these outward expressions. In the first case, the originating source is *external*, "this age." In the second case, the source is *internal*, the "renewing of the mind" as an enhancement of the indwelling life of Christ. Ponder these words carefully and prayerfully.

"Be ye transformed by the renewing of your mind." The Greek tense of both the negative and positive commands of verse two indicates continuing action. "Do not go on being conformed..., but go on being transformed...," and the mind plays a key role in either action. Your "mind" refers to the way you think, your attitudes, your philosophy. The world constantly bombards us with its "mind-set," its philosophy. Some people say that they are afraid they will be "brain-washed" by the church and the Bible — so they allow themselves to be *"brain-dirtied"* by the spirit of the world. Take your choice; there is no neutrality. Brain-washed by the Word, or brain-dirtied by the world! The Christian must be "brain-washed" every day by the Word of God, or he *will* be conformed to this age. The Word of God is the only source where we can find God's mind in order to renew our own. D. L. Moody always wrote in his gift Bibles the words, "Either this Book will keep you from sin, or sin will keep you from this Book." Scripture or sin; the Word or the world; the Savior or Satan — the choice is clear. This clearly means that a daily devotional life is not optional in the Christian life. It is standard equipment, an absolute necessity. It is as necessary to the daily Christian life as eating is to the daily physical life. No reader of these lines expects to live many days in this world without regular eating, and no Christian should allow his daily devotional habits to be erratic, either.

Salvation is instantaneous, but sanctification (transformation into the likeness of Christ) is gradual. Someone said, "It took God only one day to get Israel out of Egypt, but it took God forty years to get Egypt out of Israel." A *crisis* got the Israelites out of Egypt, but a *process* full of God, Moses, the Law, Aaron and forty years of miracles was necessary to get the mind and morals and manners of Egypt out of the hearts and habits of the Israelites. In the same way, it took God only a moment (what a moment!) to get you out of sin, but it will take a lifetime to get sin out of you! Dedication involves us in the process of being transformed. What an adventure! No other vocation is as demanding or as rewarding as this one.

According to Romans 12:1-2, Christian dedication is volitional, total, sacrificial, radical, spiritual, moral, reasonable and vocational. Is this a big life, or what?

IV. THE SURE CONSEQUENCE

Finally, Romans 12:2 reveals the *sure* consequence that follows Christian dedication. The person who dedicates himself to Christ on His terms will "prove in practice that the will of God is good, well-pleasing and complete." These three adjectives might constitute a basic study of the will of God, but here they reveal the practical outcome of Christian dedication. Note that the will of God is "proved in practice," not in speculation, or study, or consideration. Jesus said, "If any man will *do* His will, he shall know of the teaching." Christians don't *study* their way to *obedience* as much as they *obey* their way to *assurance*. It is probably true that more Christians *act* their way to *faith* than those who *believe* their way to *action*. Dr. George Truett used to say, "Act as if the Gospel is so, and it will prove itself to you." Too many people stop with naked faith if their faith did not include action from its beginning.

The will of God is proved in *practice*, not in mere proposition. Note, too, that there *is* a will of God for the Christian. God has a specific plan for your life. Surely God is no less wise that an architect who guides his work by a blueprint, or an artist who follows a plan in painting, or a shipbuilder who conforms to a pattern in constructing a ship. This will is described in Romans 12:2 by three adjectives.

The will of God is "good." It must be heavily emphasized that it is *God's* will that is so described. The will of *many* is *not* good. Have you read the book entitled The Diary of Anne Frank? It records the experiences of a fifteen-year-old girl. She was a Jewess whose family had fled from Nazi Germany to the Netherlands. Later, after having been detected by Hitler's police, the family was sent to Auschwitz, the German death camp in southern Poland. The only crime of this fifteen-year-old girl was that she was born of a particular racial stock. She described in her diary how on one occasion she had seen a group of Hungarian Jewish children in the death camp. They were standing naked in a cold and driving rain awaiting extermination in a gas chamber. They were there and subjected to such brutal treatment primarily because it was the will of one man — Adolf Hitler — that they should be there. *His* will was not good for anyone concerned. The will of many men has proved to be unspeakable evil, but the will of God has always proved to be good.

It should also be noted that even self-will is not good. Only God knows what evils have been wrought by self-will in this world. It was self-will that led Adam and Eve to commit the first sin. It was self-will that led them to think that they could elevate themselves to God's level without His help. In fact, self-will is the very essence of sin. Sin may have many other definitions, but it is basically *self-will*. And self-will is not good. Our *own* will for ourselves is bad; *Satan's* will for us is bad; even the will of our best friends for us may be bad. But *God's* will for us is always good. In what sense is God's will "good?"

God's will is good in its *beginning* in your life. The fulfillment of the will of God actually began in your life the moment you received Jesus Christ as your Savior. Any truly converted Christian will freely admit the day that God saved him was a good day in his life. Suddenly, he felt himself to be rightly related to *God*, to his *fellow men*, to *himself*, and to the *world* in which he lived. He had made the *greatest choice* ever; he had had the *greatest experience* possible to man; he had received the *deepest joy* available to man; he had begun the *best life* a human being can live. It was a good day when you were saved; the will of God was good in its beginning in your life.

Then, God's will is good in what it *intends* to do with your life. It intends to rescue you from the penalty and power and presence of your sins; it intends to make of you a person of maximum usefulness. It intends to make of you a person who lifts the lives of others and glorifies God. And when your brief life is done in this world, it intends to usher you into a life of expanding growth and service for eternity.

God's will is good in what it *produces* in the world when it is obeyed by believing Christians.

What happens when the will of God is obeyed? Where the will of God is done, the Gospel is preached, and helpless sinners hear about the dynamic of Calvary which is able to break chains that no other power can break. Where the will of God is done, churches spring up to minister to the physical and spiritual needs in their area of influence. Where the will of God is done, hospitals are established, and the healing of the sicknesses of mankind is made possible. Where the will of God is done, schools are established, and the ignorance of men is challenged. Where the will of God is done, the home is lifted out of the mire, womanhood is elevated, and children are given a chance. Where the will of God is done, social evils of every kind are challenged and arrested. The will of God is good when it is tested from the practical standpoint of what it produces.

If these things are true, then the will of God is not a course to be avoided, and it ought never to be a second choice for any of us. God's will is good, and it should be the sole pursuit of our hearts to *discover* the will of God and *do* it.

Then the text describes the will of God as "acceptable," or literally, the will of God is "well-pleasing" or "satisfying." The text does not say that the will of God is easy; it does not say that it is comfortable; it does not say that it is materially profitable; it does not say that it exempts from tragedy, but it does say that it is satisfying.

It is satisfying in that it is able to satisfy the deepest longings of the human heart. In John 4, there is recorded an incident that occurred while Jesus was passing through Samaria. He became hungry, and sent His disciples into town to get some provisions, as He sat by a well and rested. While He was waiting for the others to come back, a poor bit of wretched humanity came to the well to get some water, and Jesus began to talk to that broken women. He spoke to her about a living water, a water which would be a well of water springing up in her unto everlasting life. You know the rest of the familiar account of their conversation. Finally the woman ran back into the town to tell the people in the village about Christ, urging them to come with her to see Him. About this time the disciples returned with the food and they said to Jesus, "Master, eat." However, Jesus, caught up in the nourishment of the will of God, said, "I have meat to eat that ye know not of." The puzzled disciples said among themselves, "Do you suppose someone has brought Him something to eat?" And Jesus said, "My meat is to do the will of Him that sent me, and to finish His work."

In Isaiah 55:2, the Bible addresses this question to every human heart: "Why do you spend money for that which is not bread? And your labor for that which satisfieth not?" Why, indeed, when there is available to everyone the will of God which perfectly satisfies the deep longings of the human heart? After a life of doing the will of God, and of observing others who did the will of God and many who *didn't* do the will of God, Matthew Henry said, "A life spent in the service of God, and in communion with Him, is the most rewarding and pleasant life that anyone can live in this world." The will of God is deeply satisfying to the person who does it.

Also, the will of God is well-pleasing *even under unfavorable circumstances.* Gaze for a moment through the bars into a jail cell in the Roman colony of Philippi, and you will see this. Paul and Silas had broken up a vicious racket in Philippi, and they were put in jail because they were destroying the profiteering of some men who were exploiting a girl for money. The Bible says that they were "thrust into the inner prison, and their feet were made fast in the stocks." But "at midnight Paul and Silas prayed, and sang praises unto God." They sang at midnight! In prison! Someone called it the "first

Christian singing convention," and it took place at midnight in the dungeon of a jail! Dr. R. G. Lee, speaking about the unconquerable spirit of Paul, said, "If you put Paul in a barrel and put the lid on it, he will preach Christ through the bunghole. If you throw him in jail, he will come out of that jail with the prison door under one arm and a convert under the other!" The will of God is well-pleasing, even when it is obeyed under unfavorable circumstances. I can assure you of this: Life will be a terrible disappointment for you if you do not find and follow the will of God, but it will be unspeakably satisfying if you do.

The happiest people I have ever known in my life are those people who live with their eyes on Christ and are most caught up in fulfilling the will of God. Some of the most miserable people I have ever known are Christians who are trying to sidestep the will of God for their lives. Look at your own spiritual experience. Isn't it true that you have never had a deeper sense of fulfillment, or purpose, or abiding joy than you have had when you are most identified with the will of God? The will of God — wherever it takes you, whatever it costs you — is well-pleasing.

Finally, the text says that God's will is "perfect," or literally, "complete" or "full-grown." This means that the will of God does not lack anything that is necessary for completeness. Colossians 2:10 says, "You are complete in Christ." And I might add that you are terribly incomplete without Him. This is undoubtedly what many people need to learn. Many people refuse to do the will of God for their lives because they are afraid they will miss out on something that is pleasant or meaningful. I would be quite realistic here. The will of God will not free you from plaguing problems, and deliver you into a life of ease and ecstasy. But what you receive in doing the will of God is a thousand times better than what you forfeit.

Some people seem to think that the will of God is a puzzle to be solved or a burden to be endured, and that we would be happier without it. If it is a burden, it is the same kind of burden that wings are to a bird, or sails are to a boat. The will of God brings fulfillment and completeness to a human life.

Then the will of God is complete in the sense that it is *the ultimate achievement* that any person can accomplish in life. The greatest thing you could ever do with your life is to do the will of God. In fact, it would be utterly vain for you to be the President of the United States if it is the will of God for you to be a sacker in a grocery store. Dr. Truett used to say, "To *ponder* the will of God is life's greatest *consideration;* to *know* the will of God is life's greatest *knowledge;* to *follow* the will of God is life's greatest *pursuit;* to *do* the will of God is life's greatest *achievement.*"

A missionary said, "I have done *foreign* mission work, and *home* mission work, but the greatest work of my life is my *submission* work, and that began for me the day I decided to submit my life to the will of God for me." J. B. Phillips paraphrased our text in these words, "Let God remold your minds from within, so that you may prove in practice the will of God for you." The only way to prove the will of God in practice is by *finding* it, *following* it, *fulfilling* it, and *finishing* it.

Several years ago, Charles Wellborn told this story on the Baptist Hour radio broadcast one Sunday. He said that during the Second World War he served in Italy. One day their outfit came to a ruined Italian town which had been bombed and shelled by Allied troops. Passing by the ruins of a home they saw a little lad weeping bitterly on what had been the front porch. As they talked with him he led them to the ruins of the kitchen where lay the lifeless bodies of his father, mother, and sister.

Touched with his sorrow they took him with them; a small uniform with a jaunty service cap was provided for him, and "Tony" became the mascot of the company. Mr. Wellborn was his special friend.

Time passed and finally the word went out from headquarters that all waifs and orphans must be sent to certain central points for relocation. The company was drawn up for review and the orders read. Little Tony stood smartly to attention at the Captain's side. His friend had explained to him what must be done and had told him he must be a good soldier, that good soldiers always obey orders. When the word was given, Tony started stiffly to the jeep that would carry him away. About halfway to the jeep, however, Tony the soldier that he was trying to be gave way to Tony the boy that he actually was.

Turning back with tears running down his face, he rushed to Mr. Wellborn, threw his arms around his knees and looking up in his face said, "I can't go! I can't go with them! I don't belong to them — I belong to you!" You see, the only *logical* thing he saw to do in light of what they had done for him was to give himself to them in return. Today, many appealing voices are being heard in our world. Sounding through the din is the "still small voice" of Jesus.

When I consider the "mercies of God," I say to Him, "Lord, I can't go with them! I don't **belong** to them! **I belong to You!**" As a Christian, I am a moral personality who has chosen to belong to Christ, and I am to live and serve from now on under direct orders from Him and in the energy of His indwelling Spirit.

"So here's what I want you to do, God helping you: Take your everyday, ordinary life – your sleeping, eating, going-to-work, and walking-around life — and place it before God as an offering. Embracing what God does for you is the best thing you can do for *him*. Don't become so well-adjusted to your culture that you fit into it without even thinking. Instead, fix your attention on God. You'll be changed from the inside out. Readily recognize what he wants from you, and quickly respond to it. Unlike the culture around you, always dragging you down to its level of immaturity, God brings the best out of you, develops well-formed maturity in you" (Romans 12:1-2, The Message, translated by Eugene Peterson)

THE TRANSFORMING FRIENDSHIP

Philippians 3:10 a

"That I may know Him."

In a book that exposes a great man's great heart, the Apostle Paul is now permitting us to go with him into the innermost sanctuary of that heart, into the Holy of Holies of his very being. He is revealing to us the supreme passion of his life. He is letting us know what is his one great ambition. "That I may know Christ!" Of course, the working premise of this ambition is that Christ does not live way back in the remote centuries of a very distant past, but that he is alive and available today. Jesus is where you are, and you may meet Him and cultivate relationship with Him anytime and in any place.

Paul gave his greatest personal testimony when he said, "I know Whom I have believed, and am persuaded that He is able to keep that which I have committed unto Him against that day (II Timothy 1:12). To know a person is much more than to merely know about that person. Knowing about Jesus has a measure of value, but only knowing Him in continual personal relationship has vitality. To know His gifts is good, but this is far more. To know His blessings is good, but this is far more. To know His comforts is good, but this is far more.

No true Christian can be put off by a doctrine about Christ, or by the Book about Christ, as crucially important as these benefits may be. No Christian can be satisfied with a hearsay or second-hand knowledge of Christ. The true Christian presses through all of these things like the vestibules of a building, passing from one to another, to stand in the Loving Presence of Christ Himself. John Greenleaf Whittier said it best in these lines:

> "No fable old, no mythic lore
> No dream of bards and seers,
> No dead fact, stranded on the shore
> Of the oblivious years;
>
> But warm, sweet, tender, even yet
> A present help is He,
> And faith has still its Olivet,
> And love its Galilee."

When Paul wrote the words of our text, he had already been a Christian for over thirty years! His longing was to know the mind and heart and love and friendship of Christ in an ever-enlarging degree. We say that Columbus discovered America, but not all of America is even *yet* discovered. Even if Columbus knew he had discovered a continent, he could have no idea of the vastness of that continent that would need exploration and continuing discovery. And so it is with our exploration of the infinite Person of Jesus.

Paul also knew that this knowing of Christ had a high price-tag attached to it. In verses 7 and 8, he said, "What things were gain to me, I counted loss for Christ. Yea doubtless, and I count all things but loss for the excellency of the knowledge of Christ Jesus my Lord: for whom I have suffered the loss of all things, and do count them but dung, that I may win Christ." Author Oscar Wilde once referred to "a man who knows the *price* of everything and the value of nothing." But Paul is a man who paid the price of knowing Christ because he knew the incredible value of knowing Christ. In fact, He decided on life's greatest value, Jesus, at any price, because he recognized that the Value is always greater than the price. The value is so great that the price is not even considered.

The typical Christian vocabulary is replete with such terms as "accepting Christ," "believing in Christ," "trusting Christ," and "knowing Christ." But what does "knowing Christ" mean? Many relational metaphors could be used: teacher-disciple; master-slave; father-son; commanding officer-soldier; coach-athlete; king-subject; bridegroom-bride, etc. Each relationship presents a marvelous dimension of the Christian life, but there is one which contains the richest dimensions of all. That is the relationship of friend and friend. The Weymouth Translation of Romans 6:23 says, "God's free gift is the Life of the Ages bestowed upon us in Christ Jesus our Lord." Of course, the gift is Eternal Life, but it can be best understood as the gift of the everlasting personal friendship of Jesus with the believing heart. In fact, Jesus Himself defined Eternal Life in these words, "This is life eternal, that they may know Thee the only true God, and Jesus Christ whom Thou hast sent." So Eternal Life could be defined as knowing God through friendship with Jesus Christ. In this sense, Christianity is the acceptance of the gift of the friendship of Jesus. "That I may know Him" is simply the expression of desire for a deeper friendship with Jesus. So we are examining today "The Transforming Friendship," the friendship between a sensitive and spiritual Christian and the Great Friend, Jesus.

I. THE GIFT OF FRIENDSHIP

First, we will consider the *gift* of this transforming friendship.

1. A Gracious Gift

Friendship between Jesus and any human being is an absolute gift of grace provided solely out of the gracious goodwill of Jesus Himself. Jesus said, "*I* have called *you* my friends." The giver of the friendship is Christ Himself. No sinner could establish this friendship without the Divine initiative and permission of Jesus. Paul South said, "A true friend is the gift of God, and only He who made hearts can unite them." This is certainly true. Jesus as a True Friend is a gift of God, and His friendship is certainly a gratuity from God.

This allows us to see our only proper attitude toward Him. The proper attitude to a good gift is acceptance. If a man offers me a million dollars I do not knock him down to get it. I don't have to struggle to come into possession of it. I simply take it and go home before he changes his mind! Nor do I say to him, "I am sorry but I can't take this until I can understand the intellectual basis on which it is given." I put the money in the bank and am content to leave the intellectual basis until a later time. Now, I may never actually see the money. It may simply be placed in the bank in my name. However, if I trust the donor I go and draw checks on it and find them honored. The central experience of the Christian life is a gift which I cannot see, but which is certainly real, and mine, because I draw checks on it regularly and find them honored by God every day.

If God were unwilling to give this gift, all our striving would not make Him give it. And if He is willing to give it, there is nothing to strive for or against, except our own doubts that such a friendship is possible, and that it may be ours for the taking. With regard to "the intellectual basis" on which the gift is given, the truth is that the greatest difficulty in the matter is not intellectual at all, but the difficulty of being loyal to the Friend. And the loyalty doesn't break down through doubt, but through selfishness. We don't refuse other gifts simply because we don't understand them. Some years ago, a dear friend gave me a desktop computer. Recently, another dear friend "upgraded" the computer I presently own. I assure you that I do not understand these machines, but also assure you that I did not refuse the gifts of these friends because I do not understand the mechanics of the machine. Incidentally, I am told that they are now making a computer that is so much like a human being that when it makes a mistake, it blames another computer! I heard about a skunk that fell into a computer — and came out a stinking know-it-all! Let's see, where was I . . . Any simpleton can receive a gift. Friendship with Jesus is a gracious gift of God — and it requires a ready receiver.

The March 16, 1985, edition of *TV Guide* told the story of Lauren Tewes, an actress who was making over a million dollars a year as the co-star of the top-rated television series, *Love Boat.* Talent, beauty, and personality combined to make Lauren Tewes one of the most recognized people in the world. But despite the glamour that surrounded her public image, her private life became a struggle for self-worth from her first days on the set of *Love Boat.* Studio executives criticized her mercilessly. "I felt so insecure," she said, "I spent a lot of time trying to please people who demanded that I change myself. The public told me I was a star, but I felt like nothing."

In the attempt to escape her prison of insecurity, Lauren sought refuge in the euphoria of cocaine. But this drug eventually stole everything from her, including the last remaining shreds of her self-worth. She was fired from the series and forced to begin a long, slow struggle to rebuild her career from scratch. Only seven years after she attained television stardom, her career, her money, and her home were gone — traded for cocaine.

One morning after a sleepless night, feeling worthless and totally alone, she turned on the television and fell into bed. The screen flickered to life, and a kindly man in a red cardigan sweater smiled and said, "I'll be your friend. Will you be mine?" The parents and children of the 1960s and later will recognize the man as Fred Rogers, the host of Public Broadcasting's *Mister Rogers' Neighborhood*. Fred Rogers was an ordained Presbyterian minister with the special charge to "serve children and their families through the media," and he gently and lovingly ministered to children on public TV for years.

When Lauren Tewes heard Mr. Rogers offer and question, "I'll be your friend. Will you be mine?" she broke down in tears and answered aloud, "Yes! Yes, I will!" She later said, "I resolved at that point to get my life together. I was totally collapsed, and Mr. Rogers saved my life — with an offer of friendship."

In much the same manner, but in a far worse sense, man was totally collapsed through sin, and facing eternal destruction. But "God was in Christ, reconciling the world unto Himself" (establishing peace and friendship between Himself and the world). Jesus died, rose again, ascended to Heaven, and sent the Holy Spirit to re-present His Case to your heart. As a part of the arrangement, He says, "I will be your Friend. Will you be Mine?" What a transformation will occur in your life if you will answer as Lauren Tewes answered Mr. Rogers, "Yes! Yes, I will!"

2. A Price Paid

Another dimension of this friendship is that a high *price* was *paid* to make it possible. We must not speak glibly about this friendship, as if it were easy and automatic. No, there was a massive barrier between God and man which prohibited such a friendship as long as the barrier stood. Man's sin stood like an impenetrable wall shutting man out from God. Sin was the breach of an Original Friendship between man and God. Sin broke that friendship (fellowship) with God. And the breach was obvious in both parties. Man became God's enemy through sin, and God became man's enemy, as well. Because of sin, men are "out of sync" with God, and become "haters of God" (Romans 1:30). And God is not passive with regard to sin; He always reacts against it. Psalm 5:4 says, "Thou are not a God that hath pleasure in wickedness; neither shall evil dwell with Thee." Indeed, "Thou hatest all workers of iniquity" (Psalm 5:5). God must hate sin because He is totally in favor of its opposite. And because every sinner is identified with his sin until he is shaken by the power of God in conversion, the reaction of God against sin determines His treatment of the sinner. God hates the perversion so much that He cannot allow it in His Holy Presence (Habakkuk 1:13) — but God still loves the person! One commentator said, "This was a problem worthy of a god, and God solved it like the God that He is." This is the very heart of the Gospel of Christ: "When we were enemies, we were reconciled to God by the death of His Son; and much more, being now reconciled, we shall be saved by His life" (Romans 5:10). "The death of His Son" — this was the price that was paid to make this transforming friendship possible.

When the Bible tells us that "the gift of God is eternal life through Jesus Christ our Lord," and that we are "saved by grace through faith, and that is not of ourselves, but it is the gift of God, not of works, lest any man should boast," we might simplify it by saying that salvation is God's gift through friendship with Jesus Christ.

II. THE GROWTH OF FRIENDSHIP

Second, we will consider the *growth* of this transforming friendship. One great British Christian said, "A man must keep his friendships in constant repair." This is certainly true of the greatest friendship of all. The Bible says, "A man who would have friends must show himself friendly." This simply means that if you want to draw on the bank account of personal friendship, you must make regular deposits of congeniality and relationship. The person who *is* a friend will always *have* a friend. And this is certainly true of the greatest friendship of all.

> "One there is, above all others,
> Well deserves the name of Friend;
> His is love beyond a brother's;
> Costly, free, and knows no end.
> They who once His kindness prove
> Find it to be everlasting love."

Note in the above lines that friendship must be tried, and then it will be tested and proved. Involvement and investment are big factors in a friendship. A person may "stumble into" a friendship, or "stumble upon" a new friend, but then comes the building of the relationship into a rock-ribbed friendship. This will always involve trial and error, successes and failures, laughter and tears, but a true friendship will grow stronger with every new venture.

Henry Ford once said, "Your best friend is the person who brings out the best in you." Personally, I proudly claim Jesus Christ as my best friend! In the Presence of Jesus, men in the Gospels found a "higher, better self" emerging out of the ruins of their sinful natures. Jesus lifted men's hearts with His friendship.

1. The Law of Observation and Identification

The first "law of friendship" which we will examine could be called *the law of observation and identification*. Stated simply, this law means that you become best friends with the person you observe most closely and "hang around with" most consistently.

One of the greatest golfers in the history of the game was Bobby Jones. When Bobby Jones was a little boy, his family lived near the East Lake golf course in Atlanta, Georgia, and every afternoon after school he followed the club pro around the course, watching him play. He came to admire the golf game of this man, and he watched him ever more closely. When Bobby began to play the game of golf, his golf swing was the perfect imitation or replication of the golf swing of the club pro. It is a law of life that *we* become like what we live with and look at. Is it any accident that the word, "behold," occurs so many times and in so many settings in the Bible? Is it any accident that Jesus used the word so often, and it was used in addressing our attention to Him so often? I think not. Indeed, the only way this friendship can transform our lives is through observation of Jesus and identification with Him.

We can even go so far as to say that no one has ever properly "beheld" Jesus and truly identified with Him by faith *without* being transformed. Robert Coleman said, "No one can look very long upon Immanuel's face and remain the same," and he was right. At the end of a period of convalescence while recovering from a serious illness, the great Christian missionary E. Stanley Jones wrote, "I have spent these months looking into the face of Jesus with an unobstructed gaze, and what I see is beautiful." He was simply practicing the first law of a growing friendship, the law of observation and identification.

2. The Law of Association

The second "law" of friendship could be called *the law of association*. This law simply means that the friends who are most real to you are those with whom you associate most.

A young man went away from home to serve in the United States military. While he was away, he faithfully wrote a letter to his girl friend every single day. At the end of a year of receiving daily letters from him, she married the postman! That is the law of association.

When I was a teenager, I had a friend who lived next door. I saw him practically every day, and sometimes I saw him several times a day. We became almost inseparable companions. We ran around together. We fished together. We went to and from school together. We played together and worked together. I felt very close to him. The mutual influence that we had on each other was very real. But then I moved away. Because we were both poor writers, we didn't correspond with each other. After visiting back and forth a few times, we slowly lost contact. Today, we only remember each other from a far away place and a time long ago. Both the friendship and its failure are examples of the law of association. This law says that if two persons are to be real to each other, they must take time to be together.

If I wanted to practice the law of association in building a friendship, there are several practical things I might do. First, I would spend a lot of time *talking with my friend privately and personally*. One cannot spend extended periods in private conversation without opening windows of friendship. Apply this to your friendship with Jesus. How much time do you spend in secret prayer? Jesus said, "When you pray, enter into your closet, and when you have shut the door, pray to the Father who is in secret." How often do you converse with God? Someone said, "Prayer is simply holding open house for God." Thus, face to face contact is made, and a person-to-person association is built. In time, a friend becomes another self. In friendship with Jesus, He becomes your "other self." Aristotle spoke of a true friend as one soul in two bodies. Though the Bible says it differently, this is what union with Christ, or friendship with Jesus in its deepest sense, means.

Stanley Jones, the great missionary to India, was once visiting Copenhagen, Denmark. During his stay in Copenhagen, he visited the Church of Our Lady. While there, he viewed the famous statue created by the Danish sculptor, Thorvaldsen. He was walking silently down the aisle of the church to leave the building after viewing the statue when he was approached by a church custodian. In broken English, the man asked Dr. Jones, "Sir, did you see the Master's face?" and he gestured back to the statue. "Why, no," Jones replied, "you can't *see* His face; it is bowed to the ground." "Ah, but that's the point, "said the custodian, "if you would see the Master's face, you must first kneel at His feet." If you would see Jesus and become best friends with Him, you must spend much time talking with Him personally.

Second, I would *spend a lot of time talking with his friends.* This is a second practical step to be taken in practicing the law of association. People who are friends of Jesus help us to know Him better. Jesus said, "Where two or three are gathered together in My Name, there am I in the midst of them."

In the great account of the "Emmaus Road walk" of two disciples on the evening of the resurrection of Christ, the Bible contains this enlightening verse: "And it came to pass, that, while they communed together and reasoned, Jesus Himself drew near, and went with them" (Luke 24:15). This is precisely what happens when two friends of Jesus are in proper relationship with Him, in proper relationship with each other, and are humbly discussing the things of God. "Jesus Himself draws near, and goes with them." Dear Christian, spend a lot of time in rich fellowship with the friends of Jesus talking about Him. The law of association will operate and you will know Christ better. If we would know Him better, we must develop companionship with the right kind of Christians.

Third, I would *read a good book about Him.* This is a third practical step to be taken in practicing the law of association. Even so, if I want to know Jesus better, I must make much of His Book. God's best gift to the world is His Son. His second best gift to the world is the Bible. No one can ignore the Bible and improve his friendship with Jesus.

If I wanted to know George Washington better, what might I do? I would go to the local library in my community and get a book about him and sit down and read it. In fact, I know many of the great characters of history far better than I know many of my own neighbors — because of the law of association. I have read good books about many people from the past, and though I have never seen any of them, I have gotten to "know" them quite well. Never underestimate the power of a good book if you want to get to know someone better.

Henry Ward Beecher wrote, "I never knew my mother. She died when I was only four years of age. But one day I was reading over a lot of letters that my mother wrote to my father, and I found the letters that she wrote from the day they met until their love was one. When I read these letters, I think I understood my mother." You and I have never seen Jesus in the flesh, but we have an incredible volume of "letters" which expose His heart to us.

Gutson Borglum, the great sculptor, wrote about his technique in these words: "I studied every known photograph of the subject. I read every book about him I could find. I looked up many who had seen him, and talked with them.

Then I had my own mental picture and reproduced it." Here again is the law of association.

Pastor Charles E. Jefferson said, "I feel as though I know Paul better than any man who ever lived. I made Paul my daily companion. I read his letters over and over again. I read everything I could find which has been written about Paul; I have thought about him, and talked about him, so now I feel as if I know Paul better than I know any other man who ever lived."

George W. Truett, perhaps the greatest statesman ever to emerge from Baptist ranks, said, "If men are rooted and grounded in a knowledge of the Bible, they will go out against any sin, against any foe, against any difficulty, and they will overcome, for the Bible is a signboard pointing us to Christ."

How much time did you spend yesterday with the world and its affairs by means of your newspaper or television? And how much, by comparison, did you spend with God in the pages of His Book?

This is the law of association. If you want to know Jesus better, talk with Him privately and personally, talk with His friends, and read a good book about Him. These are practical ways to use the law of association.

3. The Law of Expression

There is a third law of friendship which is as fundamental as the others. It could be called the *law of expression*. This law means that friendship feeds on any outward expression that is given to it. If I express myself positively and practically toward another person, I get to know that person better by means of that expression. Let me suggest some practical ways to improve a friendship by means of the law of expression.

First, *follow* the friend. This is the practical side of the law of identification which I mentioned earlier. Identify with the friend in consistent association and activity. Over and over, Jesus said, "Follow me." No one can hope to be the friend of Jesus if he does not heed this admonition and take advantage of this invitation. Jesus said, "I am the light of the world. He who *follows after Me* shall not walk in darkness, but shall have the light of life." In John 10:27, He supplied two "tests of friendship" when He said, "My sheep *hear my voice,* and I know them, and *they follow me."* You improve your friendship with any person when you follow him.

Second, express yourself in some act of practical service. Genuine friendship thrives on deeds more than words. You can express your friendship in words, and you ought to, but the words will become hollow unless sometimes you let your actions speak as well as your words. The gift you sent on Mother's Day has drawn you closer to your mother. The cake you baked for your neighbor who was entertaining guests has strengthened the neighborly association. The food you fixed and sent to your sick friend, the visit you paid to the hospital, the note of encouragement you sent to the distant friend — these expressions of friendship have brought you closer to your friend. Christian, how long has it been since you went out of your way to do something for God?

I Corinthians 3:9 says that "we are laborers together with God." However, it is obvious that laborers *labor*. It is astounding to see how many Christians only read the Bible occasionally, pray occasionally, go to church (occasionally!), and then wonder why their relationship with Christ is not more real and vital. The *abiding* life of John 15 is an *active* life; the more aggressive the *action,* the more *vital* the life.

Daniel 11:32 gives us an acid test of this friendship. It says, "The people who know their God shall be strong, and shall do great exploits." Aggressive practical service for your friend is one of the great tests of genuine friendship.

The idle Christian is always in trouble spiritually. Idleness explains a thousand *doubts* and a thousand *defeats*. Even John the Baptist, the bold prophet who uncompromisingly called wicked King Herod to repent of his sin, when he was put in jail, and had a period of enforced inactivity, fell into doubt and depression through idleness (Matthew 11:2-3). Let your love for Christ begin to speak the language of deeds and you will soon have an enlarged relationship with Him.

Third, *talk about your friend* to someone else. Tell somebody what you think of him, and your relationship with him will grow. We are so constructed as human beings that no thought, no feeling, no impulse is fully ours until we have expressed it. And the more frequent the expression, the more complete the possession. This can be tested in any relationship. Just speak of your love to your parents or your children, and that love becomes more real. Tell somebody what you think of Jesus. Tell them how much you love Him. Describe Him to them, and your love for Him will grow.

These, then, are the "laws" by which friendship operates and grows. If they are practiced in your friendship with Jesus, it will be kept in good repair, and will grow.

III. THE GAIN OF FRIENDSHIP

When Elizabeth Barrett Browning was asked the secret of her life, she simply replied, "I had a friend." Anyone who knows Mrs. Browning's story can well guess that she was referring to her relationship with her loving husband, Robert, who was instrumental in bringing Elizabeth out of a tragic home background and instilling in her self-worth that enabled her to become what she likely would never have been otherwise. Whatever Mrs. Browning meant by her testimony, any genuine Christian would happily give the same testimony as the "secret" of his life. *"I had a **Friend!**"* No greater gain in life can be had than the gain that comes through a personal friendship with the glorious Son of God.

History records that Sir Philip Sidney, poet, philosopher, and soldier of the sixteenth century, fell in battle on the field of Zutphen in the year 1586. In his great distress he called for a drink of water; but as he was putting the cup to his lips, he saw near him another dying man whose eyes were fixed longingly on the cup. Lowering his hand, Sidney handed him the cup, declaring weakly, "Your necessity is greater than mine." Many acts like that made his name famous for kindness and grace. So it was not strange that a knight of that time requested that this epitaph be put above his grave: "Here lies the friend of Sir Philip Sidney." Any sensitive and genuine Christian might want these words on his tombstone: "Here lies the friend of Jesus Christ. I was one who was befriended by Him, and transformed by the friendship!"

What have I gained by this friendship? What power has come to me through it?

1. The Power of Example

A Christian's friendship with Jesus brings into his life an incredible power of *example*. No one will ever be able to testify that Jesus Christ set a bad example for Him to follow! Though Jesus has given me infinitely more than a good example, it is certainly true that He has "left me an example, that I should follow His steps" (I Peter 2:22).

2. The Power of Experience

Any friendship will inevitably mean the transfer of some power, some influence, some experience. The two friends will tend to become like one another, and both will be stronger than before. This will occur whether the strength be that of evil or of good. One nature feeds on another, and the nourishment received is the greatest in a true friendship. Normally, the weaker of the two feeds on the stronger, so that the weaker becomes stronger through the communication of personality that occurs in the friendship.

You might think of the two friends as two highly charged electric terminals, and the "spark" of power passes from the *higher* to the *lower*, or from the *positive* to the *negative*. Many people are "attracted" to Jesus Christ; many people "admire" Him. But this attraction, this admiration, bring no real gain to an individual's life. In fact, it is likely that no human being can help being attracted to Jesus when He really sees Him. But true power flows only through a solid friendship with Him.

One of the great experiences that comes through this friendship is the experience of consolidation. A believer's friendship with Jesus will run through every part of his life just as a thread runs through a necklace of beads and unites them. That thread will give to even the smallest bead an important place, a significant meaning, and a great value. Even so, this transforming friendship will focus a life into a unit and rescue it from division and waste. To follow the analogy negatively, without this friendship, the experiences of life are scattered as loose beads on a living room floor. But this friendship is like the thread that gathers up all the loose beads and makes them all part of one great whole. This friendship gives meaning and blessing to every experience of life.

Another of the great blessings of this friendship is its duration. A verse in Proverbs says that "a friend loves at all times, and a brother is born for adversity." Some people make "fair-weather friends," the kind who are not "born for adversity." Adversity is often the wind that separates the chaff of flattery from the grain of real friendship.

The Shadow once said to the Body: "Who is a friend like me? I follow you wherever you go. In sunlight or in moonlight I never forsake you." "True," replied the Body. "You go with me in sunlight and in moonlight. But where are you when neither sun nor moon shines upon me?" The friendship of Jesus does not rise and fall like the tide. It is not probated on our performance. It endures through all circumstances and threats.

3. The Power of Expulsion

One of the greatest gains of this transforming friendship with Jesus is the power of *expulsion* which it brings into the Christian's life. When this friendship has been firmly established, a lot of lesser issues are automatically settled. A lot of questions are answered, a lot of temptations are overcome, a lot of problems are resolved — by this friendship. This friendship throws the entire bias of the believer's life into an elevated course, and prevents him from wasting himself on a lower one.

> "In sin I long had found delight,
> Unawed by shame and fear,
> Till a new object struck my sight,
> And stopped my wild career."

One of the most popular hymns ever written is entitled, "What a Friend We Have In Jesus." I am quite happy and comfortable when singing it. Jesus Christ has proven His friendship to me again and again. However, it occurs to me that we are usually singing of a one-sided relationship. We are singing of *His* friendship with *us*, but not necessarily of *our* friendship with *Him*. I found that when I turned the words around and tried to sing, "What a friend I am to Jesus," I was hardly comfortable at all. I felt that the acclamation of the *first* title had become an *accusation* if I turned the words around.

Then I read in the Book of James that "Abraham was called the friend of God," and my appreciation for Abraham immediately grew. What could be more glorious than to be a friend of God? A friend of Jesus? Remember, I am a friend of Jesus only because I have been befriended *by* Him, but *how balanced is the friendship?*

Most parents can remember a time when one of their children, when small, brought into the house some neighborhood child (and it *might* have been an *urchin* or a *derelict*) and announced proudly, "This is my friend." I'm sure that Jesus makes such a presentation of me — and will reaffirm it One Day in Heaven — but the question lingers, How good a friend am *I* to *Him?* Is anyone in your community able to say about you, "That person is a friend of Jesus"?

Many years ago, a great little Scottish book was published, entitled, <u>Men of the Knotted Heart.</u> It is the story of outstanding Christian Scotsmen who were bound together by a common hot-hearted relationship with Jesus Christ. The truly fascinating thing about it is that the title is the Hebrew idiom for "friendship." Christian, *is your heart intertwined, knotted, with the heart of Jesus?* If so, then you are His friend.

We have a denomination in Christendom who are called "Friends." I am not willing to relinquish or concede the title to them. *I want to be a friend — a **best** friend — of Jesus.*

THE CLOSER THE LOOK, THE GREATER THE BOOK

II Timothy 3:16-17

"All Scripture is given by inspiration of God, and is profitable for doctrine, for reproof, for correction, for instruction in righteousness: That the man of God may be perfect, thoroughly furnished unto all good works."

Years ago, a Frenchman named Peter Roget gave to the world one of the great literary documents of lingual history. Mr. Roget's father was a French Baptist pastor, and he took the name of his book from the French New Testament. The book is like a dictionary — it has a great vocabulary, but a poor plot! We know it as <u>Roget's Thesaurus</u>. The word "thesaurus" is the word used in the Greek New Testament for a "treasury" or a "treasure." So his book was called "Roget's Treasury of Words." I think he probably knew as a French Baptist pastor's son that the *true* treasury of words is in the Book we call the Bible.

An intellectual skeptic said to an enthusiastic Christian, "How do you reconcile the teachings of the Bible with the latest finds of modern science?" The wise Christian answered, "Sir, just what are the latest findings of modern science?" You see, the "latest findings of modern science" change continuously. A scientific textbook is obsolete five years after it is published.

But the Bible is like a giant rock standing in the mainstream of fast-flowing history, with eddies swirling this way and that way and striking full up against it — and they only polish the rock and prove it. They don't change it or shake it. Isaiah 40:8 says, "The grass withereth, and the flower fadeth, but the Word of our God shall stand forever." Psalm 119:89 says, "Forever, O Lord, Thy Word is settled in Heaven." Jesus said, "No jot (the smallest letter of the Hebrew alphabet) or tittle (the smallest twist or turn of the smallest letter of the Hebrew alphabet) will ever pass away until all these words are fulfilled. Heaven and earth may pass away, but my words will never pass away."

So let's consider God's Treasure of Words. I want to do a "three-eyed" study.

I. The INSPIRATION of the Word

First, we will consider the vital matter of the *inspiration* of Scripture. II Timothy 3:16 claims that "all Scripture is given by inspiration of God." Nothing could be of greater importance than this claim. If it is not true, Christianity collapses at the point of authority. If it is true, Christianity stands in its total truth and in its significance in determining each man's eternal destiny.

When the skeptic hears this claim, he may object, "Just a minute! Some of your so-called 'Scripture' was not even in existence when this statement was written, and some of it wasn't even compiled into a Bible. So how can you apply *this* statement to all those things that came later?"

Suppose I said to you, "All rain is wet." Am I describing only *past* rain, or the little past rain that *I* have known, or all past rain that *anybody* has ever known, or all past rain whether anybody has ever known it or not, or am I actually talking about **all** rain — whether past, present, or future rain? You can make this rule — wherever it rains, it's going to be wet. Whether it was past rain, and whether you were present, or anybody was present except God, it was still wet. And when rain falls today, whether you or anybody else are present or not present, it is still wet. And when rain falls in the future, it is still going to be wet. So when the writer says, "All Scripture," he means that which God has revealed and recorded of Himself and His truth, whether it has been recorded at the time or not, whether it has been recognized at the time or not.

"All Scripture is inspired of God." I must begin our study by challenging one of the most sacred terms in the vocabulary of all Bible believers. The word "inspiration" itself leaves something to be desired in understanding the Divine origin of the Scriptures. To "inspire" means to "breathe into," and the Bible did not become the Word of God by God breathing into it. Technically, the better word would be "spiration," or simply "spired," which means "breathed." But the very best word is the word "expired" or "expiration," which means "out-breathed." You may think I am splitting hairs, but it is the failure to "split hairs" in our doctrine of inspiration which allows us to hold loose and inferior views of the inspiration of Scripture. The Scriptures were *breathed out by God Himself*, so that the Bible is the product of the breath of God. I will seek to make the difference in these terms apparent as we move along.

The Bible itself makes this claim in our text, "All Scripture is given by inspiration of God." The five words in the King James Version, "given by inspiration of God," all translate one Greek word. The Greek word is the word, ***theopneustos***. The word literally means "God-breathed." To say that the Scriptures are "inspired," or "breathed *into*", by God is to allow the possibility of a less-than-Biblical view of the Bible as the Word of God. This term permits the extremely weak "Neo-Orthodox" view that the Bible *contains* the Word of God, and that it *becomes* the Word of God *only* when God speaks to you from its page. So the standard of the Bible's value as the Word of God is existential, experiential, and empirical. I repeat, this is a less-than-Scriptural view of the Bible. But it's technically permitted by the word, "inspiration," which does not translate the word "theopneustos" with careful accuracy. There is a very real sense in which God *does* "breathe into" His Word, but this is a matter of *illumination* rather than *inspiration*.

In the two verses which bracket II Timothy 3:16, Paul gives two of the greatest objectives for which God gave us His Word. The first is to make us wise unto salvation through faith in Christ Jesus (vs. 15). These words should be weighed carefully. And the second objective is to equip the already-saved person that he may be "complete and thoroughly prepared for every (truly) good work" (vs. 17). But our purpose at this time concerns the *origin* of Scripture rather than its *objective*.

It is the claim of the Bible itself that the breath of God produced each Scripture, just as my breath produces my words, making them the vehicle of my thought.

Personally, I hold to a *dynamic plenary verbal* view of the origin of Scripture. "Dynamic" means to me that the Scriptures originated by the vital and immediate work of God the Holy Spirit. "Plenary" means that the whole Bible was so produced. And "verbal" means that God the Holy Spirit so supervised the creation of the Bible as to select the very words.

Perhaps the most definitive and exhaustive statement in the Bible of the origin of Scripture is found in II Peter 1:20-21. A word-by-word analysis of these verses would prove "profitable for doctrine" at this point. "Knowing this first, that no prophecy of the scripture is of any private interpretation. For the prophecy came not in old time by the will of man: but holy men of God spoke as they were moved by the Holy Ghost." "Knowing this first" means that this is of first, or primary, importance. The phrase, "no prophecy of the scripture is of any private interpretation," has been variously understood. The question (and it is of extreme importance) is, Does this sentence refer to the original production of the Bible, or does it refer to our present perception, understanding, and interpretation of the Bible? The key is the verb. The King James Version says, "is." "No prophecy *is* of any private interpretation." But the word "is" is an inadequate translation. The Greek word is *ginetai*, which means "come to be" or "has its source" or "comes to pass." The New International Version is accurate in translating, "For prophecy never had its origin in the will of man."

    The volition of man did not originate the Bible; it came from the initiative and creative activity of the Lord Almighty! The word translated "interpretation" is another commanding word of this passage. It is the original word *epiluseos*. It means "to untie, to unloose, to release, to unfold, to unravel, to disclose." The noun occurs in the New Testament only here. The verb form of the same word is used twice in the New Testament, once in Mark's Gospel, where it means to unravel the mystery of a parable, and once in the Acts of the Apostles, where it means to solve a problem. So the sentence could read, "No prophecy of Scripture has its source in any private disclosure." The next sentence of the text (vs. 21) echoes the negative of vs. 20 and then adds the positive side: "For the prophecy came not in old time by the will of man." The verb "came" is a form of the verb translated "moved" later in the same verse. So it literally reads, "The prophecy was not brought into being at any time by the will of man."

The last sentence of verse 21 may well be the most important sentence in Scripture in declaring the truth about the origin of the Bible as God's Word: "But holy men of God spake as moved by the Holy Ghost." Again, we will labor the words and seek the most absolute accuracy in meaning. Note that God used "men" in transmitting the truth of Scripture. This, coupled with an awareness of the unique personality which showed in the writings of each human author, greatly weakens in my view any concept of mechanical dictation in producing the Bible. Some teach that God used the writers as totally passive secretaries, but this is hardly substantiated by a careful appraisal of Scripture. In the Bible, John comes across as the mystic that he is; Paul writes as a systematic theologian with a fantastic devotional capacity; and Luke shows the concurrence of the skilled historian and the medical doctor. Their personalities are not over-ruled, though they are overwhelmed by the process of inspiration. The writers were "men", not mechanical tools. They may have been instruments, but they were not automatons.

Then, our sentence needs a slight adjustment in translation for the sake of accuracy. The text does not literally say, "Holy men of God spoke." It rather says, "Men spoke from God." Note that massive word, "from." It means *right out of God*, right out of the very depths of Deity! Men spoke out of God! Their speech was born in God; it was God-caused, God-driven, God-controlled. Friends, we must be very, very careful about our treatment of the Bible.

Perhaps the most monumental word in II Peter 1:21 is the word, "moved." It comes from the word *fero*, which means "to bear along," or "to carry along." "Men spoke from God as they were carried along by the Holy Ghost." This word is highly picturesque. It is the same word used twice in Acts 27 (verses 15-17), which records the story of the great storm at sea which struck the ship which was transporting the Apostle Paul to his trial before the Caesar in Rome. The ship was struck by "a tempestuous wind," and we read: "And when the ship was caught, and could not bear up into the wind, we let her *drive*. And running under a certain island which is called Clauda, we had much work to come by the boat: Which when they had taken up, they used helps, undergirding the ship; and, fearing lest they should fall into the quicksands, struck sail, and so *were driven*." The words "drive" and "were driven" translate the same Greek root. "We let her continue to *be carried along*." "And they continued to *be carried along*." This is the same word used in our text.

This word is also used in the description of Pentecost in Acts 2:2. "Suddenly there was a sound from heaven as *being borne along* by a violent wind." So "men spoke from God, being carried along," driven by the Holy Spirit as Paul's ship was driven by the wind. Moses, Elijah, Micah, Amos, Matthew, Mark, Paul, Peter, and the others, were all wind-swept children of God, driven by mysterious currents which they could never explain.

A solid illustration at this point might break the heavy spell of technical interpretation. I have been privileged to visit Athens, Greece, on two occasions. The second time, our tour group was assigned a brilliant female guide who gave marvelous explanations of the history and geography of that famed spot, but she was devoid of understanding of any spiritual significance. In her lecture from the Acropolis, she pointed away to the Acro-Corinth jutting up into the sky in the distance, and she identified the Bay of Salamis lying shimmering in the sun. She explained that one of the most decisive naval battles of history had been fought in that nearby bay. It was the battle between the Persians and the Greeks that wrested world supremacy from the hands of the Persians and placed it firmly in the grip of Greece. Also, it secured our civilization for Western culture instead of Eastern and Oriental influence. But even more important for a Christian is the fact that the Battle of Salamis forms a part of the background of the book of Esther in the Bible. As our guide described the importance of the Greek victory, my mind struggled to remember something I had read about that battle. I came home and began a bit of research. This is what I found.

Herodotus, the father of ancient history, has a graphic description of the tactic the Greeks employed in surprisingly gaining victory at the Battle of Salamis. They built some small warships known as "triremes," noted for their three tiers of oars. They equipped the pointed prow of the boats with sharp metal blades. When they entered the battle, they maneuvered rapidly around the larger and slower Persian warships. They quickly pressed in close to the hulls of the enemy ships and sheared off the oars that propelled the Persian boats. When one side of the sets of oars was gone, the big boats went in circles, and the Greeks then sheered away the remaining oars with relative ease. With their oars gone, the boats were *carried along* by the winds and the prevailing currents. This is a picture of the word that is used in defining the role of the Holy Spirit in originating the Bible. "Men spoke from God as they were *carried along* by the Holy Spirit!"

One last technicality from this text — and *how important it is*! The word translated "moved" is a present passive participle. Dr. A. T. Robertson, undoubtedly the greatest Greek scholar ever to come from Baptist ranks, says that it literally means, "being moved from time to time." This is an all-important tidbit of interpretation. It gives rise to one of the most important truths with regard to the inspiration of Scripture. I might add, however, that this insight is decisively true without the support of this technicality of interpretation.

One of the most important questions concerning the inspiration of Scripture is this: Where does inspiration terminate? On the *writers* or on the *writings*? In my judgment, this question is of far greater gravity that we have previously seen.

I quote from an article written by a prominent writer on "Fundamentals of the Faith" (I withhold his name to protect the *guilty!*). The article was published several years ago in numerous Baptist state papers. The article was entitled "What We Believe About the Bible." This quote is the last part of a rather lengthy paragraph: "No books will be added to the New Testament. No person this side of the eyewitnesses of the events can give the first-hand witness which is the mark of the New Testament. The writers were inspired; but this is not their uniqueness, for the Spirit of God continues to move in and upon the people of God. The uniqueness is in that these men who were borne along by the Holy Spirit also stood in the immediate presence of the once-for-all event which was accomplished in the life, death, and resurrection of Jesus Christ."

Much of this statement is quite obviously true, but it betrays two very serious weaknesses as a statement concerning the inspiration of Scripture. First, the statement that "the Spirit of God continues to move in and upon the people of God" sounds as if the writer is making the quality of the Spirit's work in a fellowship of Christians equal to the quality of the inspiration of Scripture. I cannot say how decidedly I disagree with that assessment! The Spirit's inspiration of Scripture is protected by *infallibility* and *perfection*, but no movement of the Spirit of God among Christians is so protected. In a fellowship of believers, it is the Spirit's intention to move upon them, but to work with them in their own *fallibility* and *imperfections*. So the writer does not distinguish between the quality of the

Spirit's inspiration of Scripture and the quality of the Spirit's moving in a fellowship of believers.

Second, the writer's statement about the Bible betrays that subtle weakness which is almost the hallmark of one of the "camps" which I referred to near the beginning of this message. "The writers were inspired." With this I agree, but serious reservations must be made if this statement stands alone. The writers of Scripture were not continuously or even consistently inspired with the quality of inspiration that produced their contributions to the Bible. They were temporarily inspired with that peculiar quality of inspiration that produced their contributions to Scripture; they were "moved from time to time." Peter could have written a *third* letter when he completed his two epistles which are included in the New Testament, and the third letter might not have had any of the quality of Holy Spirit inspiration that produced the two New Testament letters which bear his name. So the terminus of inspiration is upon the ***writing, not*** the ***writers!*** And again, the suggestion in the writer's article that the Spirit of God "continues to move in and upon the people of God" in inspiration, presumably of the same quality that produced Scripture, is beyond my acceptance. The quality of the inspiration that produced my Bible is of a much high quality than the "inspiration" that produced this article and its message, or any message delivered today!

An implication of this message projects itself prominently into my attention. Many spokesmen for God today are content to preach the ideas gained from Scripture while practically ignoring the words of Scripture. You simply cannot have ideas without words. It is my personal conviction that we dishonor the Holy Spirit and do a deep disservice to men when we by-pass His very words and replace them with (paraphrase) ideas supposedly built upon those words. Dear pastor, preach the words of the Word! Explore, exegete, expose, explain, and exploit the marvelous words which God has selected to form His wonderful *Word*! Take your cue from Jesus, who exploited the subtlest intonations of the Old Testament, and from Paul, who built a whole doctrine of incarnation upon an inconspicuous use of the word "seed", majoring on its singular use instead of the plural (Galatians 3:16). What warrant we have to look for "glory gleams" while turning a "verb-diamond" or a "noun-gem" in the Holy Spirit's light. I'm sure our Father would not protest our looking for a lot when we open His Book! He keeps "breathing" — and talking — after His Book has gone to press! But never independently of the truth revealed in the Book. Always within the dimensions prescribed by the Book.

Immediately some may wish to protest, "But this limits God to a book!" Yes, but this "limit" is no limitation when you realize that it is an *unlimited Book!*

For the moment, this is enough treatment of the Inspiration of Scripture. Let's turn now to another great feature in the nature and use of the Bible as the Word of God.

II. The ILLUMINATION of the Word

Second, we will consider the vital matter of the *illumination* of Scripture. You see, the same Spirit who *inspired* the Word must also *illumine* and *interpret* the Word to the believing heart. The Bible says that "the things of the Spirit of God...are spiritually discerned" (I Cor. 2:14). Illumination, or immediate spiritual enlightenment and discernment, is what the old Puritans called "the giving of the eyes." One of their spokesmen said, "When I was converted, God issued me a new set of eyes, and He has been opening those eyes ever since as I live dependently in His Word."

There are two kinds of truth, *academic* (we might roughly call this kind "scientific" truth) and *spiritual.* Spiritual truth can never be grasped by the unaided intellect of man. Academic, scientific truth might basically be categorized as an "I-it" kind of truth, but spiritual truth is an "I-Thou" kind of truth. The Biblical word for academic truth is *gnosis,* while the word for spiritual truth is *epignosis.* "Gnosis" is knowing with the mind, while *"epignosis"* is a much deeper and fuller kind of knowledge. *"Epignosis"* is a *life*-knowledge, a knowing that comes through acquaintance and relationship. With regard to the Bible, human intelligence (*gnosis*) gives you *your* point of view about the Word, while Divine illumination and insight (*epignosis*) will give you *God's* point of view about the Word. God's thoughts belong to the world of spirit; man's thoughts belong to the world of intellect. Spirit can embrace intellect, but intellect alone cannot apprehend spirit. Therefore, inspiration is necessary if God is to communicate His Word to us, and illumination is necessary if we are to properly receive and understand it.

What is the relationship between inspiration and illumination? Inspiration is both objective (produces the Bible) and subjective (through many individual writers), but it *terminates* on the *written revelation, the Bible.* Illumination is *also* objective (the Spirit utilizes the Bible) and subjective (the Spirit enlightens the mind and heart of the reader), but in this case, it *terminates* on a concurrence, a joining, a *union of the Spirit and the Word in the heart* of the humble, hungry reader, producing within the spiritual Christian a relevant perception of the written revelation. God *breathed out* the Scriptures — this is *inspiration;* God *breathes into* the Scriptures and upon our hearts — this is *illumination.*

Let's look more closely now into the matter of illumination. The Psalmist's prayer, "Open Thou mine eyes, that I may behold wondrous things out of Thy Law" (Psalm 119:18) is a perfect request for illumination. Illumination is beautifully pictured in Luke 24 in the Emmaus Road conversation between Jesus and two anonymous disciples on the afternoon of the resurrection. The two were walking sadly from Jerusalem to Emmaus. "And they talked together of all these things which had happened (concerning the crucifixion and death of Jesus). And it came to pass, that, while they communed together and reasoned, Jesus Himself drew near, and went with them." As He began to converse with them, how things began to "open up"! Before this journey began, this chapter records *the Opening of the Tomb* to reveal Christ's resurrection from the dead. Then, in verse 31, *He opened the eyes* of these two disciples that they might recognize Him. In verse 32, they testified that their hearts burned within them, while He talked with them in the way, and while *He opened to them the Scriptures.* Later in the same chapter and on the same day, verse 45 says, "Then *opened He their understanding* that they might *understand the Scriptures."* What a perfect picture of illumination! This is absolutely indispensable each time a believer approaches the Bible if He is to understand God's mind in God's Word.

In Ephesians 1:16-19, one of Paul's great prayers is recorded. It is essentially a request that the Ephesian Christians might receive a deeper and fuller illumination of the Holy Spirit. Paul writes, I pray "that the God of our Lord Jesus Christ, the Father of glory, may give unto you the spirit of wisdom and revelation in the knowledge of Him: The eyes of your understanding (*kardia,* which actually means "heart") being enlightened; that ye may know .... " Again, what a perfect picture of illumination.

Suppose you walk to a hilltop on a clear night and find several men there, gazing up at the stars. You ask, "What are you doing?" One replies, "We are counting the stars, and making a map of them." You say, "Come with me, and I will show you more stars than you can imagine. Come into this observatory and put your eye to the lens of a telescope." "What!" they exclaim. "You want us to leave the vast sweep of the heavens and peer through a one-inch piece of glass?" Exactly! If they will cease to view the heavens with the naked eye and confine themselves to the lens of a telescope, they will learn more than they ever knew before about the stars. If you in the spiritual realm will leave the little hilltop of your natural point of view and submit to the Word of God, depending completely on the Holy Spirit, God will give you supernatural vision to see into all that He has placed before you in His Word.

One of my favorite Scripture stories is the story of the "man born blind" in John 9. When Jesus entered Jerusalem with His disciples, they "encountered" a "man who was blind from his birth." The disciples saw him only as an object for theological discussion, debate, and controversy. But Jesus regarded him (He always regards individuals this way) as a subject for "the works of God to be made manifest in him." Then Jesus did and said some things that are absolutely bewildering (without illumination!). He leaned down, "spat on the ground, and made clay of the spittle, and He anointed the eyes of the blind man with the clay, And said unto him, Go, wash in the pool of Siloam (which is by interpretation, Sent). He went his way therefore, and washed, and came seeing."

Perhaps the best key to unlock this baffling account is found in the meaning of the miracles recorded in the Gospel of John. All the miracles in John's Gospel are called "semeia" or "signs." They are events that actually happened, to be sure, but each points to (sign-ifies) something beyond itself. Each miracle is a parable of Divine wisdom! When Jesus put the moist clay in the man's eyes, He was saying in effect, "Men suffer from a deeper and darker blindness than the mere deprivation of physical sight. This is why men are *really* blind. Men do not see — God, glory, grace, reality, and eternity -- because their eyes are *closed up with earth*! They are earth-bound and earth-blinded!" You see, you can take two thin dimes and totally blot out the light of the sun, if you strategically place them over the eyes of the observer. Men are blind to God because they are occupied with the "cares of this world."

    Then, Jesus told this man to "go and wash in the pool of Siloam (which is by interpretation, Sent)." What does this mean? The pool of Siloam was a pool of water near the Temple area in southwest Jerusalem. Note again that "Siloam" means "Sent." The word "sent" is one of the prominent words of the Gospel of John. Sixty-two times, the word "sent" is used in John's Gospel, and it refers either to *the Father sending the Son*, or *the Son sending the Spirit*, or *the Spirit sending the saint*, on God's appointed mission. However, it is most widely employed to refer to Jesus. Seventeen times in the first nine chapters of the Gospel of John, Jesus is referred to by this title. Every time He was asked, "Where are you from?" His reply was simply, "Sent!" Every time He was asked, "Why are you here?" His answer again was, "Sent!" *He* is the *substance* of which the Pool of Siloam was only the *shadow*. It is as if Jesus had said, "If men are ever to get rid of their earth-blindness, it will be necessary for each of them to come to Me and let Me *wash it out of their eyes!*" When the man went to Siloam and washed, he came away seeing. Even so, the earth-blinded sinner will truly *see* only as He comes to Christ and has his blindness removed and his sight restored. And the earth-bound saint will have his eyes opened to the glories of God's

Word only as he faithfully, dependently comes to Christ and is treated with the eyesalve of the Spirit.

When I was pastor of the Cherokee Baptist Church in Memphis, Tennessee, the church had a tough-minded but tender-hearted deacon named Bill Baskin. Bill managed a building crew in a construction business. One year just a few days before Christmas, he was directing a project on a construction site. He had stopped the traffic on the nearby street to allow a heavy construction vehicle to move up onto the highway. As it came up a slope that was covered with gravel, the fast-spinning wheels picked up a tiny piece of metal or a tiny stone and sent it at high speed through the air. The tiny object struck Bill squarely in his right eye. He fell backward to the pavement, his eye pouring blood. Some of his men rushed to him, and he directed them to put him in a small truck and rush him to the hospital. As quickly as possible, the hospital attendants treated the eye, stopped the bleeding and applied the necessary medical aid. Then a slow wait began. The doctors hoped to save the eye, but everything was doubtful for several days. Then, several days after Christmas, they abandoned hope and removed the damaged eye.

Sometime later, Bill and his wife went to an optometrist's office so that he could be fitted with an artificial eye and with special glasses that would compensate for the extra load now placed on his one remaining good eye. The doctor began to flash the usual examination charts on the screen, saying, "When you get to the place where you cannot see one of these charts as well as the last one, tell me." After several charts, Bill said, "Doctor, I'm not sure about this one. Put the other one back up there, and let me compare the last two charts again." Because he continued to be undecided, he asked the optometrist to alternate the charts several times. His wife, Margaret, who was sitting quietly nearby, finally said with a laugh, "Well, I'm glad to see that someone else has trouble making up his mind about difficult decisions!" Whereupon the doctor turned on the overhead light, raised his finger, and said, "That's a good point! The *fact* is, we don't *see* with our *eyes* at all! We *see* with our *minds*. We only *look* with our eyes!" Now, a Christian sees with an altogether different "set of eyes," and unless God illumines His Word and enlightens those eyes, even His child may look into the Word all day long and seldom *see*!

The story of Joseph in Genesis 41 contains a perfect illustration of illumination. The wise men and magicians of Egypt couldn't "see into" a certain matter, but Joseph did. "And Pharaoh said unto Joseph, 'I have dreamed a dream, and there is none who can interpret it: and I have heard say of thee, that thou canst understand a dream to interpret it.' And Joseph answered Pharaoh, saying, '*It is not in me*: *God* shall give Pharaoh an answer of peace.'" "And Pharaoh said unto Joseph, 'Forasmuch as *God hath showed thee all this*, there is none so discreet and wise as thou art.'" When a believer in Christ walks in the Spirit and lives in the Word of God, he becomes just such a man of wisdom and understanding.

In the year 1647, one of the most important gatherings in Christian history was held in Scotland. It was the famous Westminster Assembly, a great gathering of spiritual leaders which was charged with the task of framing a charter for the Protestant reform movement in the British Isles. Out of this Assembly came the great "Westminster Confession of Faith" and the "Shorter Catechism" of the Presbyterian Church. But there was a grave threat to the Assembly presented by representatives of the "Erastian party," a group of scholarly men who wanted to obliterate all lines, where possible, between the church and the state, and establish a strong church-state relationship. This view was ardently opposed by several Assembly leaders, but there was an additional problem. The Erastian view was advanced by Dr. John Selden, one of the greatest scholars in Christendom in that day, and the opposition did not seem to have a leader who could match his skill of mind and speech. After he had spoken powerfully in favor of the Erastian view, the conservative Presbyterians seemed to be at a total loss as to how to defend their view against Selden's brilliant arguments. Then unexpectedly there rose up in the meeting a Godly young Scotsman named George Gillespie, one of the youngest members of the entire Assembly. After securing permission to address the body, he spoke for an hour against the heresy in a most powerful and effective manner. Dr. Selden later admitted that Gillespie's speech had swept away in one hour the work of ten years of his life. When the speech was over, Gillespie returned to his seat, exhausted.

Several of his friends crowded around to congratulate him, and several reached for the notebook that he had placed in front of him as he spoke, thinking they would find his outline and the polished notes of his masterful argument. Instead, on the page they found nothing but one little sentence, penned over and over and over again as he sat in his seat before asking to speak. The brief phrase covered the page: "Give light, O Lord; give light, O Lord; give light, O Lord." Dear friends, this must be the deep, ceaseless cry of our needy hearts as we turn to God's Word: "Give light, O Lord, give light!"

We must not have a Bible that is not Spirit-related, and we must not have a Holy Spirit who is not Bible-related. To have the Word without the Spirit is equal to having rails laid, and the locomotive on them, but without any power to propel them. On the other hand, to have the Spirit without the Word, is to have the power which propels, but no rails to guide. We must have a Bible-related Holy Spirit, and a Spirit-related Bible.

The Closer the Look, The Greater the Book

Several years ago, I and three other Christians went to mid-state New York for an evangelistic crusade. Four tiny churches cooperated there, and we saw 47 people come to receive Christ that week. The morning meetings each day were held in a small church building in the tiny village of Stockbridge, New York. As I went into the auditorium of the church each morning, I noticed four unusual pictures of Jesus Christ on the walls of the room. Two were on the left wall and two on the right wall, with one at the front and one at the back of each wall. One morning, I walked over to one of the pictures to get a closer look. I made a fascinating discovery! It was a bust picture of Jesus, created by the entire Gospel of Matthew in tiny letters forming the picture. The tiny letters and words were placed closely together, making the facial countenance of our Savior. I hurried around the room to investigate the other three pictures. Sure enough, the second one was the Gospel of Mark forming a *different* picture of Jesus. The third was Luke's Gospel and the fourth was the Gospel of John, each forming a unique picture of Jesus created by the words of that Gospel. I shall never forget those four pictures! I only wish that someone would do the same thing with each book of the Bible. After all, the whole Bible is a portrait of Jesus. The Old Testament forms the background. The background of a portrait is full of shades and shadows and many dark lines, all designed to accentuate the central figure. The Old Testament is exactly like that. It has many shades and shadows and dark lines, and every page of it points to Christ and accentuates Him as the Central Figure. The four Gospels, in turn, present the actual "face" of the figure, so that we can recognize the clear contours of His countenance. The rest of the New Testament, the Acts of the Apostles, the Epistles, and the book of the Revelation of Jesus Christ, reveal the "garments of glory" worn by the Central Figure of the portrait. This is the final and most important purpose of illumination. When this occurs, the print "fades" as we read the Word of God, and the Person "emerges," and God "shines in our hearts, to give the light of the knowledge of the glory of God in the face of Jesus Christ (II Corinthians 4:6). This is true and full illumination.

> "Come, Holy Ghost, for moved by Thee
> The prophets wrote and spoke;
> Unlock the truth, Thyself the key,
> Unseal the sacred Book."

III. The INCARNATION of the Word of God

Third, we will consider the vital matter of the *incarnation* of the Word of God. Incarnation means "in-flesh-ment." When Jesus was born at Bethlehem, this was the incarnation of God in our humanity; not the Deifying of man (the elevation of man into Godhood), but the humanizing of God (the stooping of God into manhood). The Bible says, "The Word (the *Logos*, the "logic" of God, Jesus — John 1:1-3) became flesh." In that moment, God became something He had never *been* before! God afforded Himself a new experience! For the first time in His Eternal Existence, the Almighty God could look through human eyes, touch through human fingertips, walk on human feet, kneel on human knees, and speak through human lips. God suddenly became a "thing" (see Luke 1:35). He came out of the Everywhere into the Here; He got definite with us at Bethlehem! The Infinite became the Intimate; the Most High became the Most Nigh. And He became "flesh," which is a typical Biblical word for man at his *lowest*. When God came down in the birth of Jesus, He came *all the way down!* "One awful night, God walked down the stairs of Heaven with a Baby in His arms, and deposited that Baby in a cattle trough in a cowshed, among animal droppings — in Bethlehem of Judea."

But He didn't stay "cribbed"! He was "Crossed," and "Coffined and Crypted" in death, but He didn't stay there, either! He disturbed Death to death, and burst out of it in Resurrection Glory! He is alive today, and true to His Word, He is exactly where He said He would be. In the Presence of the Holy Spirit, "Christ's Other Self," He is with us and in us.

What is this really all about? God established a principle, God set a precedent, God modeled a procedure, in the coming of Jesus. His "Word-made-flesh" idea is to go on and on until the end of history. The procedure is simply, "Word to flesh to word to flesh to word to flesh" until God rings down the final curtain. With the awful modification created by my sins, my life is to be a Container and a Conveyor, a "Carrier" of the very life of Jesus Himself. When I heard the preached word of the Gospel, which was based on the printed Word of God, the Personal Word of God, Jesus, became real to me! I received Him into my "flesh," my humanity (it must have been for Him a kind of repeat of Bethlehem's birth into a filthy stable), and He literally came to live in me. So my life becomes a greatly modified continuation of His incarnation. And now, living in me, He wants to expose, exhibit, and express His continuing Life — right through me! This is a glorious part of the Heavenly Genius of the Gospel of Christ.

But this creates a question: why, then, do most professing Christians seldom re-present Christ, but instead, they show only themselves? A part of the answer is that this "Word-made-flesh" life must be daily and dynamically sustained by live and vital communication with God through His inspired and illuminated Word. And most believers apparently do not have such daily, dynamic sustenance. What can be done about this dread deficiency? I want to propose some corrective steps to enhance the incarnation of the Living Word in His people by means of the Written Word, the Bible.

First, every Christian should have *consistent exposure* to the Word of God. Hudson Taylor, a giant for God, said, "Your spiritual growth will occur in exact proportion to the amount of time you spend in the Word of God." Though there are other implications at this point which need to be explained, I believe this to be perfectly true. You, dear child of God, should capitalize on every available opportunity to hear the Word of God, and you should create your own opportunities for daily communion with God in His Word.

Second, every Christian should practice *careful listening* to the Word of God. This will require disciplined attention, reception, and retention when we are hearing or studying the Word of God. I seek to practice "spiritual personality projection" when I hear or read the Word, asking the Holy Spirit to enable me to *see myself* in the situations and truths of His Word. Also, I ask Him to "internalize" the truths received, a major step toward the incarnation of the Word. I have already mentioned the retention of the Word. This is vital! Write down what God says to men and study it over and over again. Keep a notebook of His truths which He has given to you.

Years ago, a renowned English preacher named Basil Matthews was in a Bible Conference in Calvary Baptist Church of New York City. He shared the speaking assignments with an Indian preacher from the western United States. As the conference days passed, the two preachers developed a friendship and began to share fellowship in the Lord. One afternoon, they were walking from the church back to their hotel after a conference session. The wide street was crowded with several lanes of traffic. Suddenly, the Indian stopped on the sidewalk and said, "I hear a cricket!" Basil Matthews stood beside him, bewildered by this announcement. The Indian turned, went to the nearby corner, and crossed the wide street with Matthews following close behind. Suddenly the Indian stopped. They were in front of a flower shop, directly across the street from the spot where the strange announcement had been made. The Indian preacher entered the shop with Basil Matthews following him. The Indian stopped in front of a row of pot plants and listened. Suddenly he thrust his hand into one of the plants, and pulled out a cricket. A moment later, the two of them emerged from the shop together. The amazed Matthews said, "How in the world did you do that?" The Indian quietly replied, "Sir, I learned long ago that people hear what they *want* to hear." To prove his point, he took two half-dollars out of his pocket and threw them down on the sidewalk. Matthews later said that four people changed their direction and dived toward the money!

The question is not, "Does God speak?" The question is, "Do men listen?" Do *you* listen for the voice of God every day? How *well* do you listen? What discipline and responsibility are involved! No wonder Jesus said again and again, "He who has ears, let him hear," and "Be careful how you hear!"

Third, every Christian should seek to practice *complete obedience* of what God says in His Word. A familiar passage tells us to "be doers of the Word, and not hearers only. For if any be a hearer of the word, and not a doer, he is like unto a man beholding his natural face in a glass (mirror): for he beholdeth himself, and goeth his way, and straightway forgetteth what manner of man he was. But whoso looketh into the perfect law of liberty, and continueth therein, he being not a forgetful hearer, but a doer of the work, this man shall be blessed in his deed." But sadly, we have arrived at a time in which most believers apparently equate hearing and doing, as if the entire matter were finished when we do God the favor of listening to a sermon or casually reading the Bible for a few minutes! This may give private devotional enrichment, but it is far short of the incarnation of Jesus that God is looking for.

Dr. J. M. Price, a great Christian educator, often said, "The best binding for the Bible is not morocco leather; it's a human skin." Until the Word is walking around again in me, God's will is not being done.

An old Buddhist legend tells of how Quanon, the Buddhist goddess of mercy, was showing a recent arrival in the Buddhist "heaven" around the premises. In the tour, they came to a large building. When they entered, a strange sight spread before the newcomer. The place was like a large library with many shelves, all of them filled with small, shriveled articles that looked like prunes. "What are those things?" asked the new arrival. "They are human ears," replied Quanon. "Human ears? What does it mean?" Quanon replied, "These are the ears of people who regularly heard the truth while they were on earth, but they never did anything about it. So, when they died, their ears came on to heaven, but the rest of each person went to hell!" Dear friend, what would happen — what *would* happen — if that standard were applied by God to the average attendant in our churches? There would probably be many, many bodiless ears in heaven, and many, many earless bodies in hell! How many disobediences have accumulated in your life over the years by hearing the Word of God with no obedient response to its directions and its demands? So Jesus is hidden *within* us without expression and exposure *through* us! What directive does He wish me to obey right now?

Finally, every Christian should make *constant confession* of the truths God is revealing in His Word. It is impossible to overstate the importance of this step. And how this has been overlooked in the typical Christian life. Many people come into our church buildings Sunday after Sunday, and they are no more an influence for God now than they were 25 or 35 years ago, when they were first saved. Why? Is it because they are indecent, or flagrant sinners, or that they do not believe what they are told? Probably not. The real reason in most cases is that they hear God's truth — once, and again, and again, and again — and never repeat it, never speak it, never declare it, never tell it! They don't even talk about it with their closest friends and nearest loved ones. So a vast and vital dimension of the Gospel and the Christian life is totally closed to them. I believe this with all my heart: the quality of a believer's Christian life will never rise above his vocal confession of Jesus Christ and His truth! And the other side is also true: a Christian will always rise up to follow his confession of Christ and His truth, so that the quality of the Christian's life is largely determined by his spoken celebration of the truth of God.

Someone asked Phillips Brooks, the great Boston preacher, the secret of his great church. His answer was certainly peculiar. He said, "I preach a sermon on Sunday, and 500 people repeat it as many times as they can, to as many people as will listen, all week long." Can we see the validity of that? The greatest benefit is not to the persons who heard all those repetitions, but rather to the persons who initially heard the truth — *and then repeated it over and over.* With each repetition, God materialized a greater incarnation of His Word in the life of His child.

So here is the value and vitality of the Word of God to the individual Christian, and the vocation of "in-fleshing" it in his inner life and before the world. Every believer who has had long experience with the living Word of God communicated through the written Word of God would happily testify that "the closer the look, the greater the Book." John Wesley expressed the sentiment of the faith-walking

Christian when he prayed, "Oh God, let me be mastered *by* that Book, and let me be the master *of* that Book." Oh, that this were true of me — and of every believer in Christ!

PAYING ATTENTION TO ONE ANOTHER

Ephesians 4:2; 4:25; 4:32a; 4:32b; 5:19:

"With all lowliness and meekness, with long-suffering, forbearing one another in love."

"Wherefore putting away lying, speak every man truth with his neighbor: for we are members one of another."

"And be ye kind one to another, tender-hearted."

"Forgiving one another, even as God for Christ's sake hath forgiven you."

"Speaking to yourselves in psalms and hymns and spiritual songs, singing and making melody in your heart to the Lord."

Verse twelve of Ephesians four speaks of "the body of Christ." That is one of the primary themes of the book of Ephesians—the church is the body of Christ. That figure cannot possibly be explored enough by Christians. Indeed, it is more than a figure, or an emblem, or a symbol. It is organic reality. The church of Jesus Christ is His own body. It is not merely *like* a body; it *is* His body. Then in verse sixteen, Paul mentions "the whole body" of Christ. In this chapter, Paul speaks of two aspects of the body of Christ. In the first part of the chapter, he speaks of the *larger, universal* body of Christ. In verse four, he says, "There is one body." Then, in the middle portion of the chapter, he speaks of the *local* body of Christ, the local church. There he gives ideal instructions for the proper function of the local church.

Jesus Christ operates in much the same manner in which you operate. You are an invisible, unseen personality contained within a visible, physical body. If you as an invisible personality are going to express yourself, you must do so through and by means of the body. So a person's body is the vehicle by which he can express himself and accomplish his work. His body is the means by which he becomes *functional*. Anything he does (stand, sit, walk, talk, think, write, travel, etc.), he does by means of his body. His body is also the means by which he is *recognizable*. I recognize him by means of his body, and he recognizes me by means of my body. That is the reason when I see Joe Jones walking down the street, I don't say, "Hey, there goes the *body* of Joe Jones," although his body is all I see. Instead, I say, "There goes Joe Jones," because I recognize him by his body. The same is true of Jesus Christ. His body, the church, allows Him to be active, visible and recognizable in the community where it exists.

So *each church is a mediator of Christ, because it is His Body*. Then there is a second powerful idea in Ephesians 4: *each Christian is a minister of Christ* as a member of His Body. Let me anticipate our study by stating a third principle, which is the basis for this study: *every contact a Christian has is to be used as a means of fulfilling his ministry.* Ephesians 4:12 says that the pastor-teacher of the local body is to "equip the saints (all Christians) so that they (all the saints, all Christians) may do the work of ministering." The pastor-teacher is to "fully furnish," or "outfit," all the saints to make them ready to do their job of ministering.

I. THE DIRECTIONS OF CHRISTIAN MINISTRY

What is "the work of the ministry" which Paul refers to? The work of the ministry is three-directional, or three-dimensional. My personal ministry as an individual Christian—not as a preacher, not as a pastor, not as a teacher, not as an evangelist, but as an individual Christian—is to go in three directions.

1. Ministry in an Upward Direction

First, I am to engage in an *upward* ministry, a ministry toward God. Acts 13:2 indicates that it was "as they (the church body in Antioch) *ministered to the Lord*," that the Holy Spirit told them to set aside Barnabas and Saul to form the first traveling missionary team of the book of Acts and of the world Christian movement. Every Christian should "minister to the Lord" on a regular basis, day by day and moment by moment. This ministry includes hearing His voice, praising Him, adoring Him, worshiping Him, and prayer made to Him. Surrender to Him is called our "reasonable service" to Him (Romans 12:2). In short, our primary ministry to God is the ministry of *communion with Him.* This ministry is a response to our awareness of God's goodness, mercy, love and grace in our lives. This ministry should be fulfilled both alone and in the local body, privately and publicly.

The Bible says that "God is love" (I John 4:8). That's what God *is*. Love is foundational to God's character, basic to God's nature. There are other foundational characteristics in God's nature as well, but we are here speaking of His love. The fact that God is eternally love raises a question. If love is foundational to God's character, and God lived "in the Forever" before He created man and the world, whom was He loving *then*? The Bible teaches that God is a social community within Himself. He is a three-way unity within Himself, made up of Father, Son, and Holy Spirit. Theologically, this is called "the

Trinity." For all of eternity past (the "past" is from our finite perspective), in a network of relational exchanges, the Three Persons in the Godhood of God loved and enjoyed each other member within His Person *eternally*. The Father was loving the Son and the Spirit—forever. The Son was loving the Father and the Spirit—forever. The Spirit was loving the Father and the Son—forever. Because "God *is* love," there was no depletion and no reduction of that love—forever. In that ongoing network of complete Self-satisfaction within the Nature of God, they loved One Another for all eternity.

    Now the punch line of our message. I have in me right now—at this moment—One of those Persons of the Godhead. *Do you think that the Holy Spirit stopped loving those Other Two when He came down to get inside of me?* Never! The Bible says, "The Holy Spirit has broadcast the love of God (love *for* God) in my heart" (Romans 5:5). So my heart has been flooded with the very Love that God *is*! This happened the day I was saved. How I remember it! Suddenly, in the moment of my spiritual birth, my heart was filled with the love of God. I loved Him and everybody else, instantly. I have often said that I wished then for "rubber arms," so that I could stretch them around every person on earth and carry them to Jesus so that they could experience what had just happened to me. I could simplify my life since that time by saying that it has been a contest (sometimes an intense *conflict*) between God loving in and through me, and my own desire to have my own selfish way. When I defer to the Holy Spirit, my heart becomes a love chapel. But when I choose to have my own way as opposed to His, my life assumes an overload of misery. So the first dimension, the *upward* ministry, should be easy for any Christian. Indeed, it is only difficult if we refuse to defer to the loving Holy Spirit within us.

2. Ministry in an Inward Direction

Second, I am to engage in a *between-ward* ministry, an *inward* ministry, a ministry toward and among the saints. This is a ministry inside the Body of Christ. In I Peter 4:10-11, the Christian's personal ministry inside the Body is clearly spelled out. The theme of the passage is spiritual gifts, the God-given means by which we are to minister to each other in the Body.

"As every man has received the gift, even so minister the same one to another, as good stewards of the manifold grace of God. If any man speak, let him speak as the oracles of God; if any man minister, let him do it as of the ability which God gives; that God in all things may be glorified through Jesus Christ: to whom be praise and dominion for ever and ever."

Traffic those verses again—with interpretation. "As every man (there is the *individuality* and *universality* of spiritual gifts) hath received (there is the *sovereignty* of God in dispatching spiritual gifts; you do not achieve your gift, you receive it) the gift, even so minister the same one to another (there is the intended *utility* of the gift you have received), as good stewards (there is the personal *responsibility* for the gift you have received) of the many-colored grace of God (there is the great *variety* of the gifts Christ has given to His Body; they are like a multi-faceted prism). If any man speak, let him speak as the out-speaking, or the mouth-piece, of God; if any man minister, let him do it as of the ability which God gives (there is the supernatural *ability* by which these gifts are to be used in the Body); that God in all things may be glorified through Jesus Christ: to whom be praise and dominion for ever and ever."

Here is a virtual goldmine of wealth about spiritual gifts and about their use in the ministry of the saints in the Body of Christ. Remember, we saw: The *individuality* and *universality* of the gifts, the *sovereignty* of God in giving the gifts, the *utility* of the gifts in the Body, my personal *responsibility* to use the gift God has given to me, the great *variety* of the gifts in the Body, and the supernatural *ability* by which I am to use the gift God has given.

Note that the use of these gifts falls into two categories: some are *speaking* gifts, and some are *serving* gifts (I Peter 4:11). These two ministries are *between-ward*, or *inward*, ministries in the Body of Christ, and they are to occur through the regular use of spiritual gifts in the Body. That is the second dimension of ministry in which every Christian is to be daily involved. This study is directed toward this dimension of ministry. Let me merely mention the third and final dimension of ministry.

3. Ministry in an Outward Direction

Third, I am to engage in an *outward* ministry toward the outside world. Just as I am to have all three of these ministries—upward, between-ward, and outward, so is the entire Body of Christ. The Body should be daily engaging in ministries in all three directions, just as Jesus did when He was here in His own physical body. He ministered upward, between-ward, and outward in His *first* body, and He wants to do the same in His *present* Body. As a member of that Body, are you daily ministering upward, between-ward, and outward? If not, should you not "go into the ministry" today?

II. THE DYNAMICS OF AN INWARD MINISTRY

In this study, I am discussing particularly the second of those three ministries, the between-ward ministry. I want to call your attention in Ephesians four and five to five small sentences. They are bound together by one common denominator, the term "one another." Actually, the term does not occur in the final text, but the idea is certainly there. In the Greek language, the term "one another" is just one word. You should become very familiar with these two English words, "one another," which translate that one Greek word, because these two English words are used over thirty times in the New Testament to show us our between-ward responsibilities in the Body of Christ. In this study, we will examine only six of the many "one anothers" of the New Testament.

1. The "One Another" of Toleration

The first "one another" we will examine might be called *the "one another" of toleration.* Ephesians 4:2 says, "With all lowliness and meekness, with long-suffering, forbearing one another in love." Lowliness (humility), meekness and long-suffering are supportive qualities that enrich and insure Christian toleration, and each of those words is a world in itself. The Williams translation of the New Testament translates the last phrase like this: "Lovingly bearing with one another." The Phillips paraphrase says, "Making allowances for each other because you love each other." Dear Christian, don't hurry here! Prayerfully ponder the paraphrase again, asking God to let you clearly see it and completely apply it. That is normally the last thing in the world that occurs to us in interpersonal relationships. We react to others, instead of setting the pace in bearing with one another.

If I "make allowances for you," I will give you room to stumble and fail, room to breathe, and limitless room to grow. While holding you accountable to the highest standard of Gospel holiness, I will still love you none the less when you fail. That is, I will grant to you maximum opportunity for overcoming, while making allowances for your failures. A friend sent me this great quote by E-mail recently: "Real friends are those who, when you feel you've made a fool of yourself, don't feel you've done a permanent job." These "real friends" are learning to "make allowances" for others.

I have seen this "one another" in a close-up demonstration recently. One of my dear friends worked closely in a disciple-making relationship with a young man who had been trapped in a very, very serious drug habit. His heart had been changed by the Holy Spirit, but the dread habit, like an anchor, would seduce him to failure again and again. Each time, he would come back, remorseful and as repentant as he knew how to be. Each time, my dear friend would patiently work with him, walking him through all the processes of repentance, forgiveness and restoration. His history for a prolonged period of time was like a spiral, marked by some victory and much defeat. But my dear brother "made allowances" for him faithfully, patiently and compassionately. Slowly, he came out of the deadly pattern and steadied out in a walk with God. Some time later, he enrolled in a theological seminary, and now he is pastor of a local church in another state! I wish you could have traced this example as I have. My disciple-making brother "made allowances" for his brother without compromise but with incredible patience and compassion. Many people will be benefited by his forbearance, though they will never know the cost in disappointment, disillusionment, patience, persistence, and compassion. But finally, the victory came! When I fail as a Christian, I want a friend like that.

Our verse indicates that we have four great allies to assist us in "making allowances for one another." These four allies are like planets rotating around a central body. The four allies are "lowliness," "meekness," "long-suffering," and "love." "Lowliness" (humility) is actually the word from which we get our English word "tapestry." We are to assume such a position of unassuming humility that we become as low as a rug on the floor, willing to be walked on to promote the welfare of the other person. "Meekness" means "consolidated strength," or "strength brought under control." Do you see how this characteristic is so necessary if we are to practice the "one another" of tolerance? We use the strength which, if untamed, would condemn and crush our failing brother, rather to accept and support him. "Long-suffering" is simply the ability or the commitment to "suffer with that person" in his weakness or failure for a long, long time. The word translated "forbear" here means to "hold back." You hold back your inclination to judge and condemn him, making allowances as necessary. "Love" is the word for total self-giving love, the word that only seeks the highest good of its object. When you combine these five words together—lowliness, meekness, long-suffering, love and forbearance, you see the delicate action that is necessary in practicing the "one another" of toleration.

On several occasions, I have been in the high Andes Mountains of South America. I am told that when pack animals transporting burdens there meet on a narrow trail, one animal will get down on its knees and let the others walk over it, thus passing in safety. What a picture of "making allowances for one another."

In I Corinthians 13:7, Paul said, "Love bears all things, believes all things, hopes all things, endures all things." There is hardly anything in the world more creative than one person believing in another. This verse seems to say that love is willing to go through a lot in order to preserve a relationship with the beloved. This is the meaning of this "one another," the one another of Christian toleration.

2. The "One Another" of Communication

The second "one another" of Ephesians 4 is *the one another of communication*. Ephesians 4:25 says, "Wherefore putting away lying, speak every man truth with his neighbor: for we are members one of another." Notice the negative beginning of this verse. Lying has become a way of life to many Americans. Lies are as easily told, it seems, as truth. One newspaper editorial lamented the present epidemic of lying with these words: "The curse of our legal system today is public perjury, lying under oath." The Greek word for lying here is *"pseudo,"* which refers to falsehood and deceitfulness. The positive side of the mandate is to "speak every man truth with his neighbor." Now, this does not mean that we have liberties to decimate the person under the pretense of telling the truth. Verse 15 of this chapter says that we are to "speak the truth in love." There should be a delicate balance between conviction and compassion as we speak to or about others. If you speak conviction without compassion, you may severely damage the other person. If you share compassion without speaking conviction, you may give him license to sin.

The word "truth" should be noted, also. Two women were talking about a mutual third acquaintance. One said in awe, "Tell me *more."* The first said, "Listen, I've already told you *more than I know."* There is a difference between "truth" and mere accuracy. Many things are *accurate*, but they are not "truth" in a New Testament sense. Truth has moral dimensions to it. Truth has Gospel dimensions to it. Many things that are reported accurately still have nothing to do with "truth."

Remember the analogy of the human body here. All the members of a human body are in constant communication with one another. This communication is a regular occurrence in a healthy body. The network for that communication is vast, including the bloodstream, the nerves, the sight-sound-mind exchange, etc. The same kind of sensitive communication should be occurring among the members of Christ's body at all times. This is the "one another" of Christian communication.

3. The "One Another" of Compassion

The third "one another" mentioned in the text is *the one another of compassion.* Ephesians 4:32 says, "And be ye kind one to another." The word "and" connects this statement with the preceding verse. In that verse (31), there are six deadly attitudes and actions that are the enemies of compassion. Those six things are like poisons that destroy the disposition of a Christian. The six mentioned things are "bitterness," "wrath," "anger," "clamor," "evil speaking," and "malice." Bitterness is a subtle attitude that quickly becomes a deep-set "root" in the heart (Hebrews 12:15). "Wrath" means an explosive display of bad temper. "Anger" is slowly rising, seething ill disposition which may burst forth in a show of bad temper. "Clamor" is loud speech which demonstrates an uncontrolled temperament. And "malice" is ill intent toward anyone, a viciousness of mind and disposition toward another. Obviously, these attitudes must be put aside if we are to take care of each other as Scripture commands.

"And be ye kind one to another." My first pastor after I became a Christian had a plaque on his office desk which read, "Be kind, because every one you meet is fighting a hard battle." The word "kind" is the basis for our word, "kindred," or "kinship." It seems to presume that members of the same family should be kindly disposed toward one another. That makes great sense, doesn't it? If we are *kin* to each other, we ought to be *kind* to each other.

Years ago, I saw this wise counsel, "Beware of people who have *deep convictions* and *shallow sympathies.*" It is a fine art to find consistent balance between conviction and compassion in the Christian life, but this is to be our constant quest. There are too many *good but insensitive* Christians. Mark Twain referred to them as "good in the worst sense of the word." How we need an epidemic of true kindness among us in the body of Christ! Someone said of Henry Ward Beecher, the great preacher, "No one ever felt the full force of his kindness until he did Mr. Beecher an injury." He had apparently learned the lesson of this great text. Henry Drummond, the great British scientist and warm-hearted Christian preacher, said, "The greatest thing a Christian can do for his heavenly Father is to be kind to some of His other children." F. W. Faber, another great Christian communicator, said, "Kindness has converted more sinners than either zeal, eloquence or learning."

Dr. Harry Ironside, who for years was the pastor of the great Moody Memorial Church in Chicago, traveled all over the country on preaching engagements after he retired. His wife often traveled with him. He was on one such trip one time, and he had preached four times in one day in Bible conferences in the same city. Late that night, they were driving to a nearby city where he was to preach again on the next day. As they conversed, he became irritable and spoke sharply and critically to his wife. She became very quiet in the passenger seat. The Holy Spirit spoke gently to him, and He quickly chose against himself. He said to her, "Honey, please forgive me, but you'll have to remember that I have preached four times today!" She reached over and put her hand on his and quietly replied, "Honey, I understand, but *you'll* have to remember that *I listened to you four times today!*" You see, everybody needs kindness from other people, and it is never acceptable to presume that we have a right to be unkind under any circumstance.

A Christian job foreman in an electrical business had an employee in his work force who knew that he was a Christian and was constantly testing his Christianity. He began to taunt the foreman, and the taunts became more and more intense as the foreman refused to react in anger or revenge. Others watched the demonstration of verbal venom from one man and the demonstration of Christian graciousness on the part of the other. One day, one of the other workers pulled the foreman aside and asked, "How do you take it? If it were me,

I'd fire him so fast it would make his head swim! How do you do it?" "Oh, I'm just following a lesson I learned from the moon," was the foreman's puzzling answer. "A lesson from the moon?" replied the workman, "*What* lesson from the moon? What does *that* mean?" The foreman answered, "Yes, I was reading the Gospel of Matthew one day, and I came across the statement of Jesus that we are the light of the world. I remembered that He also said that, as long as He was in the world, *He* was the light of the world. I realized that He meant that He is the *sun* and we are the *moon*. He originates the light, shines it on us, and we reflect His light to those around us." "Yes," said the puzzled worker, " but what lesson did you learn from that for this situation on the job?" The foreman answered, "Well, I arrive home late from work quite often. I have a dog that is usually out in the yard when I arrive after dark. I noticed that every time the moon is out, that dog will sit on his haunches and bark loudly at the moon, as if he is angry with it. But then I saw my lesson. *No matter how loudly that dog barks at the moon, the moon just keeps on shining as if it never noticed.* The dog's nature may be to bark, but the moon's nature is to shine. I can't speak for that other fellow; it may just be *his nature* to bark in anger. But I'm a Christian, and my nature is to shine. I can't let his bad spirit keep me from shining."

"Be ye kind one to another," and don't let anything make you stop. May God help us to consistently practice the "one another" of Christian compassion.

4. The "One Another" of Remission

The fourth "one another" of our text is *the one another of remission*, or forgiveness of one another. Ephesians 4:32 says, "Forgiving one another, even as God for Christ's sake has forgiven you." The words "even as" mean "exactly as." What a standard! The pattern and standard for our forgiving each other is in God's forgiveness of us for Christ's sake. When we think of the just reasons God might have used for *not* forgiving us, and the gracious reasons He used *for* forgiving us, surely we can use the model of His forgiveness as our example, and the resources of His grace as our means, and forgive others when they sin against us.

A Christian should always regard himself as a *forgiven forgiver*. He can never be anything *but* a forgiver because his standard is always to be *God's forgiveness of him*. Because God can be counted on to forgive, every Christian should be able to be counted on to forgive, also. God's forgiving is a model of what can happen between two alienated human beings. The dynamics are the same. God shows the way. "God for Christ's sake has forgiven you," the text says. Even so, we are to "forgive one another."

In fact, Jesus indicated several times that your willingness to forgive those who have sinned against you will determine your ability to *be* forgiven by God. This does not mean that you buy God's forgiveness by forgiving others. It simply means that if you are bound by an unwillingness to forgive others, you are demonstrating that the forgiving grace of God has never been fully activated in your own life. The "forgiveness pipeline" is the same size whether coming in to your life (God forgiving you) or going out of your life (you forgiving others).

Do not misunderstand this matter of forgiving others. Let no one think that it is easy or automatic. God Himself struggled with the matter through the awful agony of a Cross, and you will likely struggle with it, too. A teacher asked in a Sunday School class, "What does a person have to do to be forgiven?" A sharp little boy answered, "Well, first, he has to sin!" Friends, sin is one thing when it is merely done, but it is another thing when it is seriously committed *against you*.

Someone else's sins look easy to forgive—until you are in the line of fire where the sin hits the target! But this is the whole point. A Christian should aspire not merely to the *practice* of forgiveness (maybe only a one-time act), but to the *spirit* of forgiveness (a lifetime disposition, and *likely a lifetime struggle*). One wise Christian said it this way: "He who would belong to the kingdom of love as a recipient must belong to it as an agent." May God fill the Body of Christ with *agents* of forgiveness who make *good* agents because they know so well what it is to be *recipients* of forgiveness!

The need and the power of forgiveness are revealed with great poignancy in a short story by Leo Tolstoy entitled, "God Sees the Truth But Waits." It is the story of a man named Aksenov, who, although innocent of the murder of which he is accused, is condemned to exile for life. For twenty-six years he lived as a convict in Siberia; no word ever reached him of his wife and children. "His hair turned white as snow, and his beard grew long, thin, and gray. All the mirth left him; he stooped; he walked slowly, spoke little, and never laughed, but he often prayed."

Then one day among a band of new convicts Aksenov discovered Makar, the man who really committed the crime for which Aksenov had suffered. Makar was now exiled to Siberia for some petty offense. His real murder of a quarter-century ago is still undiscovered. At first Aksenov was filled with bitterness and vengeance in contemplation of his life that had been robbed from him. He tried to pray but he could get no peace. His hatred was so great that he could not go near Makar. One day, though, he suddenly had his chance to strike back. He discovered Makar digging an escape tunnel out of the prison, and had the power to turn Makar over to certain death from the governor of the prison. Makar threatened him but Aksenov retorted, "I have no wish to escape, and you have no need to kill me; you killed me long ago! As to telling the governor of you, I may do so or not, as God shall direct."

When the inquiry came, however, Aksenov only answered, "I cannot say, your honor. It is not God's will that I should tell! Do what you like with me; I am in your hands." After this Makar came begging for forgiveness: "Ivan, forgive me! For the love of God, forgive me! I will confess that it was I who killed the merchant, and you will be released and can go to your home."

Aksenov answered, "It is easy for you to talk, but I have suffered for you these twenty-six years. Where could I go to now? My wife is dead, and my children have forgotten me. I have nowhere to go . . ."

Makar did not stand up, but instead beat his head on the floor. "Ivan, forgive me!" he cried. "When they flogged me it was not so hard to bear as it is to see you now . . . yet you had pity on me and did not tell. For Christ's sake forgive me, wretch that I am!" And he began to sob.

When Aksenov heard him sobbing he too began to weep. "God will forgive you!" he cried, "Maybe I am a hundred times worse than you." *And at these words his heart grew light and the longing for home left him.* In spite of what Aksenov had said, Makar confessed his guilt. But when the order for his release came, Aksenov was already dead.

Between these two men, love had the last word and forgiveness prevailed. As forgiveness was expressed, old wounds of sin and evil were healed. As in the case of every sin, healing could not have come in any other way. Tolstoy grasped this fact firmly and clearly. God does see the truth but even He waits for the grace of forgiving love to be grasped among men. Both men in the story needed this grace. Aksenov needed to be healed of the sins of bitterness, hatred, and vengeance, no matter how "innocent" his suffering was.

Makar, in turn, needed to be healed of the sins of pride and cruelty. The only way that healing could come to either of these men was by forgiveness. Only a forgiving love could reach and change Makar's cruelty; his heart was unreachable except by love. And only the act of forgiving could bring peace to the one who was wronged. Whenever relationships between people are mangled by sin as in this story, forgiveness is the only way by which these lives may be restored to wholeness again. This is something that goes beyond all systems of justice. The miracle (*miracle*) of grace prevails through *forgiven forgivers*, people who are *broken enough to forgive* because they know they are *great sinners who have been forgiven*. This "one another" is desperately needed in the Body of Christ, and when practiced, it unleashes great waves of the love and grace of God.

5. The "One Another" of Celebration

The fifth "one another" for our study is *the one another of celebration*. Ephesians 5:19-20 says, "Speaking to yourselves (the 'one another' idea) in psalms and hymns and spiritual songs, singing and making melody in your heart to the Lord; Giving thanks always for all things unto God and the Father in the name of our Lord Jesus Christ." The entire statement has a high atmosphere of great celebration about it.

G. K. Chesterton was right when he said that "joyful celebration is the gigantic secret of the Christian." Celebration is at the heart of God's plan for human beings. The reason for this is that joy is at the heart of God Himself. The Bible calls Him "the happy God." Jesus said, "There is joy in the presence of the angels of God . . ." Notice that the joy is not merely in the angels, but in their *presence*. The joy is in God Himself. "You will show me the path of life, in Your Presence is fullness of joy, and at Your right hands there are pleasures forevermore" (Psalm 16:11). A veteran pastor, speaking from years of trial and error, gave this counsel to his people, "Go out of the way to find the 'joy pie'—and be sure to cut yourself a big slice." You see, dear Christian, you are commanded to rejoice, and God would not command it if it were not possible.

It is of interest to note that Paul wrote letters to two Macedonian churches, the church at Philippi and the church at Thessalonica. In both cities, he was heatedly abused and persecuted, being driven from both cities by those who could not receive his message of grace and forgiveness. However, in both letters to those churches, I Thessalonians and Philippians, the note of joy is loudly sounded. In fact, the book of Philippians is often called "the epistle of joy." Few things are more remarkable about the New Testament than this continual stress on joy. All information we have about the early church indicates that, from an outward point of view, there was little that could cause rejoicing. But they were "in Christ," and they had learned the truth of His words, "Your joy no man taketh from you" (John 16:22). So the word "joy" and many of it's derived forms occur with startling frequency throughout the New Testament. For example, the word for "grace" is from the root word for "joy." Also, one of the words translated "forgive" is also from the same root. Dear Christian, the Christianity of the New Testament is absolutely permeated with the spirit of holy joy. Surely your circumstance today is not more difficult than theirs. Is your life permeated with joy? If not, the reason is one of sin and disobedience.

Samuel Shoemaker, a great evangelist, said, "I have heard a lot of Christians confess a lot of sins, but I have never heard even one confess the sin of sadness. Yet the sin of sadness is the breeding parent of many, many other sins. Most sins would never be committed if the Christian were rejoicing in the Lord." Shoemaker added his opinion that the surest mark of a Christian is not faith, or hope, or even love, but the surest mark of a Christian is joy. "Joy," he said, "is the infallible sign of the Presence and blessing of God."

The English word, "celebration," comes from a Latin word that means "to frequent" something, or to do that thing very, very often. This is what worship is. It is to frequently, repeatedly, regularly recognize and celebrate God — in a positive, thankful, praising, extolling, adoring way. And we are to do it "between-ward," among ourselves, in the presence of one another.

6. The "One Another" of Submission

The final "one another" of our study (which I will only mention) is the *one another of submission*. This responsibility is not to be minimized because of my brief treatment of it. Hardly anything is more essential for the proper function of the Body of Christ. Ephesians 5:21 says, "Submitting yourselves one to another in the fear of God." Verse 22 then says, "Wives, submit yourselves unto your own husbands as unto the Lord," but it is to be noted that the responsibility of the wife toward the husband is mentioned only after the responsibility of mutual submission has already been established. In fact, most of the responsibility addressed to husbands and wives is addressed to the husband, probably because husbands are more stubborn and less likely to submit, and because the husband's assignment is bigger. If the husband takes the proper initiative in loving, leading, *and submitting*, everything else is likely to fall into place.

The word translated, "submit," is a military term. It means to "rank yourself underneath," as if to assume that the other person is your superior and you are his inferior. Christians are to do this *voluntarily*, and to do it "one to another," regardless of rank, position, or tenure. Submission is the responsibility of *every Christian*, and the submission is to be practiced "one to another in the fear of God."

Question: are you as comfortable when *you* are submitting *to another* as you are when someone *else* is submitting to *you*?

One committed Christian said, "I have tried all kinds of mission work. I have done community mission work, and home mission work, and foreign mission work — but the greatest mission work I ever did is *sub*mission work!" This is the most demanding work, and the most rewarding work, a Christian can do. If he doesn't do it, he will finally be a part of God's continuing problem. If he *does* do it, he will be a happy and useful part of God's great *solution*.

A man was leisurely browsing through a bookstore one day while waiting on his wife as she shopped in a nearby merchandise store. She appeared in the aisle to tell him she had finished her shopping, and he started out of the store with her. But suddenly, his eye was arrested by the title of a book on the shelf. It was entitled *How to Hug*. He had developed a special interest in putting some romance back into his marriage, so he impulsively bought the book. When he arrived home and examined its contents, he discovered that the book wasn't what he thought it was. Instead of a warm, romantic book, he had actually purchased a volume from an encyclopedia covering the alphabetized topics beginning with the word "how" and ending with the word "hug."

Could it be that we often cause a similar disappointment in the Body of Christ? — a disappointment to God and to the brothers and sisters around us? On the surface, we seem to be offering a warm, personal, and gratifying experience. But I'm sure that people are often disappointed with the "one anothers" they see (or do *not* see) in the local Body of Christ where they attend.

Every Christian must make a lifetime project of these "one anothers" — the "one another" of Christian *toleration*, the "one another" of Christian *communication*, the "one another" of Christian *compassion*, the "one another" of Christian *remission*, and the "one another" of Christian *celebration*. And this is only the beginning! After the four Gospels, the word translated "one another" is used 58 times in the New Testament. Paul uses it most — some 40 times. While many of the "one anothers" are repetitions, at least 22 different injunctions are given to believers in Christ.

George MacDonald, the great Scottish author, said, "Division has done more to hide Christ from the view of men than all the infidelity that has ever been spoken." Lars Wilhelmsson said, "The united Body of Christ is God's greatest weapon in fulfilling the Great Commission." Surely the Body should be united in something so important. Don't we owe it to Him — *and to "one another"?*

ADDENDUM # 1

Some years ago, I preached an extended series of sermons on the "one anothers" of the New Testament. My studies are reflected in the notes which I retained from the sermon preparation. Here are some of the notes.

The Christian life is a reciprocal life. (1) First, there is the Divine-human relationship, that of a Father and His child. (2) There is the brother-brother, brother-sister, sister-brother, sister-sister relationship. (3) There is the brother (a Christian) - other (whether an outsider or another Christian) relationship. Within the Body of Christ, these relationships are highlighted in the New Testament:

I. Commands Bearing upon Inter-relationships:
    (A) Love one another. John 13:35.
    (B) Receive one another. Romans 15:7.
    (C) Greet one another. Romans 16:16.

(D) Have the same care one for another. I Corinthians 12:24-25.
(E) Submit to one another. Ephesians 5:21.
(F) Forbear one another. Ephesians 4:1-3. Colossians 3:12-14.
(G) Confess your sins to one another. James 5:16.
(H) Forgive one another. Ephesians 4:31-32. Colossians 3:12-13.

II. The Negative Commands:
(A) Do not judge one another. Romans 14:13.
(B) Do not speak evil of one another. James 4:11.
(C) Do not murmur against one another. James 5:9.
(D) Do not bite and devour one another. Galatians 5:14-15.
(E) Do not provoke one another. Galatians 5:25-26.
(F) Do not envy one another.
(G) Do not lie to one another. Colossians 3:9-10.

III. Commands Bearing Upon Mutual Edification:

(A) Build up one another. Romans 14:19. I Thessalonians 5:11.
(B) Teach one another. Colossians 3:16.
(C) Exhort one another. Hebrews 3:12-13.
(D) Admonish one another. Romans 15:13. Colossians 3:16. I Corinthians 4:14).

IV. Commands Bearing Upon Mutual Service:

(A) Be servants one to another. Galatians 5:13-14.
(B) Bear one another's burdens. Galatians 6:2.
(C) Use hospitality one to another. I Peter 4:7-10.
(D) Be kind to one another. Ephesians 4:31-32.
(E) Pray for one another. James 5:16.

ADDENDUM # 2

The following is an adaptation of a story sent to me by a friend who "surfs the 'net" and sends things that speak to *him* to *others*. I commend him as an example to others.

Two farming brothers lived on adjoining farms. In 40 years of farming side by side, they had never had a serious conflict. But that changed suddenly in one day. A small misunderstanding between them grew into a major difference, and then it exploded into a bitter argument, followed by weeks of cold silence between them.

One morning there was a knock at John's door. When he answered the knock, he found a man holding a carpenter's toolbox in his hand. The man said, "Sir, I'm a carpenter, and I'm looking for a few day's work. Do you have any small jobs on your place that I might help with?" "Yes," John replied, "I do have a job for you. Do you see that creek running right over there?" He pointed toward his brother's farm, and the property line between them. "Last week, there was only an open meadow there, but he took a bulldozer to the river levee, and now there's a creek between us. He did this to spite me, but I'll let you help me answer him. There's a pile of lumber over by my barn. I want you to build an eight-foot fence just on this side of the creek, so I won't need to see his place anymore."

The carpenter said, "I think I understand the assignment. Show me the nails and the post-hole digger and I'll do a good job for you." John, the older brother, had to go to town for supplies, so he got the supplies ready for the carpenter and then he was off to town. The carpenter worked with great effort all day long, measuring, sawing, assembling, nailing. About sunset the farmer returned. The carpenter was standing exhausted over a finished job. The farmer's eyes popped and his mouth fell open as he saw the result. *There was no fence there at all; instead, there was a bridge* — a bridge stretching across the creek. As the carpenter had promised, it was "a good job," handrails and all. As the older brother stood shocked, his neighbor, his younger brother, approached the far end of the bridge, scratching his head with one hand and raising the other as if asking a question. The two brothers walked onto the bridge and met in the middle. The younger brother said tenderly, "I can't believe you've built this bridge after all I've said and done. But I appreciate it. After all, it's time we put this silly disagreement behind us. It was killing us and wrecking all those years of happiness we had spent together, anyway." Each put out his hand to the other, and then they embraced each other with open arms.

    They turned to see the carpenter lifting his toolbox and turning to leave. "No, wait!" called out the older brother, "I have a lot more projects around here that I need help with." The carpenter answered, "I'd love to, but I have a lot more bridges to build."

    The Carpenter came to build the Biggest Bridge of all, the Bridge of open traffic between offending men and an offended God. He used the rough-hewn arms of a wooden Cross to build this Bridge, and any of us, though we are sinners, can go home to God by way of that Cross. Once we have crossed the Bridge ourselves, we are to "traffic" it all the time as the Carpenter's Apprentices, not building walls between us and others, but pointing to the Big Bridge while building smaller bridges of communication between us and others. So be it — for the Carpenter's sake, and for the sake of men needing to cross the chasm between themselves and God.

THE HUMAN AND DIVINE INGREDIENTS IN A TRUE EXPERIENCE OF SALVATION

(Acts 8:25-40)

The entire Christian movement started when Jesus got His small band of disciples together and said to them, "You shall receive power when the Holy Spirit has come upon you, and you shall be My witnesses, both in Jerusalem, and in Judea, and in Samaria, and unto the uttermost part of the earth." Beginning at that intense moment, the Christian movement has penetrated the earth so that now there is a Christian community of believers and a witnessing group of people in every nation on earth.

The four geographical areas Jesus mentioned in His Commission in Acts 1:8 form a perfect outline of the Book of Acts. Chapters 1 through 7 record the Gospel's growth in Jerusalem, chapters 8 through 12 the growth in Judea and Samaria, and chapters 13 through 28 the growth to the uttermost part of the earth. Our text for this study falls into the Judea and Samaria section, and it provides a remarkable study of "the human and Divine ingredients in a genuine experience of salvation." It is the well-known story of the conversion of the Ethiopian eunuch, and it is a case-study of the cooperation of Heaven and earth to bring a ready soul to Christ. What are the human and Divine ingredients in a genuine experience of salvation? To put it personally, what collaboration took place to get *you*—or *me*—or *anyone*, saved?

I. A PRESIDING SOVEREIGN

First, in every true and genuine experience of Divine salvation, there is *a presiding sovereign* arranging all the necessary items in preparing for and providing the experience of salvation. Of course, God is the sovereign, and it is because of His responsibility and by His initiative that sinners are eternally saved. The command to witness and the control of the witnesses are both acts of God.

The presiding sovereign is God the Father, and both Jesus the Son and the Holy Spirit are the co-equal Agents of His administration. It was Jesus Christ who said, "You shall be My witnesses," voicing the will of His Father for the Christian movement, and it was through the personal work of the Holy Spirit that the movement was endowed and guided through the Book of Acts. In Acts chapter eight, the chapter that contains our text, God the Father "arranged" a persecution which launched the reluctant early Christians out of Jerusalem and scattered them abroad. Then, "they that were scattered abroad went every where, preaching (the word is 'evangelizing', or 'good newsing') the Word." As a part of this stress-promoted evangelism, "Philip went down to the city of Samaria, and preached Christ unto them" (Acts 8:5). A mighty moving of the Spirit of God occurred as Philip preached, and many were saved and baptized (Acts 8:6-8, 12). All of this took place under the sovereign administration of God Himself. The same Divine administration is clearly evident in the story of Philip and the Ethiopian eunuch, and by the Divine arrangements, the eunuch was saved.

The Human and Divine Ingredients in a True Experience of Salvation

It was the Holy Spirit who started the search in the seeker. The eunuch quite obviously had a prior history checkered by the work of the Holy Spirit. Here is another classic picture of prevenient grace, which is the active grace of God in the life of a lost sinner before his salvation, steadily "pushing" him toward Christ and salvation. Prevenient grace is the grace of God which protected you, provided for you, and prepared you—before you were saved!

Sometimes this prevenient grace acts within the sinner to produce a longing for "some thing" or "someone" (Someone) that wells up mysteriously within us. This longing does not spring into existence on its own. The German theologian von Hugel said, "God is always previous." In C.S. Lewis' The Silver Chair, one of his child's fantasy stories called "The Chronicles of Narnia", Aslan the Lion King explained to Edmund and the other three children from England concerning his summons to them from England into the magical land of Narnia, "You would not have called to me unless I had been calling to you." In his Letters to an American Lady, Lewis wrote this postscript to a "Mrs. Sonia Graham": "P.S. Of course God does not consider you hopeless. If He did He would not be moving you to seek Him (and He obviously is). What is going on in you at present is simply the beginning of the treatment. Continue seeking Him with seriousness. Unless He wanted you, you would not be wanting Him."

The Apostle John wrote, "We love because He first loved us." You see, God's yearning for us stirs up our longing in response (though we may not know it is God we are longing for). God's initiating presence may be ever so subtle—an inward tug of desire, a more-than-coincidence meeting of words and events, a glimpse of the beyond in a storm, or a scene, or a flower—but it is enough to make the heart skip a beat and to make us want to know more. When Saul of Tarsus was saved, the Lord said to him, "It is hard for you to kick against the goads." That is, I have been goading you to grace and to God throughout your entire life on earth, and things are now ready. The same could be said about the pre-conversion history of every sinner. It was certainly true in this eunuch's story.

It was the Holy Spirit who stimulated the service of the saint who would lead the eunuch to Christ. The Spirit-filled early believers were directed moment-by-moment and step-by-step by the Holy Spirit. He "played everything close," even to minute-by-minute, hour-by-hour, person-by-person, precision in order to accomplish His work. Fast forward to Acts 10 and re-read the account of how "Heaven's switchboard" was alive in directing the "moving parts" to accomplish the conversion of Cornelius. It is an incredible story of synchronizing of times and schedules to get the soul-winner and the seeking sinner together (suppose either Philip or the eunuch had been fifteen minutes earlier or an hour later for their "encounter"), resulting in the remarkable conversion of Cornelius the Roman centurion.

In our story, the Holy Spirit pushed the saints out of Jerusalem by a persecution, led some of them to Samaria (including Philip) to evangelize the city and the area, and then He sent an angel to personally instruct Philip to "go toward the south unto the way that goes down from Jerusalem to Gaza", etc. So the entire episode is a clear picture of the work of a presiding sovereign in preparing for and providing salvation to a prominent Ethiopian government official.

I believe that every born-again person can see the evidences of such a Sovereign governing his steps toward his saving encounter with the Son of God. In my own case, I have not the slightest doubt that Heaven was moving all of the players in the story to get me saved. "God's works are perfect," and this certainly includes His pre-conversion preparation of the sinner's heart and the timely provision of eternal salvation to that prepared sinner.

II. A PREPARED SEEKER

What a story this is! When Philip arrived at "ground zero," the place where the sinner would meet the Savior, he found a seeker who was more-than-prepared to meet Christ. Though we feel ourselves to be familiar with this man, we don't even know his name. No matter. This sexually-altered Prime Minister of Ethiopia is a very intriguing case study.

First, he was an *individual*. Philip was engaged in a big movement of "mass evangelism" in Samaria (Acts 8:1, 5-14a) when the angel of the Lord directed him to leave this exciting work and "go toward the south" where he would witness to *one person*. In the middle of a giant crusade for Christ, God said to the evangelist, "Go." Can you imagine Philip trying to explain that? "God told me to go." But when the Holy Spirit is the "Chairman of the committee on evangelism," the personal worker can trust the guidance he receives. No evangelist experiencing an outpouring of the Spirit such as was occurring in Samaria would want to leave the "crusade" where so many were being saved. But there is no hint of resistance from Philip, because he had learned to trust the guidance of the Spirit. His next crusade was to be focused on *one man*! Not very hopeful, right? But God was preparing to begin the evangelism of another continent, the continent of Africa—and the work would begin with the witness of one Spirit-filled, Spirit-led Christian and the conversion of one man already traveling back to Africa!

Second, the "prospect" in the story was an *important* man. He was "secretary of the national treasury" for Queen Candace and the entire Ethiopian empire. In those days,

"Ethiopia" was used in a broader sense to describe the upper Nile region. This was an important man.

Third, the eunuch was an *intelligent* person. Now, the fact that a person is intelligent may stand between him and God and prevent his coming to Christ, or it may be a means of his coming to Christ. People with college degrees, or post-graduate degrees, are not made more competent to understand the Bible or to relate to the real spiritual world. In fact, their educational advances may *prevent* their understanding because they lead to a misplaced self-confidence. There is no question about this eunuch's vocational intelligence. No man of little intelligence could have long held his national position. Furthermore, he was intelligent enough to want to learn more (see Acts 8:28, 30 and 31, 34). The truth is that the man who has stopped learning has stopped living, and the greatest field of knowledge is the knowledge of God. This man was intelligent enough to live on the growing edge of knowledge and the quest for God.

Fourth, he was an *intensely inquiring* person. Many Christians would call him an "inquirer after Christ." He was far ahead of most people—he knew his need was spiritual, and he was looking for a spiritual answer. His heart had been so aroused that he was willing to pay a gigantic price to find what his heart was longing for. Think of the great *distance* he traveled, all the way from Ethiopia to Jerusalem. Think of the great *dangers* he faced and the *discomfort* he endured to reach his goal. How many days was he in transit from Ethiopia to Jerusalem, and back again? Remember, he did not have an air-conditioned automobile and there were no dual-laned interstate highways, nor were there speeding jet airplanes. He traveled in a rough-riding chariot and on a narrow, rough, dusty road. *In search of God!* God had said, "You shall seek Me, and find Me, when you search for Me with all your heart,"

The Human and Divine Ingredients in a True Experience of Salvation

and here was a man acting out the human part of that Divine drama. Then, think of the terrible *disappointment* he met with in Jerusalem. He found that Judaism, the very best religion known to man, could not answer the ache in his heart. He was thwarted at every step of his search, until a stranger joined him on the seat of his chariot as he was sadly going back unfulfilled to Ethiopia.

Ah, but there was one great factor that was already moving in his favor when we come into the story. Somewhere he had gotten a copy of the scroll of the Old Testament book of Isaiah. Maybe he had heard someone read from it while in Jerusalem, and he had gone to the "bookstore" and purchased a copy of it. So he was *interested* enough to go far beyond the usual course and get a copy of this Old Testament book. You see, God was "setting him up" for Heaven, for salvation, for eternal life, and he thought all of these steps were taken because of his own independent decisions!

The story doesn't sound too hopeful when we learn that, though he was reading from the book of Isaiah the prophet, and though he was reading it aloud as if using every human aid to understand it, he still was *ignorant* of the Subject and of the Person the text referred to. When Philip "heard him read the prophet Isaiah, and said, 'Do you understand what you are reading?' he said, *'How can I, except some man should guide me?'*" Without Heaven's assistance, and often without human assistance as well, a sinner cannot understand Divine things. He is improperly equipped by his sinful nature to understand Divine things. He is like a dog trying to understand a symphony—not a chance! This man had probably kept his financial books straight, but without help he couldn't get the Divine Book straight! He kept good books, but He was ignorant of *the Good Book!* One of the tragic things in our society today is that multitudes of *ignorant* people speak as if they are *experts* about God. This intelligent man admitted that he was ignorant of the identity of the Person who was presented in the text he was reading.

The eunuch's reading of Scripture was not enough, so the Holy Spirit sent His own surrogate witness, Philip the deacon, to tell him of Christ. The eunuch was quickly *informed* of all that was necessary to be saved. We will examine the information he received in our last point of this study, but he received enough plain and simple Gospel truth to become a Christian.

The second ingredient in a genuine experience of Divine salvation is the prepared seeker.

III. THE PROCLAIMING SAINT

Finally, there must be *a proclaiming servant/saint/soul-winner* if the Personal Savior and the Prepared Seeker are to come into a saving relationship. Would the eunuch have been saved if Philip had not arrived "just in (God's) time?" No, he would not! "Other arrangements" are not an option when a presiding sovereign is orchestrating the account. Today, there may be a gracious God, and there may be seeking souls, but where are the willing workers? What part did Philip play? How important was he in the story? And what did he do to complete the transaction?

Philip was a man with an outstanding previous history before this story opened. He was a man with a previous record that showed us why he was enlisted for this desert mission.

He had a previous history of being a *servant*. Remind yourself that he was one of the original deacons in the early church (Acts 6:5). And remember that the word "deacon" is a word that describes intense and faithful service. In the early church, a deacon was not a member of a governing body for a church fellowship. I recently heard a pastor facetiously refer to his church as a "deacon-possessed church." Many churches could be so described, but there is no New Testament authorization for such a description. In the early church, the deacon didn't attend meetings; he attended to people's needs—and he did it in a hurry. The word "deacon" means "one who kicks through the dust," or "one who hastens". Philip was a deacon, and in our story we see him *running* (Acts 8:30)—and *in the dust of the desert*, no less--to fulfill his Divine assignment.

Philip also had a previous history of being a *student* of the Word of God, and a Biblically-based *spokesman* for Him. How crucial it is for a Christian steward and servant to know the full truth about Jesus Christ and the way of salvation—and to tell what he knows! Every Christian should echo the urgent request of John Wesley, "Oh, God, make me a man of Your Book!" The Bible presents Jesus Christ, but not as people guess Him to be. The Bible offers salvation, but not on the terms of man's surmising. We dare not be wrong about this things; we dare not gamble our souls or the souls of others on carnal guesswork. As Christians, we are admonished to "Study to show ourselves approved unto God, workmen who don't need to be ashamed, rightly dividing the Word of Truth" (II Timothy 2:15). Philip was called upon to give an impromptu exegesis of a critical Old Testament text about Jesus, and he had no time to consult commentaries or counselors!

Note the precision and assurance of the words of the text. When the eunuch asked Philip, "I ask you, of whom did the prophet say this? Of himself, or of some other man?" the text happily reports, "Then Philip opened his mouth, and began at the same scripture, and preached unto him Jesus" (Acts 8:34-35). The word translated "preached" literally means "He *evangelized* unto him Jesus." Even more literally, "He *good-newsed* unto him Jesus," or "He *good-newsed* Jesus unto him."

You see, almost the entire life-history and redeeming history of Jesus can be easily seen in Isaiah chapter fifty-three. His Birth is there, His Life is there, His Death is there, His Burial is there, and His Resurrection is there, and Philip surely explained all of these to the eunuch. Note that the Object of the Christian witness is always to be Christ. Christ alone, not Christ also! Christ period, not Christ plus! You see, the Spirit of God is deeply concerned that we don't substitute faith in the *saint*, or in the *servant*, or in the *soul-winner*, for faith in the *Savior*. No wonder that in a short while "the eunuch went on his way rejoicing" (Acts 8:39). Philip had a previous history as a student of the Word of God, and it was evident on this witnessing occasion.

Christian, are you a regular student of the Word of God? Have you mastered it, so that you hold "on ready call" multitudes of verses and passages of the Word of God? If so, God will likely use you to "good-news" multitudes to Jesus. If not, you will likely stand as a "very unhappy camper" at the Judgment Seat of Christ. With a Command and Commission from Jesus to engage in Total World Impact through evangelism, missions, and disciple-making, none of which can be properly and adequately done without the regular preaching, teaching and sharing of the Word of God, you instead chose to remain delinquent and ignorant of the Book of Books, or you chose to be silent about the treasures of this great Book. Perhaps *you* should face up today to Paul's admonishment to Timothy: "Study to show *yourself* approved unto God, a workman who doesn't need to be ashamed, rightly dividing the Word of Truth" (II Timothy 2:15).

Philip had a previous history of being *submissive* to the guidance of Heaven in setting his schedule, establishing his agenda, and declaring his message. The angel of the Lord told Philip to leave Samaria and go to the desert (Acts 8:26)—and he obeyed. The Spirit of God told Philip to go to the chariot and identify with the eunuch (Acts 8:29)—and he obeyed. His previous history of obedience and service established momentum for the same humble obedience here. Dear friend, you are daily building a history of selfishness, indifference, and fruitlessness, or you are daily establishing a momentum of selfless involvement with other people and fruitfulness for Christ. If you continue tomorrow on the running track you have been following, what will tomorrow bring in your life?

In this story, a saved man, a servant, a student, a spokesman for Christ, a submissive believer, led this African official to Christ. If these were the qualifications God looked for in selecting "useable witnesses," would He be likely to use *me* today? Would He be likely to use *you* today?

It is worthy of note in our story that the Holy Spirit did not tell Philip what to do when he met the eunuch. No, He just told him where to go. He already knew from Jesus what he was to do (see Acts 1:8), and he knew generally where he was to do it. The early Christians didn't ask, "What am I going to do today?" They even knew the large arena where the assignment was to be accomplished. They depended on God to send them to the *exact place* to meet the *exact person*, the person whom God had prepared.

A short time later, after Philip and the eunuch engaged in conversation over an open Bible, the eunuch had stated his new-found belief. "I believe that Jesus Christ is the Son of God," he said. You see, the confession of new-found faith in Christ is crucially important. This confession has two sides, each very important.

One is the *inner* side, what the confession means to the one confessing. Used this way (as in Matthew 10:32-33), the word means "to say the same as." Used this way, confession means to say the same thing about Jesus that God has said. And God said, as reported in Matthew 3:17, "This is my beloved Son, in whom I am well pleased."

The other side of confession, the *outer* side, is the witness borne to other people, to anyone who hears, by that confession. As a classic and powerful example, William Shakespeare, three weeks before he died, drew up a will which opens with a confession that sounds like the creed of a church council: "I commend my soul into the hands of God my Creator, hoping and assuredly believing, through the only merits of Jesus Christ my Savior, to be made partaker of life everlasting, and my body to the earth whereof it is made." Students of Shakespeare should take special note that his confession proclaims that he was a believing Christian. The same is true of the confession of the Ethiopian eunuch.

Then, the eunuch *sought baptism*, the first act of obedience of a new-born believer in Christ. Note that he didn't *resist* baptism, or *reluctantly submit* to it; no, he **requested** it! The fact that he sought baptism likely means that Philip had already begun the instruction of disciple-making, beginning with the "ABCs" of new life in Christ.

A man was playing ball with his pet dog. Occasionally the dog would become distracted and lose sight of where the ball went. He would come back to his master, tail wagging furiously and tongue hanging out. The man would say enthusiastically, "Over there!" as he pointed toward the ball. But you usually can't tell a dog where to go by pointing. When the dog sees the pointing finger, he will come to the man and sniff his finger. We may laugh at a dog's failure to understand a pointing finger, but many people have done the same thing with the Biblical truth about baptism. Baptism is a finger which points to some big truths beyond itself, but many, when they see the pointing finger, want to "sniff" at the pointer, the water itself—and thus they miss the big truths that baptism points to. I'm quite sure that Philip explained that baptism points to the new believer's identification with Christ's Death, Burial and Resurrection, as well as his total incorporation into Christ by the grace of God. No wonder the eunuch requested immediate baptism to register his testimony and his understanding of God's truth about his own new life in Christ!

Philip had joined with the Holy Spirit in publicizing Christ, in presenting the Gospel, and in promoting the eunuch's decision for Christ. Shortly thereafter, "the Spirit caught away Philip that the eunuch saw him no more, and he went on his way rejoicing" (Acts 8:39). Philip went on to new serving and preaching assignments (Acts 8:40), and the eunuch departed to begin sharing the Good News in the sprawling dark continent of Africa!

Today, I am either depending upon God, or upon myself or some other source that cannot adequately guide my life. I am either "seeking those who are lost"--for Christ's sake, or I am moving through life at a steady pace but totally indifferent to the destiny of hell-bound sinners. I am either "turning people into disciples"—that is, radical lifetime followers of Christ with total world vision, disciples who will reproduce others of the same kind and thus will multiply to the ends of the earth until the end of time, or I am spending my life with no eternal dividends to show in return.

With regard to dependence upon the sovereign God, seeking prepared sinners to present the Gospel to them, and discipling the new-borns so that they can faithfully follow Christ.

What kind of movement would the Christian movement be, If every other Christian were just like me?

The Believer's Life Style: The Quiet Time

Outline

I. The Believer's Life Style: The Quiet Time
    A. The Secret of a Powerful Christian Life
    B. The Secret of a Powerful Church
    C. Dimensions of a Daily Quiet Time
        1. Priority
            (a) Biblical Reason
            (b) Biblical Law
            (c) Biblical Requirement
            (d) Biblical Practice
        2. Place
            (a) Private
            (b) Comfortable
            (c) Conducive
        3. Period of Time
            (a) Early
            (b) Minimum
            (c) Regular
        4. Parts
            (a) Scripture
            (b) Silence
            (c) Supplication (prayer)
            (d) Singing
        5. Paraphernalia
            (a) Bible Translations
            (b) Prayer List
            (c) Globe and Operation World

           (d) Devotional Books
6. Procedure
           (a) Open With Brief Prayer
           (b) Read Your Bible
           (c) Pray Throughout
           (d) Use Your Prayer List
           (e) Vary the Place and Participants
7. Principles
           (a) Bible World is the Real World
           (b) God Ardently Desires Our Time
           (c) We Need As Much As God Does
8. Purpose
9. Protection

The Believer's Life Style: The Quiet Time

If somebody introduced to you a brand new Christian to be discipled, what would you teach him? The following study is a crash presentation to examine possible themes that might be used in building curriculum or creating curriculum for fulfilling the commission of Jesus to go everywhere among all nations and to make disciples, and necessarily disciple makers, from among all men.

The Secret of a Powerful Christian Life

In this study, we are going to look at one of the most indispensable themes or subjects or activities in a believer's life. We will examine the matter of the individual's daily quiet time. This activity has also been called your daily appointment with God, or the morning watch. The truth of the matter is the believer's daily devotional life is an absolutely indispensable aspect of spiritual life. In fact, the secret of a powerful Christian life launches in an individual's daily quiet time. The secret of a powerful Christian work launches both in the individual quiet time and in the corporate power represented by the corporate quiet times of all the Christian's involved. The secret of a powerful church involves the same thing. They all launch from the individual's personal quiet time or daily devotional life with God.

The Secret of a Powerful Church

Some years ago, I was in a powerful little church where I thought I had gone to lead them in special spiritual services they referred to as revival. However, I found to my amazement that I was actually there to be blessed more than I was to be a blessing. We had a number of people saved and Christian's lives were changed, but most importantly was what happened to me. I saw a very, very, powerful small church where great miracles took place in service after service -- things that would be hard to explain from a mere human standpoint and would require God as an explanation for them. As I was talking with the pastor one afternoon, he said, "Would you like to see the primary secret?" To which I immediately responded, "I sure would." So that afternoon he took me over to a prayer service where two older Christian ladies were praying as they did every day. They had joined up with this church when it had its first beginnings to help form its foundation and had remained over the years. Across those many years at this church, they had discipled most of the people in attendance in the matter of having a daily powerful quiet time.

Every home I went in that week I looked around upon cue, having been told what to look for. I found a small desk somewhere inside the door and I found a little stack of books on the corner of that desk. I found a Bible and a notebook that had a prayer list and devotional thoughts that were gleaned from the daily reading every day. I was told that this was the secret of the power of the church, and my life became entirely changed. I had had something of a daily quiet time, but it became much more structured in a good way to my best advantage. It became much more powerful from that point on, and I want to tell you, basically, for over 40 years, with very few interruptions, I have had a quiet time essentially at the same time every morning with some interruptions because of schedule and other demands. And if not at that time, then usually some other time during the day, every day. And I can tell you that I do not believe a person can have a viable, vital Christian life without a daily quiet time. So I want to explore with you some aspects of the daily devotional life or what others have called "the morning watch."

Dimensions of a Daily Quiet Time

As a curriculum matter, both for being a disciple and for building disciples, when I take on a disciple individually (that is, when God assigns him to me as my responsibility to build that person into a useful Christian) and I begin to teach him the matter of a quiet time, I do two or three things:

I teach him theoretically what it means to have one -- in other words, I give him a theology and a systematized statement of how to do it. But more importantly, I try to go at least one time a week over to his house, early morning or whenever he has his quiet time, and I meet with him to have quiet time with him to model to him how to do it, and after several weeks I let him then launch himself and show me how he's doing it, and I simply supervise from that point on.

And then, I think it's wise occasionally to go back over once every six weeks or once every three months just to be sure, because the greatest tendency after a person begins to have it is to drift. And the greatest veteran Christian can drift in the matter of a quiet time.

In this study, I want to explore some dimensions of the process I employ in my quiet time. Every key word we are

The Quiet Time

going to use begins with the letter "P." I am going to give you a series of English "Ps", and I hope they are sweet Ps:

1. Priority

I want you to think first of the *priority* of having a daily quiet time. The Biblical rationale for it is stated in Romans 11:16, which in the King James Bible says: "For if the firstfruit is holy, so is the lump; and if the root is holy, so are the branches."

Now notice the same verse in a different translation: "When the first handful of dough is consecrated, then the whole batch is consecrated with it."

The Biblical principle for having a daily quiet time may be stated as, "When you give the first of any succession of things to God, you are by that act, sanctifying the entire succession of things." For example, when the children of Israel went into the land of promise, God required that they surrender the first city captured in the land to Him in token of the fact that every portion of the land was His by right, and they were surrendering, through the token, the entire land into the hands of God. The same thing is true of first fruits. When the first fruits of a person's resources -- his income -- are surrendered to God, it indicates the truth that his entire resources and belongings actually are in God's ownership.

In other words, when I give a tithe, the first tenth sanctifies ten-tenths. It is not the usual Baptist idea that if I give God one-tenth that He is to stay off of my nine-tenths. No, it is rather, instead of bribing God with one-tenth, I give one-tenth in token of the fact that all of my resources belong to Him, and not a penny is to be used in any way except in a way that would advance His interest in the earth.

The same thing is true in the Biblical requirement of the Sabbath day in the Old Testament and the first day of the week in the New Testament. The idea is that when I surrender the first day of the week to God, then the entire week is surrendered to God in a token of that first day. And the same thing is true as I give the first hour of each day to God. If I do not give the first hour, then I violate the principle of first things committed to God betokening the fact that everything thereafter belongs to Him because I had surrendered to Him the first thing.

It is interesting to see how the Biblical writers, the Christians in the Bible, or the believers in God in the Old Testament, invariably practiced this. Our high profile example is Jesus himself. In Mark 1:35 we read these words: "And in the morning, rising up a great while before day while it was still dark, He went out and departed into a solitary place and there He prayed."

As for me, I'm convinced that if the Son of God practiced a daily quiet time with His Father, then it is a good standard for me to follow. And if it was necessary, as it apparently was for him to have a quiet time, then it is certainly indispensable and essential that I have a daily quiet time.

An excellent Old Testament example of "quiet times" is found in the book of Daniel, chapter 6, verse 10. However, before we read of Daniel's daily practice, let me immediately address the excuse most people use: "But I don't have time for a daily quiet time since my time gets so crowded," by reminding you that Daniel was the prime minister of a vast sprawling pagan empire. He was a man whom God had elevated to high position, and he functioned through one king after another, one rumor after another, and stood in that position for many, many, many years. Yet, pay close attention to his daily practice: "Three times a day he got down on his knees, and prayed, giving thanks to his God."

Far too often, we readily and regularly substitute public reasoning with others over private audience with the Father. It seems as if humanistic procedure moves us to think that if somehow we could put our best minds together and connive in the best conceivable way, we can come up with proper answers. Yet, it never has happened, and it won't begin with us, because we are voting against God no matter how much we connive and how brilliant our intelligence is that we use to address the problem. No, the solution is found in a relationship with God. I must understand that all that happens in my life with God is closely connected with my daily quiet time.

Since God and I know this, it should be obvious that Satan is also fully aware of the latent power in meeting with God daily. For this reason you can anticipate his willingness to stop at nothing in order to prevent us from maintaining the priority of a daily quiet time with the Lord. So don't be surprised if when you commit to having one, that you encounter constant opposition and distraction from the enemy of your soul. You will have to stand strong in the Lord and resist the Devil, while determining to daily press on and in the Lord, seeking His face, and not just His hand, passionately and persistently.

2. Place

The second word that begins with the letter "P" concerns the importance of having a regular place for your daily quiet time. Matthew 6:6 refers to this as your "prayer closet." Jesus said, "When you pray, enter into your closet," and that presumably means a quiet place shut off from all possible traffic and conducive to relationship with God where you genuinely can pray. Also take note that he did not say to his people, *"If you pray."* He presumed that a Christian will pray or he is backslidden. He said, "When you pray, enter into your closet and when you have shut the door, pray to your Father who sees and hears in secret, and your Father will reward you."

Here are some very practical suggestions. First, I would strongly suggest that you have one given place for this. For years and years now, I have varied the places, but usually there is a long period of time where I have it only in one place. For years I have had my quiet time in one place, normally either in my home or, weather permitting, very close thereby. Although one place is advisable, it should be occasionally adjusted. Second, it's wise to get up and walk for a brief while during your quiet time. It's wise to change locations for a brief period of time, even if you go back to the old standard location in order that you realize that this is a romance relationship and it is not simply that you meet with God at this given place. You are simply carrying on the spiritual eternal romance in this given place like a love seat in your house where lovers meet, but it does not mean that you do not love each other in every place and every other occasion. Third, I would suggest that your place be very private and as undisturbed as possible. It should be comfortable enough, though not overly comfortable. I would not recommend at all that you have your quiet time in bed, or your quiet time will become "sack religion" as you fall asleep while you are doing it. Fourth, I would recommend that it be a place with quiet, passive, serene surroundings and perhaps with spiritual suggestions such as pictures on the wall, and other symbols that suggest your walk with God.

On one occasion, I was in a meeting that necessitated spending the night in the home of some of the church members. I got up early the next morning and was all alone in the den, seated on the end of the couch. I had turned the over-hanging lamp on and was seated there reading my Bible taking notes and having my quiet time when the lady, my hostess, came out of their bed room dressed in a gown and a robe. She saw where I was sitting and said, "Oh Brother Herb, that's not the light you should be reading by. That's the courting light. This was one of those lights that you turn on, and it has three levels of illumination and I was operating by the first turn, which is what she called the courting light. To which I responded, "Will you kindly say that again?" She said, "Oh that's the courting light." I said, "That's exactly what I'm doing." Would to God that I could be convinced always that I am in a love relationship with the greatest person in the universe and it is actually a spiritual romance in the truest sense in which he loves me and I love him and we court one another in this eternal romance day after day. In order to aid this it requires a given, particular, and private place.

3. Period of Time

The third word that begins with the letter "P" is setting aside one particular *period of time* that you honor every day for this relationship with Father God. Biblically speaking, early in the day, whatever that may be for you, is preferable. By this I mean that if you arise at ten o'clock in the morning, your first thirty minutes or hour should be devoted to your relationship with God; if you arise at six in the morning, then from six to seven; if you arise at four in the morning, then from four to five. So by early I mean, irrespective of the time, make your quiet time the first activity of your day. If you have some chores you have to do first, of course that is a given, but right at the beginning and with meticulous protection set this time aside for God. The Psalmist said it this way, Psalm 5:3, "My voice shalt thou hear in the morning O Lord, in the morning will I direct my prayer unto thee and will look up ..." The principle behind this statement is that you ought to set it as your goal to seek God's face before you see the face of any man. Now if you quickly see another human face, then before you ever arise out of bed you ought to say your good morning "greetings" to God and determine to see his face previous to the seeing of any other face. In other words you should go into the closet with God before you go into the conflict with the flesh, the world, and the devil, because if you go into the conflict before you go into the closet, you go in unprepared for the conflict. Remember, you're reserving the most important and strategic part of the day for your relationship with the most important Person there is. That's why I call this session my briefing session, where I get my orders every day. I avow and confirm my love for him and simply report in quite often to say, "Jesus, you're good at loving, and I need to be loved right now, so I want to let you love me for a while. Let's both do what he is good at." If you can't start any other way, you can at least start like that.

    I have a pastor friend who was asked to come down to the city council meeting and lead the opening prayer that convened the morning session. They gave him a stationary microphone outside the wall that separated the observers from the council members and he stood out there and presumably they bowed their heads when the chairman asked them to have the opening prayer and when he finished and said, "amen," the chairman then said, "Now let's get down to the business of the day." This was a little more than my pastor friend could take, so he turned back and asked for the microphone again. He said, "Sir you may not realize it but *you just did the business of the day*. In fact you will never do anything more important today than you did when we bowed our heads and I called on the Lord Almighty for his attention and blessing to be upon you and, for your adjustment to be made to him today." How wise were those words, because no matter what else you may do if you do not do this business, all other is in vain as far as reality and eternity are concerned. If you do this, you may do a lot of stumbling in the other, but God will rescue most stumblings and will credit the desires of your heart as being reality even though you may stumble all the way home. So,

The Quiet Time

be sure that you give priority to setting aside a given period of time to meet with the Lord.

Another suggestion would be to set a time minimum. I don't believe that anybody could get the sounds of the earth out of his eyes and ears and the sounds of heaven into his eyes and ears in less than thirty minutes. There may be occasions when you have less time than this, but when that occurs, take advantage of the time you have to meet with God. I know a woman who called a taxi one day. When the taxi arrived, leaving her six children in the house, she went out, and got in the cab. The taxi driver asked her where she wanted to go. To which she replied, "I'm not going anywhere. I just want to sit here, put my apron over my head and talk to God a few minutes and I will pay you for the time you spend here." How wise if you can't get find a quiet place any other way.

Another important principle in regards to time is that you should have enough time to forget time. In other words, don't be dominated by time when you have your quiet time. If you are always worried about the next page that you are going to read or the next phone call you are going to have to make or the next assignment you have, you are not going to have much quality time with Father God. So have enough time to forget time and if you can't have enough time at that moment arrange it during the day where you can set aside enough time to forget time so you can give God the choice time of day. I would strongly suggest also that you keep this appointment regularly. The reason is that prayer is simply no more nor less than a time exposure to God. It is not a utilitarian thing where we get things from God, which is a bonus by-product. All of us know about unanswered, as well as answered, prayers, but that's not the purpose of prayer. Prayer is not for us to get God to adjust to us, it's rather for us to adjust to God. It's the difference between rowing a boat to shore and rowing the shore to the boat. Many people pray as if they are rowing God to their purposes instead of rowing themselves to God's purpose and God's Person.

Probably the most important quote of this study is that made by Andrew Murray as he said, "A believer's very first responsibility in each day is to bring his own soul into a happy condition before God." Do you realize the implications of this truth? Obeying its admonition would take away all negativisms out of the Christian's life, fears would be relieved, resentments would be gone, cynicism would not dominate our lives, and complaints and criticisms would all be removed immediately if we would exercise that first responsibility each day of bringing our own souls into a happy condition before God before we do anything else.

4. Parts of the Quiet Time

Having considered the priority of the quiet time, the period for the quiet time, the place for the quiet time, we will now look at the *parts of the quiet time*. We will offer some suggestions here, and you may vary them as you see best for your relationship with God.

Use Scripture. This axiom should always be followed. You must use Scripture and honor it seriously and solemnly as the Word of God. I would strongly suggest that you use the Bible the way it is written. Read it systematically. If you don't read all the way through from "Genesis 1:1 to Revelation 22:21," at least read the book you have selected systematically from front to back. Don't use the skip and dip method where you dip into a text, let the Bible fall open and just skip like a mountain bird skimming over a mountain lake, taking your choice about what you are going to get or to let chance and caprice dictate the choice of what you are going to get. No, do the honor of reading the Bible the way it was written. Read it systematically.

Now if you have never done this before let me suggest that you start perhaps with the Gospel of John, maybe with the Gospel of Mark. If you read the Gospel of John first read it at least two or three times before you read any other book in the Bible. I think that will explain itself as you read along. It clearly tells you why it was written and if that purpose is not fulfilled then all the other reading in the Bible will do no good. So read the gospel of John which is unfathomable in its riches and depth. Read it several times before you read anything else. You might want to read the action-packed account of the life of Christ as the suffering servant in the gospel of Mark and then perhaps one of the other gospels.

In addition, I would strongly suggest using an annual through-the-Bible reading plan so that you can read systematically instead of just reading it haphazardly and randomly. Justin Taylor has put together a list of through-the-Bible-in-a-year reading plans. Go to this web site and find one that is right for you:

(http://thegospelcoalition.org/blogs/justintaylor/2008/12/30/bible-reading-plans/).

Significant planned silence. A second part of your quiet time should be significant planned silence. Let me give you a standard for this: II Samuel 7:18, "... then King David went in and sat before the Lord." In other words you determine that this silence is a creed in relationship with God where you simply sit very consciously and openly before him with directed thinking -- simply telling him, "I want you to speak to me clearly and I want to listen in this silence only for your voice and cultivate my relationship with you."

Supplication or seeking God in conscious, even audible prayer. A third part of your quiet time should be supplication or seeking God in conscious, even audible, prayer. The aforementioned are just some of the parts. I'll mention other parts as we expand into this study of the quiet time.

5. Paraphernalia of the Quiet Time

The fifth "P" word involves the paraphernalia of the quiet time or the materials to be used. Let me just make a quick list in succession of possible materials to use in a viable quiet time.

Bible. Obviously, a Bible and several translations of the Bible. Now if you are unfamiliar with Bible translations, get your pastor or some more advanced disciple, some growing Christian, to help you in understanding the difference between one translation and another. My favorite Bible translations are: The Amplified Bible, and be sure to read the explanation at the beginning so that you know how to read it. It is a gold mine of wealth spiritually and in imparting God's word. Another very helpful Bible that may be difficult to secure a copy of is the Discovery Bible. If you find one, be sure and read the first ten pages of introduction before you ever read a line of the Bible. This will enlighten you as to what those things mean in the text as you are advancing through it. Then acquire at least two good Bible paraphrases. For the New Testament my favorite is J.B. Phillips Paraphrase which is actually a commentary/translation/paraphrase on the text which is very alive. J.B. Phillips said when he translated it, it was like putting a wire into an old main that he thought had been disconnected but he found it very much electrically alive. Another of my favorite paraphrases is The Living Bible, which, although it is not a translation, nevertheless, it is truly a living word. In fact one of the most anointed meetings I ever attended in my life was led by a man who read out of nothing but The Living Bible. As he read, I kept wondering, "What is that translation he is reading out of, it is so powerful." Eventually I discovered that he was reading segment after segment from The Living Bible.

The Quiet Time

This motivated me to begin immediately to open my own quiet time using The Living Bible. Having said all this, let me challenge you to get several Bible translations.

Prayer List. Create and employ your own prayer list. If you have to use documentation from other prayer lists, or other prayer suggestions, or your church prayer calendar, don't hesitate to do so. I have followed this standard, somewhat erratically, for years. For example, on Monday I let the M stand for men and I pray for God's men; on Tuesday I let the T stand for texts and I pray for my texts; on Wednesday for specific workers whom I am aware of in strategic positions doing strategic work for Christ. Thursday is a time of thanksgiving; on Friday, specifically for my family; on Saturday, for saints and sinners; and on Sunday, when I spend less time praying than any other day of the week probably for obvious reasons, I pray for the services and the sermons.

Your pastor ought to be included on that list at least in the men of Monday, the workers of Wednesday and the saints of Saturday and the sermon and the services of Sunday, thus praying for him at least five times a week.

So you ought to have a prayer list and use it regularly. If it gets too lengthy or out of date, then rework it. An up-to-date-prayer list will rescue you from the monotony of praying over the same things every day.

Devotional Books. Another great aid for your quiet times is devotional books.

In my opinion, one of the best, and one that I have used for several years, is entitled Streams in the Desert. Another great devotional book is Awake My Heart by Dr. J. Sidlow Baxter. But if I had to choose just one, my favorite, although in some places it is hard to use, is My Utmost for His Highest by Oswald Chambers. If you look into Chambers' teachings carefully you will be staggered again and again how they have tier upon tier, level upon level, of profound insight.

I would also suggest Charles Spurgeon's two great books, one entitled <u>Morning and Evening</u> and the other <u>Faith's Checkbook.</u> They are usable documents which you may use year after year in your daily quiet time.

A Hymnal or Sing-Along Type Digital Music. No believer should be without a hymnbook that is filled with the greatest songs of Christian history in it. Almost all of these all-time favorite hymns are available on an mp3 player or an Ipod or Ipad device. Somewhere in your quiet time, you should sing along with the songs you play on your media devices. There is a biblical precedent for this found in many places in the Bible. The following are but a small sampling of the many places the Psalmists speak of singing to the Lord:

Psalm 59:16, *"I will sing of your power, O Lord, yes, I will sing aloud of your mercy in the morning."*
Psalm 13:6, *"I will sing to the LORD, because he has dealt bountifully with me."*
Psalm 61:8, *"So will I ever sing praises to your name, as I perform my vows day after day."*
Psalm 104:33, *"I will sing to the LORD as long as I live; I will sing praise to my God while I have being."*

Christians rob themselves by failing to sing aloud in celebration of God's great person, purposes, provisions, and goodness.

Materials. One final suggestion about materials that aid one's quiet time. Include *a small map of the world,* preferably a globe that one may spin on its axis with a copy of the book <u>Operation World</u> open before him. If the purpose of being a disciple and making disciples is to impact the world, then the first mandate is to be knowledgeable about our world. So I would strongly encourage you to use <u>Operation World</u>, which

The Quiet Time

is a daily prayer guide for the nations of the world one by one, day by day.

For example, the country of Afghanistan is in the news daily due to our military involvement there. Turning to Operation World, we learn that this great mountainous country that nestles between Hindu India and all the Hindu and Buddhist lands to the east and then the Islamic world block of nations forms a tremendous cross road for world evangelism with ten million people. Because of its location, it would not be significantly difficult to evangelize many of them and yet they have never heard the gospel. Operation World informs us that most of the inhabitants of Afghanistan have never heard the name of Jesus even once. Becoming aware of this, you are given specific issues to pray for in order to see the gospel message bring forth fruit there.

6. Procedure to Follow

The sixth "P" involves a *procedure to follow*. This procedure should follow steps like the following:

Open your quiet time with a very brief prayer. For many years, erratically and spasmodically, but with some degree of regularity, I have used one line in scripture, Psalm 119:18, *"Open thou mine eyes that I may behold wondrous things out of thy law."* At times I may pray James 5:8, asking the Lord for wisdom. On other occasions, I may pray over Ephesians 1:15-19, asking the Lord to open the eyes of my understanding, or of my heart, so that I may see what is mine in Christ and what my responsibility is as a Christian, and thus learn how to cultivate an ever-deepening relationship with him.

I have also prayed for years, negatively, Psalm 28:1 which says "... be not thou silent unto me O God lest if thou be silent unto me I become like those who go down into the pit ..." because the most dangerous thing that can ever happen to a Christian would occur should God stop talking to him.

Likewise, the most significant thing that ever happens in anybody's life, saved or lost, is when God speaks to them. It should be a regular, daily, momentary occurrence that God speaks to his child which he is longing to do all day long every day. His speaking should only be interrupted consciously by the mandate that the child of God do other things, and even then he ought to be aware that God is present and is speaking. With this attitude, the child of God should then tune in as quickly as possible to what God is saying.

Read your Bible and use part of the reading time to read it audibly. Someone well said, "Bible reading is the listening side of prayer, if the ear side, or the listening side, is right then the tongue side, or the speaking side, will necessarily be right and we will learn to pray according to the will of God." This quote basically sums up all that needs to be said about the importance and imperativeness of reading your Bible, daily and even audibly.

Pray -- pray throughout your Bible reading time, pausing to echo back to God what He has said to you. In fact, the best way to pray is to hear from God and then do not allow yourself to change the subject. I would recommend that you mark passages in your Bible and pray those favorite passages back to God. If you can't do it any other way, paraphrase them as you look at the page and transfer them to your own lips and thank God for speaking those to you and ask him to incarnate that in your life. Dr. Price was right when he said the best binding for the Bible is not Morocco leather, it's a human skin. So ask God to incarnate this in you as he did in Jesus, modified by your limitations, sins and inabilities, but as much as God can do it.

Use the prayer list every day. Instead of going first to men on God's behalf, go first to God on men's behalf. So we go to the man by way of God's throne of grace instead of going in any other direction any other way which will be basically useless.

Now occasionally I would suggest that you vary the place of your quiet time as well as the procedure of your quiet time and the participants. In other words, occasionally have a disciple or a discipler to join you in your quiet time. Or go to some believer's house and get a group together and have a quiet time with them. It will encourage everybody concerned.

On one occasion, I was in a church in northwest Louisiana where I asked the pastor's permission to ask the people to honestly tell me how long it had been since they had a viable quiet time. I assured them that their responses would be held in confidence, with only the pastor and me being privy to their answers. The answers amazed both the pastor and me. One of the most dismaying responses came from one of the leaders of the church, a deacon, who confessed that he had not had a viable quiet time for eight years. No doubt it would be staggering to find out in our churches how the few of the persons in leadership and leading spokespersons in the body do not have a viable quiet time with God every day. This is tragic. It despises the cross of Christ, deprives the church of Christ and prevents the cause of Christ from the advance God wants it to have. I do not see how anybody can disobey the Bible and call themselves Bible Christians at this point.

7. Principles Behind the Quiet Time

Briefly, let me give you some principles that are behind the quiet time:

The Bible world is the real world. I John 2:17 says this world is passing away, but 2 Corinthians 4:18 says the things which are seen are only temporary, it's the things that are unseen that are eternal. Thus, when a person spends time alone with God he is in constant contact with the ultimate reality that runs parallel with and intertwines with what we call the real world, which in reality is passing away.

God ardently desires our daily fellowship. In John 4:23, Jesus said to the woman at the well in Samaria, "The hour is coming and now is when the true worshiper shall worship the Father in spirit and in truth, for the Father is seeking such to worship him." Let it be underscored in your thinking, draw circles around it, highlight it every conceivable way, God wants fellowship with you. He is seeking for people who will take time to build relationship with him. What is the basis of that? Any good father can answer this because he knows that a father wants to spend time with his children. Sometimes he wants to spend time with all of them in a group corresponding to public worship but often he wants to spend time with each of them individually as you do with God in your quiet time.

We need the quiet time as much as we need anything else we ever have in our lives. Let me remind you again of Daniel, who was prime minister of an empire but who had to have those check point times with God where he refreshed himself in God's presence. This daily time with God made him the mighty man of God that he was, despite living in a pagan land. Spending time with God gave him a wisdom that caused other leaders to always be consulting him in regards to great decisions.

8. Purpose of the Quiet Time

Another principle that begins with the letter "P" is the purpose of the quiet time. First, we will state it negatively. The quiet time is not for the purpose of primarily gathering principles or gleaning produce such as blessings either from the Bible or for an answer to prayer or whatever, but it is to meet with and cultivate relationship with a Person. It is to have a heart that is occupied with God himself. It is to behold Jesus in his glory and to allow no distractions to keep us from seeing him.

I heard the account of a young Christian who went to his pastor one day and said, "Pastor, I want to sadly confess that I hear all of these people around here talking about what they are getting out of their daily quiet time. But it has not produced that for me. I read my Bible and pray seriously and don't seem to be getting anything out of it. What is wrong with me?" While he was asking the question the pastor was quietly praying, in what Guy King called the "sky telegram" prayer, i.e., he sent a quick prayer up to heaven and asked the Lord for the answer to this question. Immediately, when the boy finished the question, the pastor had his answer. He said, "Son, do you see that wicker basket on my desk?" "Yes sir," answered the boy. "Empty the papers out of that wicker basket," said the pastor. Puzzled, nevertheless the boy did as he was told. Then the pastor instructed him to take the wicker basket out into the hall to the water fountain and bring it back to him full of water. The boy just stood there puzzled and looking at the basket and then at the pastor thinking, "what in the world does this mean?" Then he said, "Pastor this basket won't hold water." The pastor said, "Never mind, you obey me and go out and take it to the water fountain and bring me back a basket of water." The bewildered boy walked out into the hall, went down to the water fountain, and ran the water into the wicker basket, which of course spilled through almost as quickly as it poured in. The lad came back with a dismayed look on his face and said, "Pastor, I told you that this was crazy because the basket won't hold water." "Yes," said the Pastor, "But son, even though it didn't hold the water, the basket was a lot cleaner just from being washed by the water flowing in and out of it."

The point is, don't worry about what you are getting out of your quiet time. I don't check up on my relationship with my wife all the time to see what is happening in our relationship. If I did it would become a very uneasy relationship. I rather presume on growth in that relationship without taking it for granted and I take it for granted without presuming on it. In other words, I cultivate it but I'm not always checking up on it to see if it's occurring. The same thing is true with your relationship with God. So, the purpose is to be daily cultivating an ever-deepening love relationship with the Father, the Lord Jesus Christ, and the Holy Spirit.

9. Protection

If we have only ten minutes to give to God, most of us will say we can't get anything out of such a short time, so we won't spent any time at all. This is the very root of our problem. Rather than seeing time with God as moments with a friend, we see it as time during which we accomplish something or get something only for ourselves. We need to give those minutes to Him rather than say I can't get anything out of them. You see the most important thing God can give you is a deepening love relationship with himself through your quiet time. For this reason we must be deliberate and careful to kept this meeting with God or we will not have it at all, or will eventually drift out of it.

It would be staggering if honesty would force us to admit how many people there are in the church, including church leaders everywhere, who do not have a daily quiet time with God. Those who live in this manner are like a deep sea diver on the deck of a ship preparing to go down into the deep, who has his diving suit on, but forgets or neglects to connect the air hose. What do you suppose is going to happen to him?

The same thing is true of a Christian. He may fake his way all of the way through. In the process he may increase his

The Quiet Time

time and effort to gain productivity, but as far as eternity will be concerned it counts for nothing. What a wonderful day it would be if the church would suddenly stop in its tracks, take it's bearings, and Christians everywhere would re-determine to assist each other in having a vital, viable daily quiet time using every inter-networking means possible. One suggestion would be to have the whole church occasionally come together in the morning and have one of the leaders teach and demonstrate to the others how to have a quiet time, and then follow up with breakfast served afterwards.

In the last church I pastored, at least once every three months I had a quiet time with my people on Wednesday night, and occasionally on Sunday night because there were people there on Sunday night that were not at the Wednesday service. I would go into the services without a message, call for somebody to open his Bible, and hand me the Bible from the pew where they were sitting. I would then proceed to have a quiet time teaching my people how to do it.

At the beginning of my pastorate at the last church, when I preached on a quiet time, many people there had never heard of this before in their lives. Seeing such lack of understanding of this essential aspect of the Christian's walk with the Lord, I asked in the invitation how many of them would stand pledging themselves as best they could do to begin and to continue in the pattern of a daily quiet time. Perhaps only around one-fourth of the congregation stood up. I appreciated the honesty and the reluctance of the other three-fourths and then I made a discovery out of the one-fourth who made the commitment.

About a month and a half later I was walking down the hall in the Sunday school time and the lady who had stood up that morning stopped me. She said, "Brother Hodges, if a proposition is made such as you made about having a daily devotional life every morning, I will never again stand to my feet and pledge myself to such a thing." Knowing that this was a kind gracious woman, I said, "May I ask you why?" She said, "I cannot do it." I said, "On what grounds can you not do it?" She said, "I don't know, I simply cannot do it. I took your suggestions, got my Bible, started a prayer list, and read a devotional book, and I simply cannot do it." To which I responded, "Let me ask you a question or two. If you want to go to the bank do you have any trouble doing it?" She said, "No, I just go." "If you want to go to the grocery store do you have any trouble doing it?" "No, I just go." I said, "If you want to go, and I named a number of other places, do you have any trouble going there?" She said, "No." I said, "Then what does it tell you when you tell me that God wants an appointment with you every day and you cannot keep it. You are telling me how important Satan and your flesh say those things really are. They are more important than going to the bank, more important than going to the grocery store, more important than going to the closet for the clothes you wear today, or breathing the air you breathe. And Satan will oppose it every step of the way."

Let me illustrate from the scriptures what it will be like if you undertake to have a daily quiet time. In II Samuel 23:11-12, there is a man named Shammah, who was one of David's mighty men. The setting of the text reveals that the Philistines were gathered together into a troop or as an entire organized army around a piece of ground where lentils were being grown. The reason the Philistines came for a piece of ground where pea and beans were being raised was in order to cut off the Israelite food supply and to steal food for themselves. All the Israelites in that area had fled in terror except the one warrior named Shammah. He stood in the midst of that plot of ground, declaring, as one of my friends preaches it, "I have left my pea patch for the last time." He defended the land, slew the Philistines who were attempting to take it and the Lord brought great victory.

The point is that if you commit to having a viable and vital quiet time this is exactly how it will happen. There are Philistines everywhere gathered in a troop against you because they know how important this is. However, we must have the attitude and posture of Shammah, who stood in the middle of that plot of ground, closed his hands around his weapon, and declared, "I will die before I give up this ground to these Philistines." When we do, we can expect the Lord to bring a great victory in that day. Christian, the Philistines will come at you from every side. But when you do hold the Sword of the Spirit, the Word of God, like you are going to have to have your hand pried loose from it when the judgment comes and you say, come and get it because here I stand, and in the name of God a great victory is going to be wrought here this day.

God bless you as you work at having a viable, vital, powerful quiet time that will be a blessing to you and will be an honor to God and a channel for his power to be displayed in the earth.

Taking the Wheel for Disciple-making